ENDURANCE

The Extraordinary Life and Times of Emil Zátopek

Rick Broadbent

John Wisden & Co Ltd
An imprint of Bloomsbury Publishing Plc

50 Bedford Square   1385 Broadway
London   New York
WC1B 3DP   NY 10018
UK   USA

www.bloomsbury.com

WISDEN and the wood-engraving device are trademarks of John Wisden
& Company Ltd, a subsidiary of Bloomsbury Publishing Plc

First published 2016
This paperback edition published 2017

www.wisden.com
www.wisdenrecords.com
Follow Wisden on Twitter @WisdenAlmanack
and on Facebook at Wisden Sports

British Library Cataloguing-in-Publication Data
A catalogue record for this book is available from the British Library.

Library of Congress Cataloguing-in-Publication data has been applied for.

ISBN: PB: 978-1-4729-2023-2
ePub: 978-1-4729-2024-9

2 4 6 8 10 9 7 5 3 1

Typeset in Adobe Garamond Pro by Deanta Global Publishing Services,
Chennai, India
Printed and bound in Great Britain by CPI Group (UK) Ltd, Croydon CR0 4YY

To find out more about our authors and books visit www.wisden.com.
Here you will find extracts, author interviews, details of forthcoming
events and the option to sign up for our newsletters.

To Debs, for her endurance

A NOTE ON THE AUTHOR

Rick Broadbent is an award-winning journalist and author. He has been staff writer at *The Times* for 15 years and spent 2007–13 as the paper's athletics correspondent. He has written nine books including *That Near-Death Thing* and *Ring of Fire*, both shortlisted for the William Hill Sports Book of the Year. He was also the ghostwriter of Jessica Ennis's bestselling autobiography. He lives with his wife and two children in Dorset.

@ricktimes

Also by the author:

Looking for Eric
Seize the Day (with Baroness Tanni Grey-Thompson)
The Big If
Rocket Men (with Ron Haslam)
Ring of Fire
Jeremy & Amy (with Jeremy Keeling)
That Near-Death Thing
Unbelievable (with Jessica Ennis)
Feel (with Freddie Spencer)

Contents

1

The Brown Paper Package (Prague, 1966)

On 18 July 1966 a plane touched down on the black tarmac in Prague, and a bronze face peered from the oval window. Ron Clarke pulled his bag from the overhead rack, thanked the stewardess and emerged on to the steps into the Czech night. It took him a while to realise that the figure with his hand extended on the runway below was Emil Zátopek, older now, tufts of hair bookending a bald pate, but with eyes still alive and enquiring.

Clarke smiled. The Australian was a handsome man in his prime, with thick, jet-black hair and sun-smoothed skin. It was a fortnight since he had set the new 5000 metres world record in Stockholm and he was in demand. During his annual European summer tour, Clarke would run as many as 30 races in 50 days, but when word came through from the Czech Republic that Zátopek wanted to meet him, he changed his schedule. It was a meeting between athletics legends, and that pitted tarmac was actually a bridge across the generation gap.

Clarke was an amiable man prone to introspection, but resilience had been the sap that filtered down the family tree. His great-grandfather, Thomas Clarke, had been a gold miner in Victoria when the great Australasian mine was flooded by an underground river. The workers had continued to stave away at the walls as they knew they were close to a rich lode of gold, but the mine collapsed and water gushed in. Thomas escaped and spent 53 hours incessantly pumping water from the underground prison. Twenty-two men drowned but, as the scroll of honour that the Amalgamated Miners' Association of Victoria later presented to him stated: 'Your almost superhuman efforts were at last successful in reducing the water, enabling the relief party to reach and rescue your five famished mates who had miraculously been able to survive, sealed up in a remote part of the upper level.'

His son had also worked in the mines, and was crippled by them and then laid off from them, but his own son, Tom, Ron's father, forged a new path as a sportsman, becoming a star in the religious fervour of Australian Rules football.

It could be said, then, that Ron Clarke came from the sort of stock that breeds champions. He had broken 11 world records in 1965 and was an elegant presence on tracks around the world, but it had all gone wrong at the Tokyo Olympics in 1964. Mining for his own gold, he had been the victim of one of the Games' great upsets when Billy Mills, a half-Sioux Indian from the reservation and the Marines motor pool, had powered past him on the home straight of the 10,000 metres. That had been a brutal and physical race. Mohamed Gammoudi had clawed at Clarke and Clarke had shoved Mills off balance; when Clarke came home third, only a second behind Mills, he was sure that he would be disqualified. He smiled anyway because it had been a great race and Clarke liked running almost as much as he liked winning.

It got worse for him. In the 5000 metres final, Clarke led for 4000 metres but the tactics of his rivals upset his rhythm and belief. 'Damn it!' he said to himself and mentally quit. He knew he should have roused himself and fought on but he couldn't. He was only ninth, and people began writing about his lack of a killer instinct. In the marathon he soldiered on manfully, but was a spent force, barely able to put one foot in front of the other. He was ninth again, but he had entered all three distance events and, really, who but Emil could expect to do that and thrive?

The cost of running intrigued Clarke. Ultimately, it was all about gold. Billy Mills' success had even seen him rewarded with a ring forged from genuine Black Hills gold. The elders of the Oglala Sioux, the descendants of Crazy Horse and Red Cloud, gave it to him along with warrior status, something unprecedented for a half-breed. The flipside was those who failed: men like Kōkichi Tsuburaya, the Japanese runner who had finished ahead of Clarke in the 1964 Olympic marathon but would suffer career-ending injuries and then kill himself by slashing his right wrist with a razor blade. The note he left said simply: 'Cannot run any more.'

Clarke came from gold-mining stock, but had been left with only world records in his panning dish, and these feats rendered conflicting emotions. He called each historic mark 'a peculiar sense of disappointment' and said the exhilaration would drain away, leaving only dejection and profound weariness. He likened it to turning 21 and finding out that, when the party ended, this milestone was much like any other.

So he was in Prague to meet a hero and find some answers. Zátopek had sent word that if Clarke would agree to run a 3000 metres race in Prague then he would meet him and, despite being some 15 years older, even join him on a training run.

Zátopek marched Clarke through customs, flashing officials a panoramic smile and waving to everyone. He was a terribly erratic driver, but somehow they made it to his home, where he introduced

Clarke to Dana, his wife, and after an hour-and-a-half discussion on manifold subjects then took him to the track for the race.

Clarke was tired after his travel but he beat a man known locally as 'the Head Waiter' and Zátopek took him to his hotel, cheerily informing him that he would pick him up tomorrow at 5.30 a.m. 'We went up to the small track in the woods, north of Prague, where he had run two successive 10,000 metres faster than almost anybody else had run one, [and] where he had set the 30,000 metres world record,' Clarke recalled. 'He ran me hard through the hills and he was full of enthusiasm. He told me about Fartlek training and we spoke about lots of things – politics, his early career and his training experiments.' Clarke was pleased to hear Zátopek explain that he would run between lampposts holding his breath. Then he would try to make it to another lamppost. 'I did something similar back home in Australia, where I'd try to see how far I could swim underwater. We had a really pleasant morning.'

After the training, Zátopek said, 'You can't go home without getting some Czech crystal.'

'So he drives us down into the main street in Prague. It's lunchtime and there are policemen everywhere. Emil parks up and had this habit of being able to whistle loudly through his teeth. A policeman came charging up with his pad out ready to book him. Then he sees that it's Emil Zátopek. Emil signs the pad for him and hands the keys to the policeman. We go into a couple of shops and I find a beautiful glass bowl that I still have. We must have been in there for about half an hour. Then we came out and there was no car. I look around and am a bit confused but then I hear Emil whistle again. Instantly, from nowhere, the car speeds up to us and the policeman gets out. I thought, "This is really something, this is true fame – being able to get an on-duty policeman to go off duty, park your car, wait for you while you go shopping and then bring the car back. Jeez." Then he took me to the airport and walked me through customs without stopping. He even took me out on to the tarmac and on to the plane again.'

It had been a brief meeting, but one which still resonated with Clarke when we spoke early in the summer of 2015. Zátopek had been long retired back in 1966, but Clarke still had an Olympic Games to go. Yet both men knew that the altitude of Mexico City in 1968 would jeopardise Clarke's hopes of victory.

In 1968 Clarke was still the world record holder at both the 5000 and 10,000 metres, but he was a worried man. British experts had predicted deaths in the endurance events. Billy Mills called the physiological differences the 'gulp gap', while Dr Roger Bannister, famed for breaking the four-minute mile barrier but also an eminent neurologist, said athletes would be seriously endangering their health in Mexico.

Clarke tried to do all he could to compensate. His friend and sports medicine doctor, Dr Danny Zimmerman, known as 'Zim', had relatives in Mexico City and got hold of all the scientific data he could. They travelled there together the year before the Olympics to conduct experiments. Clarke ended a 5000 metres trial race with an ashen face and sunken features, reporting palpitations and a searing pain behind his eyes. His time was the worst since he had been a junior. Tests showed he had suffered a 16 per cent drop in haemoglobin, the red corpuscles carrying oxygen in the blood.

Clarke had a habit of remembering the races he lost rather than the ones he won, and the defeat to Mills in Tokyo festered. He knew, because Mills had been fading, that he should have gone harder with a few laps left. He had let the Sioux Marine off the hook and suffered for it. On other occasions, it went brilliantly and he experienced what modern athletes would call 'flow', that other-worldly state where instinct and ability merge to form a perfect physical storm. It had been that way when he set the 10,000 metres world record in Oslo in 1965. His wife, Helen, had gone home early because her mother was dying of cancer, but she had won her race and got back to Australia just in time to say goodbye. Clarke had only one race left before he could go home to see his family. He was demob happy and in wonderful shape. It felt like the endgame. 'All the stars were in the right place in the universe that day,' he said. 'It felt so good.'

But in Mexico City it would be very different. 'I'd have been better off waiting for 1972,' he said. 'In the 10,000 metres it was like being in a sort of curtained room. You have to tippy-toe within yourself. Normally you keep pushing the curtain, but once you step beyond it you can never come back.' He ran with care but when runners started to pass him on the last lap, and he saw more gold fading away, he was, in his word, 'history'.

His heart stopped on the line. Dr Brian Corrigan, president of the New South Wales Sports Medicine Association, was a friend. He had predicted that unacclimatised athletes would suffer an 18 per cent decrease in performance or, put more bluntly, it would be like depriving a person of a pint of blood and asking them to run a mile. Corrigan saw Clarke struggling on his last lap and jumped the perimeter moat, which was no mean feat, protected as it was by barbed wire. He did not have the required pass but shoved someone aside. People had been circulating the arena with oxygen tanks to attend to runners as they keeled over. Corrigan grabbed one and ran to his stricken friend. He saw his face go from white to green and feared that he would die there and then. 'It was a tragedy waiting to happen,' Clarke said. 'I would not have pushed myself that hard normally – I'm not that mentally strong – but it was the last lap of an Olympic Games. That was all I could think about.'

Corrigan probably saved Clarke's life, and he recovered sufficiently to play a cautious, supporting role in the 5000 metres, but he was nowhere near the Olympic medals again. He never ran as well and struggled to be extraordinary any more.

When he broke down in training he needed walking sticks to get his legs moving again. After a lap or so they would warm up again and he would discard the props. Before and after every race, he would be in agony until he finally retired in 1970, with no gold medals but with 18 world records, more than almost any man in history other than Zátopek. Later Clarke found that he had damaged a heart valve in Mexico City and would be plagued by health problems for the rest of his life, reclaimed for the ordinary.

Back in 1966, with the wind blowing down the Prague runway and Zátopek holding his overcoat firmly against himself, both men sensed something bad was in the ether. Zátopek said goodbye and, as he shook Clarke's hand, he smuggled a small brown paper package into his grasp. 'You deserve this,' he said, and then he began to leave.

Clarke looked at his package, clumsily tied together with old, yellow string, and thought, 'He wraps presents like I do.'

'Thanks, Emil,' he said.

He was seated in the first row and looked out of the window again, a portal into another age and another world, the golden era of the 1950s and the mysteries of the Iron Curtain. 'What the hell is this?' he thought, as he felt the package in his pocket. He told himself he would plead ignorance if the customs people found it on him, but he wondered just what he was being asked to courier away from Czechoslovakia.

As the plane neared Heathrow, the co-pilot clicked on his radio and warned of turbulence. There would be a delay in landing, and finally Clarke's curiosity got the better of him. He pulled out the package and began to unwrap it. To his amazement it was an Olympic gold medal. There was a scrap of paper underneath that simply read:

Emil Zátopek, 19 July 1966.

Emil knew inside that Ron could not win in Mexico, and this was his compensation: a medal won not in one race but through the admiration of another created by a lifetime's work. In some ways, it meant more to get a gold that way.

Zátopek and Clarke both knew that the rarefied air would smother the life from the fading trail of an Olympic dream. What they did not know was that these two pre-eminent figures of post-war endurance running would both suffer such savage fates at the time of the 1968 Olympics. Clarke would collapse and suffer health problems for the rest of his life until he died, shortly after our interview in 2015. Zátopek's fate would be much worse.

2

Emil the Wimp

Usain Bolt may have redefined the parameters of human possibility with his record-breaking madness, but science is not easily seduced, and raises one pertinent question: why are we so obsessed with a man who cannot beat a squirrel?

Daniel Lieberman, a professor of human evolutionary biology at Harvard University, is not one of those blown away by Bolt's munificence. Instead, he points out that, in relative terms, the Jamaican's feats are utterly pedestrian, whereas elite endurance runners are truly incredible.

'The maximum sprinting speed of Bolt is around ten metres per second, which is well below the maximum galloping speed of most mammals,' Lieberman said of the Jamaican sprint star. 'Bolt would be beaten by any dog, or even a squirrel. A lion could go twice as fast for much longer. We suck. The truth is, as sprinters, man is pathetic. We did not evolve to do it. We were hunters and so what makes us special is our ability to run long distances.'

By contrast with Bolt, elite marathon runners run at a pace of up to six metres per second for 26.2 miles. Lieberman pointed out in his paper, *The Evolution of Marathon Running*, written with Dennis Bramble, that this meant that, over long distances, man could outrun all mammals, even horses.

This is partly down to our ability to keep cool. Most mammals slow down after short distances because they rely on panting as a cooling mechanism, and that interferes with respiration. By contrast, we have become what Lieberman terms 'specialized sweaters', meaning we can get rid of heat via a higher density of sweat glands.

The upshot of all this is that endurance runners are true masters of the universe, whereas sprinters are abject failures.

Emil Zátopek is probably the greatest of these masters, but the first were the Finns. When Zátopek emerged on the international scene, Finland had won five of the last six Olympic gold medals in both the 5000 and 10,000 metres. It was a curious phenomenon. In the early 20th century running was deemed an ungentlemanly pursuit, even lazy, as it involved the use of labour that could be put to more practical uses. For these reasons the first big names of distance running, the Kolehmainen brothers, would turn training into a clandestine affair and would work out at night in overcoats. That all changed in 1912 when Johannes, a vegetarian bricklayer, went to the Olympic Games in Stockholm and won three gold medals. That he expressed his anger at hearing the Russian national anthem played in his honour only made him more popular at home. When Finland finally gained independence from Russia in 1917, 'Hannes' became a totem for national pride, the very embodiment of Finnish *sisu*, loosely meaning guts and spirit, even when he moved to the USA and competed under the winged fist of the Irish-American Athletic Club. In his review of the 1912 Olympics, James E. Sullivan, the outspoken former secretary of the United States Olympic Committee, wrote, 'I have been an official at five Olympic Games since their revival in 1896 and I have seen all the great distance runners from America and Europe, but never have I had the pleasure of seeing such a phenomenal piece of human machinery.'

Sullivan may have been biased, having suggested England would become 'athletically degenerate' after griping his way through the 1908 London Olympics, but there was no debate about Kolehmainen's successor.

Paavo Nurmi was the son of a carpenter who suffered from a weak heart and died young, leaving his teenage heir to grow up fast. Kolehmainen's success had inspired a generation of Finnish boys to run, and Nurmi committed himself to a monastic regime. He joined this throng and then joined the army, where he confounded his commanders with the speed with which he completed a 20-kilometre march while clad in full combat gear, complete with a 30lb backpack. The following year, 1920, he went to the Olympic Games in Antwerp and duly won the first of nine gold medals. His 10,000 metres rival, Joseph Guillemot, of France, had just finished his lunch because he was unaware that the King of Belgium had requested an earlier starting time for the final so that he could attend an arts function. No sooner had he crossed the line behind Nurmi than he vomited on the winner's shoes.

Throughout his life and career, Nurmi's achievements would also be besmirched by critiques of his personality. The 'Stoneface' moniker was well-suited and, in 1924, the French journalist Gabriel Hanot wrote, 'He is ever more serious, reserved, concentrated, pessimistic, fanatic. There is such coldness in him and his self-control is so great that never for a moment does he show his true feelings.'

Yet he did embrace fame and went on a lucrative tour of the USA, where the media loved his mystique and painted him as a figure cut from folklore. Contenders had to be found to be beaten. On one dramatic occasion Nurmi was taken to Los Angeles to take on eight Hopi Indians. *The Real American* newspaper remarked on his 'stolid' features as it gave him top billing in its edition of 1 May 1925, flanked by Sitting Bull's Indian Smoke column: 'Paavo Nurmi, the famous Finn whose frail legs and stout heart have made him the most talked about athletic figure in the world today, thrilled a crowd of more than 45,000 persons at the Coliseum last Saturday in the greatest track and field meet ever staged in America.'

By that time Nurmi was acclaimed as the biggest star in sport. His refusal to give interviews only led to a melting pot of myth and gossip, but it was the 1924 season that truly cemented reality into rock-solid legend.

Nurmi was now the best runner at every distance, from 1500 to 10,000 metres. He was an irresistible metronome, winning each race by running even pace, regardless of the situation, nonchalantly ignoring all rivals and only glancing at the watch he held in his hand. This unique signature would end with him hurling the watch into the infield as he sped to the line on the last lap.

Olympic chiefs were concerned that his dominance would devalue the Games and turn the global celebration into a one-man exhibition. Thus, they scheduled the 1500 and 5000 metres finals just 55 minutes apart. Nurmi was nonplussed and, three weeks before the 1924 Olympic Games, embarked on a trial run in Helsinki. He started the 1500 metres at a ferocious pace and duly broke his own world record with a time of 3 minutes 52.6 seconds. Fifty-five minutes later he returned for the 5000 metres. To the astonishment of all watching, he set a second world record in a shade over an hour, clocking 14 minutes 28.2 seconds. These feats were made more remarkable by the fact he had seriously injured a knee in a fall that Easter. He had still been suffering with it when the Olympic trials were held and Ville Ritola had set a new world record in the 10,000 metres. Ritola was one of 20 children and had emigrated to America when he was 17. Now the Finnish officials decided not to risk a confrontation between their two stars on the first day of the Olympics and so only Ritola was entered for the 10,000 metres, leaving Nurmi to remain fresh for the shorter distances. For Nurmi this was nothing less than a betrayal and, beneath that stone face, his emotions boiled and bubbled towards a cathartic revenge.

Ritola duly won the 10,000 metres in a world record time of 30 minutes 23.2 seconds. Such was Nurmi's anger at his snub that he was said to be running a 10,000 metres of his own, alone on a training track, at the same time. Legend has it that he completed it in 29 minutes 58 seconds.

That was not enough for him and he needed the public to see who was best too. Four days later his chance came. First, he won the 1500 metres. It was no contest as he held his stopwatch until the last rival had been vanquished and then tossed it away. As the crowd celebrated his Olympic record, he calmly picked up his watch and disappeared to prepare for the long-awaited 5000 metres and his duel with Ritola. It was an enthralling battle. The field, including a certain Herbert 'Johnny' Johnston, from Britain, had decided to start at a gallop to take advantage of Nurmi's perceived tiredness. Finishing times for races generally plummet with the passing of years, so it was a sign of true speed that the first 1000 metres were covered at the same pace as the 1972 Olympic final. Nurmi hung on. And then he shed the race of its bit-part players and he and Ritola took centre stage. Nurmi led throughout those latter stages, but Ritola was his shadow. On the final lap, stopwatch finally discarded, Nurmi dredged his anger for more fuel. Ritola tried to pass him just 30 yards from the tape, but Nurmi held firm and won.

Ironically, it was only Nurmi, after winning five Olympic golds in 1924, who met film stars and was fêted in America. He had his photograph taken with Mary Pickford, the Hollywood siren, and was courted by media barons. Ritola, who had actually lived in America for seven years and had won a staggering six medals at the Paris Olympics, went back to working on construction sites.

Each man would beat the other at the 1928 Olympics in Amsterdam, Ritola taking the 5000 metres gold and Nurmi winning the 10,000 metres, but history has polarised their achievements.

What is unarguable is that these Flying Finns were part of a cultural phenomenon. According to Jack Schumacher, a 1930s German writer, 'Nurmi and those like him are animals in the forest. They began to run because of a profound compulsion, because a strange dreamlike landscape called them with its enchanting mysteries. Their awe-inspiring times are a way of giving thanks to Mother Earth.'

An overblown appraisal, perhaps, but it is one that hints at the mythology that began to swathe Finnish running in the 1920s and 1930s. Indeed, in his book *Running*, the Norwegian folklorist Thor Gotaas points out that between 1912 and 1940, the Finns set more than 70 world records at distances beyond 1500 metres. But Ritola went back to manual labour and Nurmi was banned by the IAAF (athletics' governing body) over allegations of professionalism. The Finnish Athletics Federation investigated and said that there was no evidence 'of "padded expense accounts" relating to races in Poland, Italy and Germany', but the IAAF disagreed. In truth, they were right. Athletics would not officially go professional until 1982, but promoters had long been finding ways to circumvent athletics' amateur status to entice the best to their meetings. The conflict meant Nurmi did not get the chance to end an unprecedented Olympic career by following in the 40,000 footsteps of Hannes Kolehmainen, who had signed off with a gold medal in the marathon in 1920. Nevertheless, Finland was the centre of the running universe. Who, on earth, could stop these superhuman Flying Finns?

***

The boy standing by while his brother ran away in a wheat field did not seem a likely usurper. Emil was one of seven children and his brother Bohus was deemed the best runner when it came to escaping from their father, František, a struggling carpenter. František did not rule his household with a rod of iron so much as a 12-inch carpenter's ruler. Previously, he had used his belt to issue beatings, but his wife, Anežka, had burnt it in an attempt to save her sons. 'When Father called us from the courtyard we knew our escape was over,' Zátopek recalled in the book *Dana a Emil Zátopkovi vypravují* (*I Declared*): 'One after another we had to go there and offer our hands, and when Father started hitting we would all shout and scream and jump about. The worst thing of all was that, at these executions, the little boys and girls of the neighbourhood rushed out and for us it was terribly shameful to cry in front of these spectators.'

Bohus decided he had suffered enough that day and took off, pursued by František and assorted voyeurs. They could see the raised arm edging through the wheat field that lay adjacent to the house in Kopřivnice, a small town in the Moravian-Silesian region of Czechoslovakia. Just in front of František the wheat swayed with the unseen movements of the desperate Bohus. It was, perhaps, the first race of the Zátopek family: father versus son, with blood, sweat and tears at stake. Ultimately, František tripped over a large rock and fell, allowing the shifting wheat to usher in Bohus' victory. As the father made his way back to his house, the neighbours watching and pointing, a woman approached him with a wry smile. 'Well then, Mr Zátopek,' she said. 'Who won?'

Emil developed a different tactic based on evasion rather than escape. Hence, he kept his distance and, whenever his father shouted 'Emil' and he had to make his way to the courtyard, he gave in to a fit of histrionics. The shouts and screams would spring the neighbours from their daily routines, and they would round on František and tell him not to beat his boy so savagely. František tried to explain that Emil was faking it – exaggerating for the very purpose of eliciting sympathy – but it was to no avail. Emil got away with a couple of symbolic swipes on the bottom. The only downside was the children in the neighbourhood began to refer to him as 'Emil the Wimp'. Time-travellers seeking prescient landmarks on the road to international fame and a dominant role in Czech history would have been frustrated.

Emil was born on 19 September 1922 in a house in Kopřivnice. His mother was so poor that, when she was pregnant with him, she asked her doctor for financial help. He refused, saying he could be struck off. Instead, he offered her some rudimentary medical advice to make the baby come, which was to jump off the kitchen table. Emil would tell that story for ever.

In 2015 I visited the town for memories. I went to the Technical Museum, where there is a small exhibition on Zátopek, and was directed to a black and white barn, a mile up the road. I had paid 700 Czech koruna (about £18) to see a private Zátopek archive, but after making my way through a potpourri of deer heads, folk instruments and farming relics, I found a balding man in shorts who told me he had only ten minutes. He dumped a file of Czech newspaper cuttings on the table and set his watch.

Despite his unhelpfulness, I gave him a lift to the foot of the street where Zátopek was born. He bade me a fonder farewell than our fruitless meeting had merited and went to pick up his daughter from school. I looked around. Kopřivnice is an industrial town, best known for tractors but also for producing bricks and steel. The landscape was pockmarked by bright-coloured concrete blocks, like a Communist Legoland, but an air of ennui and jaded hope lingered. I found Zátopek's old house. It was small and attractive, with an orange slate roof, white pebbledash and two brown-framed windows parted by a small, gold plaque

V tomto dome se narodil a žil
EMIL ZÁTOPEK
+19.9.1922 – 21.11.2000
Čtyřnásobný olympijský vítěz
Ve vytrvalostním běhu

Občané čtvrti Luhy

I looked for the wheat field, but it must have been built over long ago. The Czechoslovakia that Zátopek grew up in went through at least two revolutions. The vista would change beyond all recognition and Zátopek would be there, with a box seat in the vanguard of change, redefining sport and even nationalism before juddering clashes between the personal and the political. In this house, then, empty now as evinced by the letters piling up inside the door and contrary to the claims of the museum man who said a niece still lived there, a private revolution began its slow-burning arc.

In his early years Emil the Wimp showed few signs of what lay ahead. His father would introduce him to guests as 'the last arrival', although another brother, Jirik, was later born. He attended athletics sessions where the register would be a source of rich amusement.

'Zátopek?'

'Present.'

'Zátopek younger?'

'Present.'

'Zátopek younger still.'

'Present.'

'Zátopek the youngest.'

'Present,' Emil replied, although Franta, another brother, reminded Comrade Hornicek that the clan had another member at home.

'Then bring him too – the more the merrier,' the trainer replied. And so Jirik began training before he went to school.

This was the time of Sokol. Meaning 'Falcon', Sokol was a sports organisation set up by a Czech art historian who had fought on the Prague streets during the 1848 revolution and boasted of taking a bullet in his cap. These were largely sport and gymnastic groups designed to promote democracy and Czech nationalism. They would hold mass competitions known as *slets* and, despite being disbanded during the First World War, had close to 700,000 members by the time Emil Zátopek was a teenager. Ironically, the Czech Sokol system put emphasis on grace and decoration, rather than the disciplined repetition that was the trademark of the German version – qualities that would be distinctly lacking from the running style of Zátopek. As Red Smith, the great American sportswriter, would put it, 'He ran like a man with his noose around his neck, the most frightful horror spectacle since Frankenstein, on the verge of strangulation.'

Zátopek and his brothers – only one of whom would survive until his 18th birthday in those hard times of high mortality rates – would marvel at the great circus artists of Sokol and would try to copy their elaborate movements, often in rivers and streams, the water cushioning their falls. However, when he was only eight, Zátopek had to spend a month in hospital after a serious bowel operation. When he emerged he threw himself back into football, later admitting that his high-energy performances were forged from a need to prove himself fit and able. 'I cultivated some quality good for future competitions,' he said, but if team-mates would say, 'Emil is everywhere,' they would temper their appreciation of his ubiquity with an acknowledgment that he was no footballer. 'Because of all that running around they put me in attack in my class team,' he said. 'I ran obstinately the whole match but I never scored a goal.'

Running without frills would become his métier. The date of his very first race is a subject of conjecture. His friend and peer, Jindřich Roudný, said Zátopek told him it was in a cross-country race. His Communist biographer from the 1950s, František Kožik, said it came aged ten, when a bunch of Kopřivnice youths decided to run around the block. In the guise of a yesteryear Forrest Gump, Zátopek completed the first lap in the lead, but kept on running, rounding the block for a second and third time before collapsing on the grass and having his forehead wiped by the bemused and beaten. There was also another race that came from a challenge from a friend named Gal, the best runner in the street behind the white house with the orange roof. Gal won the race to an oak tree and back, but it was close and Gal was several years older.

However, the race that forms the genesis of the Zátopek legend happened on 15 May 1941 when he had moved to Zlín to take a job working at the Bata shoe factory. As Zátopek put it: 'The childhood games ended for me when I was 14 and I finished school. I had to find a job, not an easy thing in those days.' In the end a family friend visiting from Zlín told him that he could sit exams in Zlín and get a job at the Bata company. And so his father took him to the station and within a couple of hours he was 200 kilometres away from home. The new surroundings fascinated and terrified the teenager: 'There were modern buildings everywhere, a fantastic organisation and a rigid regime I wasn't used to.' The rules were so strict for interns that an unmade bed or toothbrush placed the wrong way up in a glass produced severe consequences.

The Bata story itself is worthy of a book. Founded by Tomáš Bat'a in Zlín, a small factory with ten employees grew into a multi-national phenomenon which soon had 300 Bata shops in America, 1000 in Asia and 4000 in Europe. Innovative mechanised productions lines fuelled the growth, but in 1932 Tomáš died in a plane crash close to Zlín. The business passed to his half-brother, Jan. The success continued, but it was marred by controversy and the nods and winks of suspicion. Deals with Mussolini and the presence of a slave-labour camp at Chełmek, where Auschwitz Jews were made to clean a swamp for the benefit of the Bata factory, helped tarnish the name. However, these events are at odds with the role Jan Bat'a played in relocating thousands of Jewish employees around the world when the Holocaust began. Indeed, documentation shows that Bat'a set up the Kotva company and used it as a front to relocate employees. One of those owing his life to his good deeds was the British playwright Tom Stoppard, who was relocated to Singapore when a toddler on the same day that the Nazis invaded Czechoslovakia in 1939.

Bat'a had tried to appease the Nazis, even meeting Hermann Göring, one of Hitler's right-hand men, in Berlin. Göring flattered Bat'a and suggested he would be a fitting man to lead the Czech nation after President Beneš' resignation. However, it is clear Bat'a was playing a very dangerous game with the Nazis, and his own family was placed under house arrest in March 1939. His wife, son and youngest daughter fled by car through Slovakia months later. Bata employees helped smuggle his other daughter into unoccupied Europe via train. Yet in 1941 Jan Bat'a was blacklisted by Britain and America for cutting deals with the Axis powers and fled to Brazil. He was tried *in absentia* and sentenced to 15 years in prison for failing to support the anti-Nazi movement.

In May of that year, against this backdrop of pervading doom and debated heroism, the teenage Emil Zátopek lined up for his first true race. He had not wanted to run, although he had been an active child. The story goes that his mother remarked on the problems in fattening their geese because they would meet Emil on his way home from school and he would run them ragged around the fields. His father shared the views of the Finns in the Kolehmainen era, that running was evidence of a lazy spirit. 'Sport is an unnecessary time-waster,' he told his son. 'If you've got nothing to do, go and fetch catkins for my bees.'

The spring race through the streets of Zlín was a PR stunt dreamed up by the factory directors, with the runners wearing the Bata logo on their vests. 'I don't know why but our manager gathered the whole team together and ordered all those who were not sick to run.' Zátopek was working in the technical school at first and hopeful of gaining a job in the shoe factory. He stayed in one of the company hostels where he was told he must run in Sunday's race. Zátopek was slow to warm to the lure of factory-organised sport and feigned a knee injury, but when a doctor declared him fit, he had no choice. His manager was furious at his unwillingness, but Zátopek was equally annoyed.

He tried to fade away. First he sloped into a reading room, but his friends found him and reminded him that protesting might harm his prospects within the company. And so, on 15 May 1941, Zátopek, aged 18, stood at the start with around a hundred other boys. His old biographer, Kožik, suggests it was the mantra of his father – 'a thing worth doing is worth doing well' – that drove him on that day. That seems highly unlikely, given that his father later sent him a telegram warning him to cease running or risk damaging his health.

Emil was uninhibited when running, though, and moved naturally, with an ugly rolling gait and flailing arms, tongue lolling, face contorted. He was also fast. He ran from the bunch and forged ahead, impressing the streets throbbing with workers. After a kilometre only a man named Honza Krupička was ahead of him. He caught him and they ran alongside each other as the spectators cheered. Zátopek liked that but, as he smiled, Krupička took off. Try as he might, Emil could not cross the gap and came home second. His manager basked in the appropriated glory and told anyone who would listen that he trained champions. Zátopek was more phlegmatic. 'But I didn't win,' he protested.

Krupička told him that he must keep training. 'You're a born runner, Emil,' he said. Zátopek was less impressed and said it was a one-off, but, having been dubbed Emil the Wimp at home, he must have enjoyed the kudos. He had a fountain-pen for his trouble and had blown his cover. His manager carried on with his dreary monologue. 'Next week we'll need you for the relay team,' he said. Like it or not, the die was cast.

While his country hurtled towards calamity, Zátopek began his athletics career in tandem with his work. He started out corrugating the stuck-on rubber soles with a cog-wheel. He would work for eight hours a day at 'the circle' followed by four hours of evening classes. Then the factory was taken over by the Germans and the focus shifted to footwear for the military. Instead of turning out 2200 pairs of tennis shoes a day, the workshop became a cog in the Nazi wheel of industry.

Zátopek and his friends thus found themselves unable to get hold of running shoes. Instead, they would pick up discarded boots that had leather inners missing and nails protruding from them. This meant they hurt, but at least they provided some grip in the winter months when the soil was frozen. On one such training run, Zátopek scraped his right instep with his left boot. The wound festered and became infected. It led to a long spell in hospital and a temporary end to his running. It made him realise how much he actually liked it.

When he finally did return, he joined up with his friends and faced another problem. Jindřich Roudný, his peer and later a European steeplechase champion, recalled an incident that told of his idiosyncrasies. 'We went together to run in the surrounding woods beyond the boarding school. There was a fenced garden that we had to run around, in which a huge German Shepherd was on permanent patrol. Like all dogs, he hated it when someone ran and he would begin barking furiously and showing his teeth as he ran at the fence. We were very afraid that he would jump over it because it was only about two metres high, so we tried walking slowly, but he was allergic to us and nothing worked.

'When Emil returned from hospital, he had to start very slowly, and so he joined us. When he first walked past the fence the dog started to act up again. We continued walking away, but Emil didn't follow us and went directly to the fence. With horror we expected the worst. The dog was hysterical. Then, Emil stood quietly and calmly peed on the dog's nose. The dog just whined, put his tail between his legs and dragged himself, whimpering, back into the shed. Emil turned around, smiled and said, "Now he knows whose territory it is." The dog never troubled us again after that.'

Another shaggy dog story: Emil loved nature and would run in the forest for hours. He developed favourite routes, but one day, as a prank, a colleague dropped his shorts and defecated on the trail. Soon after, Zátopek arrived and almost jumped out of his skin. The memory irked him so much that he changed his route, but he was not about to let the slight go unavenged. And so, after finding out who had done it, he surreptitiously slipped a frozen piece of dog dirt into his peer's rucksack. That night, on the bus trip home, the heating had worked its malodorous mischief. His friend doubled up. Zátopek smiled at revenge served cold.

Zátopek had a talent for chemistry and would conduct his own experiments. He became renowned for a special concoction of lemon juice and chalk. He told Roudný that Vitamin C, alone, takes calcium from the teeth. So he made a toothpick from a coat-hanger and, from a kilo bag, added minute doses of chalk. He said teeth saturated in his solution would prevent decay. His peers thought it sounded unlikely but gave it a go. Emil also stressed the need to drink properly and to take extra minerals. He used magnesium and said carbon dioxide neutralised fatigue. He told them that he had graduated from high school with honours in chemistry and recommended they drink three bottles of Luhačovice's (heavily mineralised) Vincentka water a day.

'As the war went on the diet was getting worse,' Roudný said. 'We had a motto – "Don't care about quality, we want quantity." The food we could get was poor in fat, vitamins, sugars and so on. Emil pioneered the idea that we needed to eat much larger helpings to get the elements necessary for energy. We stole raw potatoes from the canteen because they contained starch, and Emil said that was important in changing into sugar.'

Zátopek also noticed that the administrator would send his maid to the canteen to get food for his dog named Sony. Hence, Zátopek got there first on several occasions, brandishing a mess tin and telling the chef, 'For Sony.'

The quest for food even extended to his love life. After a date with the prettiest girl in his section, whose father happened to run a butcher's shop, Emil told Roudný that the night had ended on a sour note. 'She wanted to kiss but she didn't bring a piece of sausage,' he griped.

They were not on the breadline, but Bata was not the answer to their prayers. All Bata employees had their earnings documented in a yearbook with the aim of saving 10,000 Czech koruna within four years. Those in charge of distributing wages were strict. Roudný explained: 'There were situations where a young man asked for permission to buy a wedding shirt, or a worker in machinery asked for a slide rule, and they were denied. As a result we tried to cheat on our payslips as much as we could.'

Despite the war it was a simple enough time, until 1942 when life in Czechoslovakia shifted to a new, less innocent plain. Finding himself bereft of sympathetic neighbours, President Beneš had resigned in 1938 and the German Protectorate of Bohemia and Moravia was created. Beneš then led the Czech Government-in-exile in London, officially recognised by Britain and then the USA and the Soviet Union. However, months after Stalin sided with Beneš, Hitler made a move that would have horrific implications for the Czech nation when he appointed Reinhard Heydrich as *Reichsprotektor* of Bohemia and Moravia.

3

Ali

The mass killings began in 1942. Reinhard Heydrich was among the most amoral killers in Hitler's army and had been given the responsibility of finding the Final Solution to the Jewish problem. However, with it looking as though the Allies might be close to winning the war, the exiled Czech president sought a single, dramatic act to show solidarity. The outcome of this search for a grandstanding act to safeguard the future was Operation Anthropoid, a plot to assassinate Heydrich. A Czech, Jan Kubiš, and a Slovak, Jozef Gabčik, were selected to shoot the *Reichsprotektor* as he made his daily journey to Prague Castle. The assassination was a botched affair, with Gabčik standing in the road with a jammed sub-machine gun and Kubiš throwing a grenade that only caught the back wheel of Heydrich's car. The Nazi leader was able to return fire with his Luger pistol but had suffered injuries that led to complications from which he later died.

When news reached Beneš he denied involvement but still sought credit. However, the repercussions were beyond even his worst nightmares. All Czechs aged over 15 were forced to register with the police. Failure to do so would result in death by firing squad. A million marks reward was offered for the capture of the assassins. They were still at large when, the day after the funeral in Berlin, the Gestapo stormed into Lidice, to the north-west of

Prague, erroneously believing the assassins were linked to the village. They then shot 173 men and took 196 women to a concentration camp. Eighty-eight children were gassed and the village was burnt to the ground.

Finally, a Czech paratrooper took the million marks and betrayed the plotters. The Gestapo raided the flat of the Moravec family in Žižkov. A 17-year-old boy named Ata was stupefied with brandy, tortured and shown his mother's severed head in a fish tank. Finally, he cracked, leading to the dramatic denouement in the cathedral of Saint Cyril and Methodius in Prague in which Kubiš was killed in the prayer loft and Gabčik committed suicide in the crypt. In the aftermath Nazi persecution escalated further, and it was not hard to see why the likes of Zátopek would grow up to be both Communists and staunch nationalists.

Jan Haluza was born in 1914 in Sternov. His father was a mason who had eight children. Jan completed his law studies at Masaryk University in Brno days before the Nazi occupation. The Germans immediately closed the university. 'It was during the Protectorate and there were lawyers everywhere,' he said. 'Nobody wanted a lawyer and so I was unemployed. My father was worried that I was a university graduate and couldn't find work, so I told him I will apply at the construction site in Brno. I was the only graduate there but there were about 200 people that couldn't finish their studies because Hitler had closed all the universities.'

His working life had been troubled. A job as a German teacher and working in the gym at Archbishop Grammar School in Prague ended when the Nazis also closed that in the wake of the assassination of Heydrich.

'It began the Zlín chapter of my life,' he would recall. 'They offered me a place in the inspection department of the Bata factories, which I then had the honour of representing at sport.'

He was good if not great. A committed member of Orel, the sports movement that had Christianity, patriotism and culture at its heart, he won national championships and was named athlete of the year in 1942 by Czech reporters. He also got married to Věra. Life looked good. It was also in Zlín, while working for Bata's stock company, Kotva, that he competed for SK Bata and first came across a dog-bothering runner with an eye-catchingly eccentric style.

Haluza was a small-scale star in Zlín. His name was often in the Monday morning papers. 'Every boy in Zlín recognised him and he was very popular,' František Kožik would write. Tall, with matching high cheekbones, he had Aryan good looks and swept-back blond locks. He was a deep-thinker and had already developed links with the Czechoslovakian People's Party via his association with Orel. Like Sokol, Orel was banned during the war due to the belief it fuelled patriotism. Members were imprisoned and even executed as the Nazis took a stranglehold on the social and cultural lives of the cuckolded Czechs. Haluza, though, was asked to train some of the Bata boys and obliged.

It was a friend named Štěpán Hrstka who alerted Haluza to Zátopek after that fabled race around the Zlín streets in 1941. He told Haluza, 'A boy came to the start and he ran as if he was crazy; he is from some village somewhere; take a look at him.'

Haluza did. 'If you would like to, come to the stadium tomorrow evening,' he told Zátopek. 'We can train together.' Zátopek jumped at the chance to train with a man who was already a champion at 1500 and 3000 metres. Haluza had a natural kindness that drew the young man to him. 'Today the race track seemed like a festive carpet,' Kožik said of their first training session. Haluza stared at his stopwatch but did not tell Emil his times. That confused the rookie runner, who assumed he had done badly. He went back to cutting up strips of cellulose in the factory and reasoned his career was over before it had really begun. And then the phone rang and Haluza's cheerful voice asked him how he had slept and what he had eaten for breakfast. The words, 'I've been thinking about you,' were enough to forge a bond. Haluza's interest showed a natural paternalism, exposing something missing from his own childhood. When Haluza rang Zátopek to ask how he slept and extolled the virtues of sleep as a key component of the athlete's armory, the apprentice was seduced by the level of interest.

Haluza's nickname was Ali, and Zátopek was soon using it. At the time Zátopek's best time for the 1500 metres was a mere 4 minutes 20 seconds. However, under Haluza's tutelage, he made steady progress as they worked on the Zlín track, swathed in smoke and soot from the adjacent heating plant. It was far from an ideal facility on which to forge an Olympic dream, but fitted with his day job where he now breathed in silica dust in the research institute.

'Emil did not have much lust for racing to start with and saw his future in the chemistry lab,' Haluza said. 'But I quickly managed to awake a militancy in him. He came to the track as soon as he had finished a tough job, and it was a pleasure to work with him. He never lost his optimism and was always cheerful and honest. The big problem, however, was a lack of food. I often felt sorry for the boy when he begged, exhausted, for the last piece of bread and I could not give it to him. Everything was on ration cards. It was hard to get shoes for him so that he did not destroy his feet.'

František Kožik recalled a 1500 metres race run in nearby Batov in 1942 when Ali won in a time of 4 minutes 14.2 seconds. Zátopek was a mere two-tenths of a second behind. He was only 19 and catching a seasoned winner.

Some people criticised Zátopek for only entering races in which Ali was also running. 'You'll always come second if you compete with him,' they said. Zátopek was nonplussed. He was learning. Haluza was different, more spiritual than most people he met in the factory. Indeed, Haluza's own mentor was a priest named Prevovsky, who had recruited a raft of clergymen from around Zlín and got them jobs at Bata, thus evading the Gestapo and the concentration camps.

Much later in his life, Emil would say there would be no Zátopek without Haluza. Ali was the first person to embrace his talent and work to nurture it rather than neuter it. The duo formed part of a Zlín 4 x 1500 metres relay team and set a new national record. Then Zátopek went to Prague for his first national championship. Ali was the winner and Zátopek was fifth in a time of 4 minutes 13.9 seconds, well ahead of a man named Václav Čevona, who would run 20 seconds faster when he made it to the Olympic Games in 1948.

Zátopek also improved. He was clearly an innovator and brought a semi-scientific approach to his training. His use of interval training would become renowned, but Roudný says the Swedish Fartlek system, by which faster and short sections were intertwined in the same run, was a secret until 1948. Zátopek was developing his own form of this in isolation.

Over in Britain, from the Achilles Club at Oxford to their privileged upper-class peers at Cambridge, men like Roger Bannister and Chris Chataway held a snobbish disdain for training too hard. Rest was considered far more important and certainly more gentlemanly. In some ways they were the descendants of the dyed-in-the-wool Finns who forced Olympic heroes into long overcoats and nighttime excursions.

Zátopek, though, felt he needed speed more than endurance and so would run harder and faster for as long as possible. Merely jogging interminably was not helping. Inevitably, his methods were frowned upon and even mocked, driving him increasingly to run alone. He also grew frustrated that he had not yet won a race. 'Dr Haluza taught me many useful things,' Zátopek said. 'But my improvements were never enough to win. Years passed and I still didn't know what victory meant; boys started to call me "Emil the Second".'

However, his ascent was underway if not bound to an inexorable course. A milepost came in the autumn of 1943 when he competed in the Bohemia–Moravia match with a talented and established runner named Tomáš Sale. The pair entered the 1500 metres and Sale's reputation as a fast finisher preceded him. His rivals set off at a blistering pace – 'I had never been in such a savage race,' Zátopek recalled – and he dragged his reserves to stay in touch. He began the last lap in third place behind well-known runners named Dolensky and Fucikovsky. With each step Zátopek expected the thunderous steps of Sale's experience to pass him. With 200 metres left he threw caution to the wind and asked himself, 'What if I sprinted?' So he did. The fans in the grandstand saw the bolt for home and roared their approval. 'I cut for the winning tape. Late that night, coming home, I picked up the next morning's newspaper and it said "Zátopek – 1500 metres – 4.01". I liked that so much I read it over and over all night.'

Emil travelled to Prague in July 1944 and again lost to Václav Čevona over 1500 metres. 'If you had run the 5000 metres the championship would have been yours,' Čevona told him, but Zátopek was still loyal to Ali's advice. A few months later he lost to Čevona again in the Grand Prix of Přerov. Čevona won again but, in the space of two weeks, Zátopek had firmly proved that he was no mere provincial runner from a soot-doused track that was not even regulation length.

His speed training – repetitions of 10 x 100 metres, 10 x 200 metres and 6 x 400 metres – had given him a sense of belief. He asked a friend called Mirek Zdráhala to time him over 2000 metres. Inadvertently, Zátopek broke the Czech 2000 metres record in that training run, leaving Zdráhala staring at his watch in bemusement.

The president of his section at the factory had heard about his exploits and congratulated him. However, he said that for a record to be valid it had to be done in a race. 'Get ready for Saturday,' he added. 'We've announced an attempt on the 3000 metres record.'

Zátopek was annoyed by that because he was not convinced he could even run that far. Until now, his ability had been a private thing, shared only by a few people and his guide, Haluza. Now he was being billed as a show pony, with the beauty of running reduced to the prosaic target of 8 minutes 42 seconds.

Nevertheless, he turned up on the Saturday and marked off points on the track so he would have a better idea of his pace. Sale, now a firm friend, said he would shout out the split times, while a small bunch of cynical spectators watched from the grandstand. The run was a precursor to a familiar sight: a body contorted with pain, frantic movements seemingly betraying an inner fight, and the rocking head that made it look as if he was in desperate straits. Yet the time was 8 minutes 34.8 seconds. He had set a record, in Zlín, by the heating plant, on an oversized track. In *Dana a Emil Zátopkovi vypravují*, he said: 'I felt like a hero and they all wanted to congratulate me and give me prizes. No cups or trophies, though. Someone gave me two pears, another some bread and butter, a third some apples.'

The feat impressed the spectators but made only murmurs further afield. A week later Zátopek was back at the same venue at the behest of his club chiefs and watched by his friends from the laboratory. He took a huge 20 seconds off the Czech 5000 metres national record with his time of 14 minutes 54.9 seconds. His revolutionary method of preparing for long-distance races by focusing on sprint repetitions in the week beforehand was mystifying to many. So much so that Prague flatly refused to believe it. This sounded like a clerical error. Zlín was an industrial backwater, known only for shoes and Jan Bat'a's remarkable office, which was placed in a central elevator and could be transposed to any floor. It did not know about sport and athleticism.

Zátopek, then, found himself invited to Prague. It was not so much a celebration of his achievements as a search for proof. The cognoscenti simply did not believe his times. Zátopek was frustrated by this centralised supremacy but was pragmatic and proud enough to know he needed to silence the dissenters. So far his records had come from the wishes of his superiors. This one was for himself. He broke the 2000 metres in Prague in a time of 5 minutes 33.4 seconds and set tongues wagging and typewriters tapping. He had set three national records in less than a month.

Haluza knew he was no longer needed. Most record books state that Zátopek never had a coach, but that is not true. Haluza certainly helped him along the way in his early years, as Zátopek himself acknowledged.

Božetěch Kostelka, a friend of Haluza, explained: 'Zátopek was pretty quirky and very often did not let anybody advise him, but at the beginning there was a need to work on a number of things, mainly on breathing and technique. The key thing with him was his willpower. He was a child from the mountains.'

Zátopek clearly had the talent and imagination to develop on his own, but the role of Haluza in his learning years should not be underestimated. He encouraged, advised, cajoled, taught, mentored, criticised and nurtured one of the most singular talents sport has ever seen. 'At the stadium, they cared about me,' Zátopek said decades later. 'I got the tracksuit, the sneakers and I even got the instructor, who was a double winner of the Běchovice run. Dr Haluza trained me and I grew.'

Despite the horrors of Lidice and the disappearance of Jan Baťa, the Zlín workers become inured to the dangers of war. Zátopek crushed silicates in Building 56 while Roudný worked on the pneumatic machines in Building 67. Separated by only 100 metres, they would meet by the rail crossroads and wait for a truck to take them to the mountain suburb of Kudlov, two miles away. Wearing tracksuits under their work clothes, they would head straight for the small football stadium, stripping as they went.

They were well used to the sight and sounds of US aircraft overhead with their baritone hums. Whenever the alarm sounded the factory had to be evacuated, but sometimes they ignored the sirens altogether. On 20 November 1944 they pushed their luck a little far. 'That day, when we observed the "silver spoons" high above us. Something started to fall from them,' Roudný recalled. 'It began to whistle and we understood it was serious. We fled to the grandstand as the first bombs started to fall. They fell into the factory very close to us. They hit the power station. From a nearby garden, cabbages and other vegetables came flying at us. And then, in the stadium itself, two bombs exploded on the grass surface. When the raid passed, we looked at the mess with frightened eyes.'

All around Europe, the war was touching disparate lives that would become entangled in the years to come; distinct strands were being woven and left ready to be plaited in peacetime.

And so over in Britain, on the North Downs, on the southernmost part of London, where the city sprawl faded to lush green hills, a young Yorkshire-born boy named Gordon Pirie, with black hair and spidery limbs, saw the war as a huge adventure. When planes crashed, boys would flock to the scene, hopeful of stealing some memorabilia before the guards arrived. Once a Spitfire plummeted to the earth and destroyed the tennis courts some 50 yards from the air raid shelter where Pirie and his brothers were gathered, playing cards. On another occasion a V2 rocket struck a house near to one where Pirie lived in Meadway Street and killed the entire family. Pirie was only 13 when Zátopek was setting his Czech records, and although his father was a stalwart of the South London Harriers, he was more focused on exploiting the war for his own boyish fantasies than running. He collected bullets and bombs and hand grenades. When a flare descended into the Old Coulsdon Wood, Pirie and his friends chased after it. One boy helped himself to the parachute, another to the inflammable core, and Pirie took the timing fuse. The complicated figuration, with a red steel tube and two plungers, intrigued him. Alas, on this occasion the police caught up with the boys and they were herded off to Wallington Juvenile Court, where a kindly female magistrate took pity and let them off with a caution and 7 shillings costs. This was war. It was a time of excitement and, just as Zátopek and Roudný would run and look to the American bombers above, Pirie and his friends would often spot German fighters as they did their cross-country runs on the Downs.

In another part of southern England, Jim Peters was carrying on with his life. He had been born just days after the end of the First World War and was a sickly child who suffered from anaemia and was a regular visitor to hospital. On the advice of the family doctor, his parents moved from the cramped streets of Hackney to a new housing estate named Becontree, now part of Dagenham. Peters left school aged 15 and took a job as an office boy at a printers' and set a London Federation of Boys' Clubs record for the mile in 1936. Then, with the onset of war, he found himself on a train with 600 other teens heading for Boyce Barracks near Aldershot, now a number as well as a name: 7366379, Private J. Peters of the Royal Army Medical Corps. He noted the Battle of Dunkirk with some trepidation, and feared imminent invasion, but Peters had a gentle war. He had taken an apprenticeship with a firm of opticians before the fighting started and was now in charge of issuing Mark 3 steel-rimmed spectacles to more than 35,000 troops. 'There was nothing exciting and no feats of bravery about my job,' he would write in his book *In the Long Run*.

The contrast with another strand in the Zátopek story could not have been more marked. Ali Mimoun Ould Kacha had been born in French Algeria in 1921, the year before Zátopek. He later became known more simply as Alain Mimoun, a sign of his allegiance to France and De Gaulle as well as his desire to thrive in his adopted home. Yet, like many others would find, that idealism was undermined by an inherent racism in French society. Doors were closed and he was forced to live a peripheral existence, which is probably why he joined the French Foreign Legion after war broke out. His military exploits were far more exciting than anything the young Pirie or the sickly Peters could imagine. From the Maginot Line to the trench warfare of the Belgian front, Mimoun, an angular man with a small, thick moustache, fought for his country, whether they liked him or not. Conditions were so bad that he took clothes from prisoners as he spent nine months toiling against Rommel's troops in Tunisia. Yet there was an interlude that hinted at a different future. During a posting to the town of Bourg-en-Bresse, Mimoun had watched local runners circling a cinder track. Intrigued, he had taken off his thick army jacket and joined in – but an old man with a beard had accosted him after only a few laps. After a few admonishments for churning up the track with his thick army boots, the man, a Monsieur Vilar, said he would lend the soldier some cleats and a black vest. When Mimoun turned up for a race, in front of large weekend crowd, his triumph was met by huge cheers. *Le Progrès* paper even proclaimed him a 'born marathon runner'.

Yet those memories seemed like mirages when, in 1944, he found himself below a rocky hill, topped off by an abbey in which Saint Benedict had founded a monastic order in his name. The settlement was called Monte Cassino and it would be one of the most botched and bloodiest conflicts of the entire war. It began when Allied radio hams misinterpreted a message that confused the word 'abbot' with the German abbreviation for battalion. Given Monte Cassino's strategic location, dominating the road to Rome, and a previous agreement not to touch the sacred site, the Allies were furious enough to wage a relentless bombardment. More than 1000 tonnes of explosives were dropped on the abbey, destroying it and indiscriminately killing monks, women and children. Ironically, it was not until the abbey lay in ruins that the Germans approached it and set up camp, leading to four bloody battles and 75,000 casualties. One of them was Mimoun.

Blood streamed from his foot and he had shrapnel in his thigh and leg. He was slung in the back of the truck as a huge storm blew through the valley. US doctors looked at the ragged figure, bound up in dust and blood and shredded skin, and decided to amputate his leg, but a French medic stepped in and said it could be saved if they transferred him to a French hospital in Naples.

Hindsight would damn Monte Cassino as one of the most reckless campaigns of the war, a throwback to the wilful sacrifices made by absentee commanders in the First World War. An eyewitness described the lucky ones who survived: 'It was more than the stubble of beard that told the story; it was the blank, staring eyes of men so tired that it was a living death. They had come from such a depth of weariness that I wondered if they would quite be able to return to the lives and thoughts they had known.'

Mimoun was just another number. 'People don't know about Monte Cassino,' he said. 'They don't care. They kept the shrapnel in my body because it moves around for 25 days. It was hell but I was alive. It was fate.' A number with a saved leg thanks to that French medic, and although he later saw six friends blown to pieces, and he would recall how he wandered into the streets one night because of insomnia and saw women pushing carts full of dead children, he escaped from his personal apocalypse with a pain in his leg and a scarred mind. His athletics career, though, was surely over before it had begun.

All were touched by the war, some lightly, some brutally, but life went on. In Zlín, Roudný now lived in room Number 19 at the second Bata boarding school. A group of keen runners decided they should share their dormitory because of their unusual hours and regimes. There were three engineers, two hosiers, two shoemakers and a *gumar* (a man who worked with gum and rubber). This was the Zlín athletics team, bound together by nicknames ranging from 'Shrub' (Roudný) to 'Badger' (Zátopek), and under the stewardship of Rudolf Juranek, the section chairman who arranged inter-club races and promotional races in Moravia where, to the room-mates' delight, they were provided with a free lunch. Although Zátopek still, technically, lived in boarding house Number 5, his visits were so frequent that a bed was kept free for him. A communal diary was left on a table in which the runners penned slogans. A one-crown penalty for the use of bad language was imposed, causing a man named Tocan to ask if he could use the word '*sranda*', a colloquial word for fun derived from a vulgar expression. As it was slang and Tocan pleaded that it would be hard for him to not use it, the friends unanimously approved his request. The friends also wrote down their dreams for the future. One day Emil read some entries. '"The war will be over"; "the Olympic Games will take place again"; "it is possible that Emil will be one of the top runners. He could win 5km, perhaps the 10km, and what if he won the marathon?"' Emil turned away, embarrassed. 'I took these naïve ideas as a joke.'

He was a popular figure in this group. His running ability was a small part of it – Roudný was also remarkably talented – but it was his personality that bound the small band of brothers. Before they fell asleep at night, Zátopek would often recite poems, some of his own making and others that he had learnt such as Kipling's 'Mandalay'. He would tell stories with props, and loved to sing. He also seemed to have a penchant for mischief and calamity that enlivened monotonous factory days. After the winter bombing of Zlín in 1944, which meant there was no power for heating, Mr Juranek helped the young runners by providing them with a small heater, which they christened 'Pikolik', meaning bell-boy.

Roudný explained how they not only used this for cooking, but also upgraded it into a sauna. 'We laid logs between two beds,' he said. 'Then we sat on the beds and doused Pikolik with water. The stoves created a wet steam.' One day, Zátopek had started a fire and, when the men started adding water, the steam erupted into a geyser. Zátopek caught the brunt of it and jumped back, burning his genitals and then his back as he collided with a hot pipe. It took him several months to recover from his burns, but when he emerged from his hiatus he had a new way of training.

Roudný said: 'In the penultimate week before a big race, he would double the dose of mid-trotting. Then, in the final week, he would halve the dose and take a day's rest. By then he was already training alone because no one was as good as him. Even later, when he volunteered for military service and was in Uherské Hradiště [a small town on the Morava river], he trained by himself and so this method remained a secret, but it was so phenomenal that he began improving at record times and was in the perfect condition before races. Later, we discussed this kind of preparation with Václav Čevona and we decided Emil was transforming quantity into quality. We compared the human body to the battery, which runs down during training but is recharged overnight by rest, diet and sleep.'

It is clear that, even in the war years, long before the advent of sports science, Zátopek was using himself as a guinea pig for natural experiments. He was already aware of the importance of things like metabolism, fatty acids and hydrocarbons to his running. He deduced that the ratio between fatty acids and hydrocarbons shifted as he increased his training. More oxygen was needed and he reasoned he could get this from increasing his fatty-acid stores, which would then be metabolised into energy. It was a rudimentary grasp on physiology, long before it was an industry and vocation, and showed that he was far more than an instinctive runner who merely trained harder than the rest. According to Roudný, if Zátopek had not decided to finish training on Thursday, before a Sunday race, he would never have been at his peak because the battery would be dead and the fatty-acid reserves depleted.

He held other beliefs that were more philosophical. Zátopek told Roudný that a life of 'stereotypes', or routines, as we would interpret it, was good for the normal working person. However, he claimed it was anathema to the athlete and that 'stereotype is like poison'. Roudný recalled that his friend found an intriguing antidote and so, the night before a race, he would often go to a dance or simply get up and do something unusual: 'He called it an increase in hormone levels and this little thing pushed him a few more metres ahead of his opponents.'

For Zátopek the war ended on 2 May 1945, a few days after Hitler had killed himself and a few days before the military surrender was signed off in Reims and Europe celebrated VE Day. Kožik lauds the heroic Red Army troops for liberating Zlín on 2 May and paints a romantic hagiography of Zátopek as the conscience of a town hiding in cellars. Zátopek, himself, recalled the Germans burning documents so they could escape back 'to their native empire' like 'innocence personified'.

He walked from the sports ground as the earth shook with the last echoes of war. He saw lorry loads of fascists fleeing out of town by the graves of the newly fallen. Zátopek ran along a ditch by a stream to meet the first Red Army troops at the footbridge. 'Comrades, you are here at last,' he said. Zátopek picked up a shovel and helped dig trenches. The Germans still attacked the town from afar and Emil accompanied the soldiers to the town gates where the last bloody battle ensued, with mortar bombs and guns and a wounded man whom Zátopek tried to help amid the 'hell-fire'. The Russians were well-equipped and the Germans were fighting from memory. All hope had gone. The war was over and, as Kožik put it somewhat simplistically, 'life was suddenly much more beautiful'.

Zátopek confirmed that he gained so much pleasure from helping the artillery men dig their trenches that, within a week, he knew he wanted to join the army. Roudný said there was a more prosaic reason: 'He could get better food if he signed up.'

Older athletes tried to dissuade him. 'Don't talk rubbish,' one said. 'It will be the end of your sporting career. In the army nobody cares about results.'

Yet Zátopek felt not all at Bata cared deeply either. Once, he had asked for a Saturday off to run in Prague, and was reminded that he was not a young boy and that his mission was to be a chemist. Zátopek wanted to run now and the army could help him. 'I was grinding silicates in the research department where there was as much dust as around the grinding stone of a mill. The doctor scared me about silicosis and advised me to either stop running or change job.'

In this new state of rose-tinted bliss, Zátopek decided to become a soldier and help his new country take roots and grow. He would call it the 'best change of my life' and say that it allowed him to combine morning exercises, gymnastics, parades and runs in the fields. He also admitted that the food was, indeed, better.

But Zátopek did not enjoy an entirely blissful time in the army. During an inspection an army sergeant looked inside his trunk and was unimpressed by the cluttered assortment of athletics trophies. Eager to impress, Zátopek gave the trophies away, but at the next inspection was criticised for having a barren trunk and told to sit on it for 12 days as punishment.

His obvious talent also meant he became a plaything for the powers-that-be. In Vyškov, on training exercises, the commander called him in and said he needed a message delivering urgently to the garrison. Zátopek took the letter, put it inside his coat and ran seven kilometres through the fields to the garrison, whereupon the superintendent casually opened it and, without appearing to read the missive, told him to return immediately. 'Go back quickly and say all is OK,' he said. When Zátopek emerged through the final field, he noticed all the battalion's commanders waiting for him with interest. He wondered what was wrong. Then, his own commander appeared with a broad grin. 'You haven't disappointed me,' he said before explaining that the commanders had been betting on how long it would take him to run the 14 kilometres. The note had merely told the superintendent to send Zátopek back at once. 'Nobody believed me when I said you could run it in less than an hour,' his commander said. 'And you came back in 48 minutes. I'm proud of you.'

Without the threat of war and invasion, Europe was breathing a sigh of relief. Gordon Pirie was 14 years old and was training with South London Harriers at Coulsdon South Station, where the assorted athletes would fill tin baths with water and leave them on the stove to heat up while they went out to run. His school years were an academic waste. He admitted he would rather play table-tennis than study, and only a teacher's taunt that he might as well not sit his chemistry exam lit some competitive ire and propelled him to memorise formulae and gain a pass. Later, he would admit, 'We were always playing the field and laughing about crazy things. My school days were never serious enough.'

In another part of London Jim Peters was looking at his stomach. His war had ended early, with an early release number due to his length of service. He had arrived home in a civilian suit armed with only a cardboard box containing his possessions. He was married to Frieda and they had already shared the birth of a son and mourned his death. Now they were forced to live in a room at his mother-in-law's house. He had got his old job back, but moved to another firm of opticians and was now contemplating his future and his girth, with only one of them seeming in any way big at that point. He decided he needed to start training again, if only for his self-respect and physique. Frieda was against this, but she agreed to come and watch him in a three-mile race and thus see whether he was wasting their time or not. He clocked around 16 minutes for the distance and Frieda was unimpressed. 'Don't you think it's time you gave way to the younger ones and just get used to the fact you were a runner *before* the war?' she said. Peters was 27 and determined to prove her wrong.

Alain Mimoun had dragged his bad leg across the Vosges mountains between France and Germany, and suffered –26°C temperatures before the armistice was signed. He had done his duty but was now demobilised and moved to Paris. He was regarded as a foreigner rather than a war hero, but his running ability at least alerted the local clubs. Stade Français found him a cold, dark apartment, but that enticement gained him a three-month ban for infringing his amateur status. Years later, as an elderly man, Mimoun would return to the apartment for a French television documentary. He told the interviewer that people made pilgrimages to see his home and that the 40-year-old Portuguese landlady spent her days telling people about the former tenant. However, more poignant is a clip that shows Mimoun meeting another pensioner at the apartment. She says she remembers him and adds, 'You were sad.' That may have been down to being a top runner but having to work as a waiter to the wealthy customers at Racing Club's restaurant in Bois de Boulogne, a huge public park on the edge of the 16th arrondissement, beloved as a playground of Parisian high society.

For Jan Haluza, the war brought an end to his athletics. 'In the summer of 1945, when we could begin sport again, I felt that the time of my end had come. I used to joke that Emil is a grateful pupil, but will be an ungrateful athlete. For a long time I'd been motivating him with words, that he must work very hard to beat me soon, and that happened in 1944. At the end of the war I was

30 years old and wanted to take care of my wife and business. Emil did not want a [new] coach and he did not need one.'

Haluza was also chairman of the youth section of the People's Party in Zlín. As the months passed, he would become increasingly politicised. It was a development that would have devastating repercussions and serve to underline the different paths undertaken by Zátopek and the only man who could ever claim to have coached him. The war was over. The troubles were just beginning.

4

Born to Run

After Finland came Sweden. The trends of international endurance running were changing. Part of this was down to natural selection, a shrinking of the globe and the advent of science. Some of it was down to a farmhand and a teacher in a country that remained neutral during the war and, thus, could let its runners flourish, without the inconvenience of conscription.

The Swedes did it differently. Whereas Paavo Nurmi had ushered in a new era of athleticism with his exaggerated hip and shoulder movement, and his ever-present stopwatch reducing his runs to the mechanical, the Swedes believed in conserving energy. So they ran shorter distances and varied the tempo. In a nutshell, this was the Fartlek method of interval training. Sweden would forever be known as the birthplace of the Fartlek, but varying the tempo of runs had been utilised by runners from the days of the ancient Greeks and, over in Germany, Woldemar Gerschler and Herbert Reindel were the coach-scientist team taking the methodology to the laboratory.

Yet the greatest wartime stars of track and field were Swedish. Gunder Hägg was born four years before Zátopek and, although the farmer who owned the land where he worked was awestruck by the way he handled the plough, a double dose of pneumonia in 1939 had doctors warning him to give up sport at once.

He ignored them, became a soldier close to the Finnish border – almost a symbolic posting – and ran through thick snowdrifts in running spikes. He would usually run 2.5 kilometres in the snow and then walk the same distance. It toughened him. He broke the 1500 metres world record in 1941, but received a nine-month ban for taking 350 Krona to take part. That punishment, the result of a jealous whistleblower who managed a football team and was worried about dwindling attendances, was a portent of things to come.

Hägg set a new world record for the mile on the day his ban was lifted. Absence had made the heart grow fonder and his appearances attracted a sort of mania out of kilter with the Swedish psyche. He broke ten world records in 80 days in 1942, toured the USA and seduced people with his fluid style, rather than Nurmi's cold mathematics. While he was away on tour, Arne Andersson, a tall and handsome man who worked as a teacher at a boarding school, was close to supplanting him at home. He set world records for the 1500 metres and mile too and, just as people had been romanced by the man-from-the-woods folklore of Hägg, they swooned for this gutsy runner who had lost his mother to flu on his first birthday, but came from stock where his grandfather, the fabulously named Long Johan, was the strongest man in his province. They ran against each other and they won and lost in equal measure. In July 1944, the two had one of their most memorable meetings at a sold-out stadium in Malmö. Thousands of people formed a disappointed cordon outside the arena as the duellists fought over a mile. The loudspeaker relayed the news to the fans outside. After taking over from the pacemaker, who had reached halfway in 1 minute 55.9 seconds, Hägg led for most of the race. And then came Andersson, limbs scrambling for any semblance of momentum, effort spilling out of the deep crevasses in his face. He just got ahead by the line. The time was 4 minutes 1.6 seconds. In 1945 Hägg went quicker still. A decade before Sir Roger Bannister would break the four-minute barrier, two men from Sweden were showing that it was eminently possible.

The great Arne Andersson, who had found that running in the forest had a soothing effect on the problem children at his school, visited Prague in 1945. Zátopek ran against him twice, first in the 2000 metres and then the 1000 metres, and was well adrift in both. He could scarcely expect better. The following month Andersson and Hägg were among those who admitted that they had breached the sport's rules of amateurism. The Sports Association (of Sweden) had carried out an audit of finances in Sweden's clubs and found that expenses had been fiddled and subsistence loans inflated. The public was in thrall to its two heroes and scarcely cared, but both Andersson and Hägg received life bans. The theory went that the Swedish authorities were embarrassed that, while the world was at war, Sweden had carried on running away and had been taking illegal payments to boot. Hägg made light of his ban, but Andersson had already started to think about the next great goal – now that the war was over, attention was turning towards the 1948 Olympic Games which had been awarded to the heavily bombed city of London.

Andersson visited Prague again in 1946 as an ex-runner. He watched Zátopek win and shook his head. 'Oh, the lucky Emil,' he said. 'How happy I was at his age before I knew anything of fame.' Andersson actually stayed in Czechoslovakia and began coaching athletes. When a Czech team went to Stockholm for a meeting later that year, he walked on to the track alongside his young charges only for a Swedish official to approach him and say, 'We know who you are and we don't want you here.' He was forced to leave the track and arena and stand outside. This myopic treatment of sporting stars by the authorities would be another portent that would hover over Zátopek's rise, and there was both symbolism and irony in these two men becoming firm friends.

The end of the war had brought peace but no cure. Within a year of Zlín being liberated by Red Army troops, the Communist Party was far and away the largest political body in the country. The Nazis had effectively destroyed the middle class by closing universities, sending Czech Jews to death camps and attacking intellectuals, leaving a rump population ready to be manipulated. The wounds of war were still dominating society two years later when Jozef Tiso, the leader of the First Slovak Republic, was hanged for treason.

Thousands of Czechs were locked up, degraded and persecuted, so it was understandable that people had little sympathy for the 44 SS guards given lethal injections by a single doctor as paranoia ran riot in post-war Czechoslovakia. On his return to Prague from a Gestapo concentration camp, a man named Nikolaus Martin saw a group of German-speaking individuals stripped to the waist, swastikas daubed on their foreheads. Elsewhere, women had their hair torn out and were forced to lick swastikas off the pavement. Martin, whose father was German, saw the electrocuted bodies of three Gestapo agents dangling from a lamppost.

In this troubled climate, the Communist Party created the StB, short for Státní bezpečnost. A plain-clothed secret police force, the StB was used by the Communists to spy and repress political opponents. Files were quickly built up on those with businesses or property. Everyone had reason to fear they were being watched, especially those like Zátopek who travelled to foreign countries.

StB agents and informers were drawn from all walks of life and ranged from government officials to elderly women. The

Orwellian idea was to enable the state to know precisely what everybody was doing. Years later people would find out close friends and even family members had spied on them. For athletes travelling abroad, civilians would often go with them and pass on details to the StB. These so-called agents were often marked by a lack of education, and the spy network was far less sophisticated than the popular portrayal of such activities. Sometimes, under pressure from their superiors, agents would simply make things up. Files would also be doctored to implicate targets. Yet, as time went on, the StB became a far darker and more malevolent presence in the shadowy corners of Czech consciousness. At the higher levels, torture, blackmail and sexual degradation were part and parcel of their methodology, and these agents' nefarious work would impact directly on the lives of Zátopek and his friends.

The first entries in the StB files for Emil Zátopek are trifling matters, but the very fact that his travels abroad were being monitored highlights the culture of suspicion.

By the summer of 1946, Zátopek was the bona fide star of Czech running. He had broken the national 3000 and 5000 metres records three times apiece, but was still some way short of the world's best. His first real test came in August 1946 when he was picked for the European Championships, which were being held for the first time in the distance-running hotbed of Scandinavia, in Oslo. Zátopek initially refused the call-up, saying 'whatever for?' when asked if he would like to travel to Norway, but that papered over the more prosaic truth. The Czechoslovak Union of Amateur Athletics was broke. Allied to the fact Zátopek was struggling to get leave from the army, who were not always helpful to his ambitions, his place in Oslo looked in doubt. Originally, 20 athletes and nine officials had been named in the team, but now that was dramatically reduced with some hopefuls told they would need to pay their own way through club whip-rounds or public collections. Jindřich Roudný was fortunate that Bata's technical director saw the merit in the trip and paid up. Not only that, he also provided the modified Junkers bombers, used by the Luftwaffe during the war. Roudný and Tomáš Sale travelled to Prague with the pilots, while Zátopek had to wait until the last minute to gain clearance.

Zátopek hailed the trip as the first time he got to meet the best European athletes. He added that he had gone pale when the old Junkers engines fired. He found the diary that a travelling journalist was writing. The entries are little more than milestones on a landmark voyage for Zátopek:

9.20 a.m. – the start in Ruzyně [airport].
9.30 a.m. – down – Mělník, junction of Labe and Vltava rivers, in the background the mountain Říp.
9.40 a.m. – Mácha's lake, Bezděz castle, Ještěd mountain.

Zátopek looked out of the window and saw the Krkonoše mountains as the plane crossed the Czech border. The list of locations in Mrs Nedobita's diary ended at 11.50 a.m. when she simply wrote, 'The sea.'

Always alert to the chance of a prank, Zátopek took a pen and added some entries of his own:

12 p.m. – The sea
12.10 p.m. – The sea
12.20 p.m. – The sea

The mood turned when storm clouds swallowed the plane and the pilot announced that the radio had broken and they had no connection to air traffic control. Hence, they would fly below the clouds and use a simple compass to navigate. Anxious faces mirrored fear at each other. Then one of the twin engines stuttered to a halt. Roudný was terrified as the plane flew in this uncertain corridor between 'the raging sea and black clouds above'. The plane travelled on with all ears straining for changes to the engine's rhythm. The athletes shrunk to silence, until Zátopek broke the vacuum and, given the likelihood of crashing into the sea, said, 'Well, I'm getting undressed.' The gallows humour worked. The plane made it to Copenhagen, where the team stayed while the plane was repaired.

Jim Peters was still in England and wondering why he was not going to the European Championships. He had won the coveted AAA title in the six-mile race on 19 July and had been approached by Jack Crump, the British team manager, afterwards. 'Where have you come from?' he said. 'I've never heard of you.' Peters had just cause to believe he would now be selected for Oslo on the back of his success, but when the team was announced his name was missing. 'Though my winning time was not a record, or even a very brilliant one, at least I was the AAA champion. I was completely at a loss to know why I was not selected, and I received a considerable amount of sympathetic and sometimes indignant comment from the national press and athletes themselves.' It was not his way to complain. Jim was a small, pale man with hair receding on the sides and he did not relish confrontation. In a sporting world of super-confident athletes and assured Oxbridge graduates, he sometimes struggled to be heard. Later, Peters learnt that he was deemed too inexperienced, despite being almost 28 at the time.

In his absence the undisputed star of the British team was a bespectacled former public schoolboy who now worked as a solicitor. Sydney Wooderson was nearing the end of a career of what-ifs. He had suffered a broken bone at the 1936 Olympic Games and then, having set 800 metres and mile world records, found his chances curtailed by Hitler and the onset of war. Fragile in build and standing only 5 feet 6 inches tall, he coined nicknames ranging from 'Syd the Cyclone' to 'the Mighty Atom', but he was the epitome of British decency and fair play. Everyone felt that he would have won Olympic gold if there had been no hiatus, and that he might have broken the four-minute mile barrier to boot. Indeed, he was as popular in Britain as more enduring sporting heroes such as Stanley Matthews and Denis Compton, as proved by the sense of occasion that marked his 1945 clash with the Swedish duo of Andersson and Hägg in front of a sold-out 45,000 crowd at White City in London. Interest outweighed expectation as Wooderson had spent months in hospital with rheumatic fever and had only run in a sporadic low-key events beforehand.

Thousands of fans burst through the sold-out signs on the gates to see the duel. It was a gutsy affair with Wooderson taking the lead on the last back straight. Among those watching was the 16-year-old Roger Bannister. 'We all have our sports heroes and Wooderson from that day became mine,' he said. 'I admired him as much for his attitude to running as for the feats he achieved.' Despite setting a new British mile record of 4 minutes 4.2 seconds, the feats did not extend to beating Andersson, who inadvertently bundled the waspish Wooderson aside on the run-in.

The European Championships were a chance for Wooderson to get even and get another medal to go with the one he won back in 1938 in Paris. Like Zátopek, he was based at an old German anti-aircraft station in Smestad. The Germans had used the site to prevent the Allies from dropping supplies to the Norwegian patriots hiding out in the hills. In a sign of the somewhat stiff attitudes of the British hierarchy, Crump recalled how the women's quarters were separate but close enough for the men to visit and get the ladies to make their tea and hang out their smalls. Crump also revealed that the 48 hours on a boat trip to Oslo with Britain's leading ladies had cured Harold Abrahams, the broadcaster whose gold medal run at the 1924 Olympics would be immortalised in *Chariots of Fire*, of his snobbery towards women's athletics.

Zátopek clearly felt he was in an Aladdin's cave and, when the action began, he was riddled with nerves. He was racing against Viljo Heino, the last of the Flying Finns and the breed upon whom he had modelled his commitment. Finland was in raptures that summer and these championships would be seen as the high water mark of sport in that country.

As ever, the 10,000 metres came first. A scheduling mix-up meant that the 10,000 metres and the marathon finished on the track at the same time. The track runners ran in one direction and the marathoners another. Heino won his gold and Finns took the top two positions in both races. Zátopek, who had watched the race, wandered up to the great Finn and touched his arm. Heino turned in surprise. 'Hello,' he said. 'What's this all about?'

Zátopek smiled. 'I just wanted to make sure you were human.'

Heino laughed. He would have suffered anything in the aftermath, as it had seemed that he might be unable to take part at all after more allegations of breaking the sport's amateur status.

A Swedish official had bumped into Jack Crump on the eve of the race at the Bislett Stadium and asked how he and Wooderson felt about the news that Heino had been cleared. Crump said that he had been found not guilty and so that was the end of the matter. The Swedish official frowned and told him that it was certainly the wrong decision and that Heino had been paid.

'How do you know?' Crump asked, quizzically.

'Because I'm the treasurer of the club that paid him,' he replied.

Wooderson was just as edgy as Zátopek ahead of the 5000 metres. Crump had arranged for a late meal of steamed fish to be served, but the athlete nibbled at it and then pushed it away. He knew he was the emotional glue of the team and that anything less than a win would be a disaster for morale. Added to that, he had to take on a stellar field, including Heino, Willy Slijkhuis of the Netherlands, and a man whom Abrahams described as 'probably running out of his class' – Emil Zátopek.

It was the apotheosis of the little man. Few runners have debunked athletics' Adonis analogies quite as dramatically as the fragile 8-stone solicitor who was so in thrall to the amateur ethos that he would return even a few pennies to the AAA if he felt he had been paid too richly for his travel expenses. Wooderson could run and this was as good as it got. The pro-British crowd roared his name at the start and Zátopek reasoned that the sensible move would be to track him. He knew Wooderson had a fast finish and so reasoned that he should stay with him. When the names were called, he looked for Wooderson and was surprised to see a serious-looking man with receding hair and glasses. He asked himself, 'Is this the favourite?' He looked like a myopic professor.

However, in the early stages the experienced Wooderson stayed behind the machismo of the pack. Zátopek looked over his shoulder and wondered whether he would be sacrificing his own chances by staying with a man who may be ailing or injured or simply too close to the endgame. No athlete really knows when the tipping point is coming, but it can be a sudden and devastating process. In one race, egos and reputations and belief could be washed away by the faster spikes of younger men and left as rubble on the cinders.

Zátopek wondered if Wooderson was there and decided to stay with the leaders. Slijkhuis led and looked strong. Zátopek was learning to read the body language of opponents and, even without noting the three-kilometre time of 8 minutes and 33 seconds, knew he was in with a real chance. Heino was also there, pumping his arms like a bantamweight boxer, but Wooderson was somewhere behind, a memory then a shadow and then, finally, a threat, rounding Zátopek's shoulder and tracking the Dutchman. 'I followed the leading group,' Zátopek said, 'and lost interest in Wooderson. I overtook one after the other until I exhausted myself and finally Wooderson went past me like the wind.' There was dirt on his glasses but, with around 250 metres left, Wooderson trusted his past and began one of his renowned sprint finishes. He churned up the grey ash and the muffled thud of ambition ushered him down the straight. Zátopek was some way adrift now and beaten, but he toiled away as hard as he could. Ahead, he saw Wooderson edge away from Slijkhuis. By the tape the lead was five seconds. And another athletics crowd got that unique sight of a face contorted in effort. Emptiness and pain suddenly subsided in a smile. It was as if a switch was flicked. They loved to run, but they loved to stop even more.

Wooderson's time was 14 minutes 8.6 seconds. Only Hägg had ever run a faster 5000 metres, back in 1942. Heino was out of the medals in fourth and Zátopek finished in fifth place in a new national record of 14 minutes 25.8 seconds. Gaston Reiff, another of the greats of distance running, was a full 37 seconds adrift. It was a race that lifted Wooderson to new heights and plunged hugely talented opponents to depths of despair. For the first time, Zátopek tasted the drug of the grand occasion.

He went home to the academy. His commanders did not reproach him because they reasoned a new national record was a worthy effort, but others did. 'Ten times a day I would hear, "What happened in Oslo? At home you win every little race and when we really expected something you go and blow it." It was not worth going all the way to Norway for a fifth place.'

Zátopek had made an early decision to push for officer status rather than being a NCO. His success did not go unnoticed and his commanding officers told him to travel to Berlin for the Allied Forces Championships. He set off, alone, on the day before the event, arriving in Dresden at midnight. The street softly ticked with the remnants of a thunderstorm and he winced at the half-destroyed buildings rising like stalagmites from the ground. He spoke to a Soviet lieutenant who was intrigued by his uniform and was told the next train to Berlin did not leave until 3 a.m. Exhausted, he crashed on a bench on Dresden station, catching a brief sleep before taking the train to a city still symptomatic with the Third Reich.

They did not know him in Berlin. When he made his way to the stadium he had to convince officials that he was the entire Czechoslovakian team.

'But there's only one of you?' said the captain in charge of entries. He then pointed Zátopek in the direction of a lorry which took him to a place where he could get a meal and coffee.

He returned to the Olympic Stadium the following day. The ornate grandeur of the coliseum had witnessed some of sport's most unforgettable moments, not least in 1936 when Jesse Owens, the black American, had won four gold medals and exposed the sinister vacuity of Hitler's beliefs.

Each team had a standard-bearer, a soldier given the duty of carrying a national banner before the athletes. When Zátopek told the man designated Czech duties that he was the sole representative, he was met with a disappointed scowl. Embarrassed to be leading a team of one into the mighty Olympic Stadium, the soldier shrugged his shoulders and did his best to ignore the laughter from the stands. Zátopek noticed the guffaws and finger-pointing too, and went to sit down in the shade. He got talking to an American soldier who asked him what event he was taking part in. When he replied 'the 5000 metres', the soldier looked aghast. 'They've already called that one,' he said. 'It's about to start.' Roused, Zátopek tore across the infield to the start. His name was not on the start list and the official was going to bar him from competing, until several other competitors vouched for him. 'Oh, I suppose it will do no harm,' said the man with the pen and clipboard.

If Zátopek's passage to the race had been unusual, he was also in a different league from the others and duly won in a good time. The soldiers gathered after the race and were impressed. 'Have you ever raced before?' some asked. His standard-bearer was happiest of all, slapping his back and forgetting his previous disgruntlement. For Zátopek these two events were important. He had stood shoulder to shoulder with genuine greats of the sport at a major championship and he had been inside an Olympic stadium. There was a gap and he was still a relative unknown, but slowly, almost subconsciously, running was taking over his life. As countless others would find in the years ahead, he needed to run. He might even have been described as born to it.

5

Horseplay

The post-war election of 1946 was a watershed in Czech history, but its claim to be democratic was a half-truth. The StB was now increasingly active and drew up lists of people who should be barred from voting. Certain parties, including the Slovak branch of the People's Party, were not even allowed to stand. The Communists won a crushing victory and set about bringing Slovakia, where there was more support for the democrats, into line. This was done with increasing savagery and a form of ethnic cleansing, as relations fractured between German democrats, Hungarians and Communists favouring a totalitarian state.

For Zátopek, studying to be an officer at the academy, running around the barracks and down the corridors, and trotting along the 400-metre cutting he had found in the wood, life was simple. Politics happened somewhere else. His regime at that time involved marking out a 12-kilometre course on the road when the weather was too severe to hit the woods. He would do 20 runs over 250 metres one day and 20 over 400 metres the next, as well as the four kilometres to and from the barracks. By this point, he tended to work alone, although military athletics clubs were growing and physical exercise in the army now had its own separate department. By the time that ATK, the army gymnastics club, was established in 1948, Zátopek was a lieutenant and able to preserve his amateur status while enjoying a fairly professional training regime. His soldier's life and his athletic one dovetailed and he continued to progress.

His friend Milan Svajgr met him when he was training at the academy in Hranice. He remembered those days fondly and had a different take on Emil's motivation for joining up. 'I'm from Opava, but after the annexation in 1938 we had to leave,' he recalled. 'My father was a financial officer and we moved to Hranice where he unfortunately died. I was doing track and field and then, after the war, Zátopek came there. He had raced for Bata Zlín, but during one race he had his trousers stolen. He looked grotesque and said, "I will join the army." So he did and that's where we met and we would run together along the Bečva river and into the town of Lipník.

'The military academy was a set of buildings that were almost a kilometre long. They were connected and, when the snow fell in the winter, he would run inside.'

Jindřich Roudný, his old friend, was serving two years in a college of engineers in Litoměřice, 40 miles north of Prague. He bumped into Zátopek at various races and, in September 1946, was called up for the same team to take part in the Allied 'Britannia Shield'. The friends were reunited for two weeks before departure at the army barracks in Stará Boleslav. 'We trained in beautiful pine forests twice a day,' Roudný recalled. 'One day it was raining terribly and so we decided to go jogging in the indoor riding hall, where jockeys were based and tasked with looking after two or three horses. The jockeys were supposed to ride them out in the morning, but they could not be bothered to saddle them and so they herded them into the main arena and then chased them around. One poor guy chased them around and was hot and sweaty and the horses were smart and lazy, and so they would stop when they had got out of reach. When we saw this Emil and I thought this would be good training for us. So Emil took a little birch whip and stood me in the other corner. He then slapped the horse's rump and drove him back towards me before running back. Then I took over and drove him to Emil. In the end we trained six horses this way and the jockeys were very happy. And we figured out that we had run a total of around 30 150-metre straights as well as 30 mid-trotting straights. It was a good bit of interval training for us.'

There were six athletes training for the Britannia Shield but only five places. The weakest in training was named Marcinko, but the army chiefs insisted that they have a trial race to see who should drop out. The athletes were not happy with having to run a pointless 12-kilometre race and so hatched a plan in which they would tear away from the barracks and hide in the woods until due time had passed for them to emerge and have a genuine three-kilometre race to finish with. However, a problem arose when a Colonel Lecher, a renowned dressage champion, said that he would follow the runners on his horse. Zátopek tried to dissuade him, spinning a yarn about how the first Olympic marathon was not measured because the timekeepers' horses could not keep up with the runners. He felt sure the same would happen now. Lecher was indignant and said that was nonsense. 'We could not convince him and so the race started,' Roudný said. 'We followed our plan. We ran, turned in the woods, hid and watched the colonel riding past. We waited for about 30 minutes and then we gave Emil a lead of about 300 metres, to make it look real, and then followed him.' The race result turned out as expected, with Marcinko missing out. After a while the colonel came out of the forest, pulling his lathered horse behind him.

'It's impossible!' he cried. 'I have nearly killed my horse and I have not seen you.' Zátopek smiled at Roudný but they said nothing and headed for the showers.

The Czech army was in the process of rebirth after the war and supplies were scarce. When they got to England, one of the team's security guards, Dolenský, wore an old German jacket that reached almost to his ankles. An English policeman was taken aback by the uniform and looked at Zátopek. 'Is he your prisoner?' he asked.

The Czechs were popular in Britain, thanks to the exploits of their pilots during the war, and Zátopek and Roudný enjoyed their taste of the nation where the Olympic Games were due to take place in 1948. The race itself was a cross-country affair that took place in thick fog in Ascot. Roudný was hampered by deciding to hurdle the metre-long grass while Zátopek just ploughed straight through it. Among the field that day was Alain Mimoun and two other French-Algerians. At various points Mimoun would turn back and urge on his two compatriots who were jostling with Roudný. Zátopek won by a huge distance with Roudný ninth out of the 54 competitors.

The Czech cross-country team won their race and the team, including fencers, boxers and riflemen, took the overall title and a curious shield depicting London's bombed City Hall. They were also treated to an audience with Queen Mary at Buckingham Palace. The athletes stood in a semi-circle and marvelled at the red velvet and gold-leaf splendour. Then the Queen edged forwards and said, 'I know Czechoslovakia very well. Zátopek and Pilsner beer.'

Roundý heard Zátopek mutter under his breath: 'Damn, how can this woman know everything?'

Queen Mary saw his lips moving but had not heard the words and so she repeated, 'Yes, Zátopek and Pilsner beer.'

Zátopek smiled and bowed. Then the party was ushered away and given a flying tour of London, from the crown jewels to Westminster Abbey and then on to Eton.

When the group arrived home in Czechoslovakia, the chief of the army staff, General Bocek, welcomed them. He thanked them for the great Czech representation overseas and then approached Zátopek. 'So you're the famous skier, then?'

'No, I'm not a skier, sir,' Zátopek said.

'Ah, so you're the cyclist?'

Eventually, the general was enlightened, but Zátopek and the rest left with a slightly bitter feeling. As Roudný said, 'Emil was better known in the UK than at home.'

The following year the Allied World Championships took place in Hanover. This was a big deal given it was less than two years since the war and was a chance for Germany to show a more humble face. Hanover was part of the British-occupied zone and the trip would be another that illuminated the wastelands of post-war Europe. When the train stopped in Nuremberg, Zátopek noted the people still clearing the streets, but a group of American soldiers looked after them and treated them to a rich dinner topped off by fruit compote and whipped cream. Zátopek felt the marked contrast with the misery on the streets.

Hanover was worse still. The entire city seemed to have been razed and singed, with jagged edges forming macabre silhouettes on the horizon. Zátopek watched a bulldozer clear tonnes of bricks and piles of detritus so that trams could make staccato progress. As they walked along they heard singing coming from a pub down a side street. They walked in and, at once, the place fell silent. Zátopek looked around and noted that the place was full of soldiers, some still wearing their German uniforms. 'They were not particularly friendly,' Roudný recalled. They forgot their beer and left in haste.

The race was due to take place at a horse-racing track, and the Czech contingent decided it would be shrewd to go and check out the course. It was an eye-opener, with thick bushes covering an early part of the course before it thinned out into a narrow bank where it would be impossible to pass. Zátopek told his team-mates that they had to get to the bank first or they would be held up.

The runners were herded into the iron starting gates, like horses, and then a switch flicked and 45 athletes were unleashed. It was a frenetic, brutal start, with elbows and spikes to the fore, but the Czechs' training with Zátopek set them in good stead. Roudný managed to stay among the front runners along the bank, by which time Zátopek had all but disappeared due to his high tempo. It was good enough for the Czech team to win ahead of a French military team, including the revitalised Mimoun, whose wartime injuries did not seem to be hampering him any more.

That night the Czechs were once again the toast of the British, with Zátopek's display drawing particular attention. The wife of the British commander of the occupied zone demanded to be introduced to the 'sensational runner in red shorts'. She gushed and blushed. 'No horse has raced as well as you and you excited me very much.' She flirted with Zátopek and added, 'Indeed, for me, horses have now lost their glamour.'

In the next few months Zátopek's cover would be blown once and for all. The paucity of newspaper coverage during the Cold War meant it was hard for anyone but the most obsessive of sports watchers to take note. However, the breakthrough into the wider consciousness was coming, and it started on 25 June 1947 at the Rošický Memorial meeting in Prague.

The event was held in honour of Evžen Rošický, a Czech runner and journalist who had been involved with an anti-Nazi resistance group called 'Captain Nemo' during the war. In 1942, along with his father, he was arrested and then executed.

It was a lustrous day in the vast Strahov Stadium in Prague. When Zátopek lined up for the start of the 5000 metres – he was still to try the 10,000 metres – women fanned themselves in the grandstand. Against a good field, containing Swedes and Finns, Zátopek ran like never before. He lapped in around 68 seconds. By mid-distance a soon-to-be familiar cry was reverberating around the stadium like an aural domino effect: 'Zát-o-pek! Zát-o-pek! Zát-o-pek!'

By the ninth lap of 13 he was a good 100 metres clear of the Finns, Väinö Koskela and Evert Heinström. The result was not in doubt, only the time and Zátopek's battle with himself. So his head was cocked to one side, as if too tired to remain upright, and his tongue lolled between his parted teeth. His crooked arms looked ungainly but the legs moved with speed and grace, like a bizarre hybrid. He slowed on the penultimate lap and was troubled by a strong wind, but with the finishing line nearing he sprinted and covered the last 200 metres in just 30.2 seconds. The time was 14 minutes 8.2 seconds. That was faster than Wooderson had run when winning the European title, faster than anyone else except Hägg, the world record holder. A year away from the Olympics and Zátopek was now one of the elite.

There was little time to bask in any glory before he was told to go to Helsinki to race against Koskela and Heinström once more. The return visit had been part of the deal that saw the Finns travel to Prague, but there was a surprise in store for Zátopek, with Heino also slated to run. Emil travelled to Finland with Koskela and Heinström, the former teaching him some pidgin Finnish and recounting his life as a farmer, complete with various animal impressions. As he finally made his way to his base on the island of Santahamina, Zátopek felt strangely tired. Only when he looked at his watch did he realise it was actually close to midnight and the bright sunlight was down to being so far north.

As Zátopek stood with the others on the start line, he surveyed the faces but failed to locate Heino. Then came an announcement and Heino came trotting across the infield to the rapturous delight of the crowd. He was the undisputed star and the man the entire meeting had been arranged for. This was to be Finland's revenge and proof that *sisu* endured.

Koskela had taught Zátopek to count in Finnish, and that would prove a valuable asset. By 1500 metres Zátopek heard the announcer call out 4 minutes 8 seconds. It was fast, Heino refusing to give an inch or betray any inkling of fatigue, Zátopek matching him stride for stride. The crowd was on its feet as the combatants lapped and got nearer to the finale. And then, with the place in uproar and every desperate breath drowned by the sonic boom of adulation, Zátopek just managed to get his shoulders in front. It was a crucial victory by two-tenths of a second.

The devastated Heino skulked away and refused to appear on the victory rostrum, until the catcalls of the crowd forced him out of hiding. Nevertheless, he was severely disgruntled at such a narrow but important defeat.

Zátopek was in sufficiently good spirits to arrange to meet some Swedish journalists for an interview the following day. They woke him at 6.30 a.m. and took him to the Nurmi monument where they asked him countless questions about his life and running. Only when they had finished did they reveal that they were actually rivals of the journalists who had arranged the meeting. Later, those journalists found Zátopek and made him go on a boat trip where he was forced to run around the deck in the same way Gunder Hägg had once done on his way to the USA. Zátopek was becoming a man in demand.

He could be eccentric. In the summer of 1947 he was part of a team that made a problematic trip to Holland for an international match. The flight was delayed by two hours because a minister had taken their plane to Bulgaria. They were given no food and, when they finally made it to Holland, suffered a coach crash on the way to Enschede, near the border with Germany. That led to a missed train and a disgruntled bunch of athletes waiting in the reception of a large hotel. Zátopek sat on his suitcase and, to the amazement of the hotel staff, proceeded to eat an entire cucumber for effect. When an official then said their places were ready, Zátopek did not bother to tell them that they were not staying there and so the athletes duly helped themselves to a meal laid on for a wedding party that was still to arrive.

The race was held on grass, a novelty for the Czech team, and hence something of an advantage for the Dutch. The Dutch star was Willy Slijkhuis, dubbed 'the poetry of motion' by the British media, but he was no match for Zátopek, despite the modest time. Roudný recalled, 'After the races we sat in a semicircle on the grass and a local photographer started taking pictures. We were about to leave but a woman waved at us to stay. She stood in front of us and the sun shone right through her skirt. Inevitably, this led to a bit of titillating comment, and so we were surprised when the photographer said goodbye to us in perfect Czech.' They had been rumbled.

Later that year, 1947, Zátopek once again travelled to London for the Britannia Shield race. Roudný was in the team again, as were other members of the SK Slavia Praha club. One of them was Ladislav Kořan. The son of a chemistry engineer and a businesswoman, Kořan was something of a radical. He had been affected by the assassination of Reinhard Heydrich, like everybody else in Moravia, and when a curfew curtailed many activities, including a ban on bicycles, he started to run. He could have no way of knowing that, as Zátopek moved effortlessly towards the Olympic Games, he would soon be wrenched from the team in brutal fashion.

Kořan was oblivious to what lay ahead as he got into the twin-engine Dakota plane that had previously carried parachutists during the war. However, the StB was growing and keeping watchful eyes on anyone who was not a dutiful comrade. One night the phone rang at the home of Milan Svajgr, who was married to an athlete named Věra. She picked up the phone and listened to the dull voice. 'I am obliged to watch over you,' the voice said. Svajgr remembered, 'There was always someone with you.' Like Kořan, he had already attracted the suspicion of the StB. He knew he was playing with fire and fell foul of Václav Mudra, a police colonel, as they trained together. Svajgr's anti-Communist asides scandalised Mudra, who told him, 'I'm going to denounce you immediately.' Only the head of athletics, named Vykoupil, saved Svajgr on that occasion, but he admitted, 'I had the mark of Cain. I was an enemy of the regime.'

In the files that would remain lodged in the Ministry of the Interior for decades, a letter from a Czech admirer of Zátopek in the USA was stored away. A magazine from his travels was also added. These were taken by plain-clothed civilians tasked with keeping their eyes on him. Report No. 3783 reported that Zátopek said that he did not meet many people during his travels, but this network of amateur spies, gossips and uneducated informers meant that nothing went unnoticed, and for Svajgr and Kořan, who ran a successful small business selling guitar pick-ups, the suspicion was mounting. Another rising runner, Ludvík Liška, who would become a close friend of Zátopek, said a 'special attaché' would travel with overseas teams: 'They rode with us and we knew exactly who they were and we were careful. They were often a bit poor and rarely knew a language. They often could not even speak English. And in that Emil, who spoke many languages, had the upper hand. Sometimes Emil had a long talk with local people and they were wondering what he said. He would very merrily mistranslate it for them.'

On the plane Dr Topinka, the team doctor, provided a veritable feast with five jars containing apples, pears, grapes, plums and an assortment of pastries. The plane was also jammed full of other athletes – fencers, archers, boxers and swimmers – and was uncomfortable. Zátopek was phlegmatic about the mode of travel and attached his hammock to the bare ribs of the plane, while the pilot dipped and rose with worrying erraticism. Several athletes were sick with the altitude changes and vomited into brown paper bags, but Zátopek just swung gently in his hammock.

With growing inevitability, he won the Britannia Shield race and moved into Olympic year as an emerging star. In 1947 he had run 12 5000 metres races and won them all. He had beaten Heino and was the fastest man in the world. Indeed, he had not been beaten over the distance since Wooderson's bow at the European Championships. His time was coming.

6

Dana

Six hours after Emil Zátopek was born on 19 September 1922, a soldier and his wife celebrated the arrival of their daughter in the town of Fryštát on the Moravian–Silesian border.

Fryštát would become famous for two people. The first was Henryk Flame, a dashing Second World War pilot who was shot down during the war and went on to form an anti-Nazi resistance group, later becoming a Communist infiltrator. His life was as colourful as any *Boy's Own* war story and he wriggled free from death on many occasions. During Operation Lawina, some 200 of his men were drugged and stripped and then murdered in a Polish forest. Flame, who went by the moniker 'Bartek', escaped, but his penchant for embarrassing Communist authorities meant he was still a sought-after scalp long after the war. On 1 December 1947 he was assassinated while dining in a restaurant. His legend would grow as the years passed, as would that of Fryštát's other famous alumnus, Dana Ingrová.

She, too, had suffered a troubled occupation. 'My father was arrested during the war,' she said when we met in her flat and drank a bottle of Moravian plum brandy in the summer of 2015. Her eyes still had a watery veneer as she recalled those days some 60 years beforehand. 'When the Germans came they arrested all the lieutenants. They took him to Dachau. It was very hard, of course. He was there for two years, but we survived.'

Dana also roused the suspicion of the authorities due to her family's military connections. As well as her father's time in Nazi concentration camps, her link to General Jan Ingr was also a source of contention. Ingr was a diplomat who chose to stay abroad during the war and serve the Czech government-in-exile before joining a counter-intelligence group in the United States. It was believed that he was Dana's uncle. He was actually her godfather. Either way, the relationship was too close for comfort in the world of Cold War paranoia.

Dana followed a similar path to Emil in terms of her athletics. She joined Sokol and excelled at gymnastics before concentrating on handball.

One day she was in Zlín visiting a girlfriend, who had a brother who was an 800 metres runner.

'Can you see that boy over there?' her friend said.

Dana looked and saw the figure. He had black shorts and a white T-shirt stained grey with sweat. 'His hair was cut very short because he was already in the army. It was the first time I saw him.'

Her friend said, 'My brother says he is very hard-working, that boy from Zlín. He is talented and my brother is sure that he will touch something great.'

Dana did not think much of that first sighting, but two years later she finished her studies in physical education and moved to Zlín, where she joined the same club. However, at that time Zátopek was more enamoured with another athlete called Adela, who happened to be Dana's room-mate, but as time went on his affections shifted.

'I remember it was my first meeting for the club because I had started doing the javelin,' Dana said of the nascent romance.

'I had been a handball player beforehand, but started doing the javelin and I loved it. In 1948 it was our first meeting together because the club was organising a competition. We were told we all had to be there because Emil was going to make an attempt on the Czech record for the 3000 metres. They needed a crowd, and so we were all under orders. The javelin was the first event, and I set a new Czech national record. I was delighted and he came over to me and congratulated me.' Soon afterwards, Dana returned the compliment as Zátopek set a time of 8 minutes 7.8 seconds for the 3000 metres, curiously in a 4000 metres race.

Zátopek would remember that meeting for the rest of his life, and later wrote about it in his diary. 'The girl in the javelin I liked the best. I liked her from the start.' After Dana's success, he approached her and said, 'It was a beautiful throw.' Their respective feats gave them a common bond. In a short space of time, they went from strangers to confidants and found they did not need athletics victories as an excuse to talk.

'What are you doing tonight?' he asked her after one event. His heart was racing. Confident on the track and in company, asking a woman on a date was still a daunting prospect, especially when so much rested on her answer. 'Would you like to go to the cinema?'

Dana replied, 'I'm going to Hradiště.'

'Hradiště!' said Zátopek, surprised. 'I did my military training there. I like it a lot. I'll come with you and return tonight.'

Unbeknown to Zátopek, his commanding officer when he was a raw recruit in southern Moravia was Dana's father. He had heard people say he had a beautiful daughter, but had never seen her.

As they made their way from Hradiště station a familiar figure marched into view. It was Zátopek's commander, who had a habit of finding his soldier and congratulating him after every athletics triumph. Zátopek opened his mouth to greet him, but failed to get the words out before Dana said, 'Hey, Daddy!' The commander smiled and kissed his daughter, but was as confused as Zátopek. Emil was surprised that Dana was from an officer's family, as he found her answers vague and lacking military precision. It was that way when he asked when she was born.

'September,' she said, laconically.

'Really?' Zátopek replied. 'Me too. What day?'

'What day?' she repeated, as if trying to remember. 'The 19th.'

'Oh, come on,' Zátopek said. 'Me too. What year?'

'1922.'

'You are pulling my leg! Were you really born the 19th September 1922?'

'It's true,' Dana said. Still dumbfounded by the coincidence. Zátopek arranged for them to meet as soon as possible with their birth certificates. He then mused, 'We were born the same day. What if we got married the same day?'

The relationship blossomed on a coach trip from an inter-club meeting in Bratislava. 'I was the new one and Emil was not a member of our club,' Dana said. 'That meant he was not allowed on our bus, but he did not care much for that. He "attacked" the bus and forced his way on.'

He sat some way behind Dana, but she could hear the commotion as he struck little deals with athletes to swap seats and edge closer. Finally, he got to Dana's row and her friend quickly vacated her seat. Emil plonked himself down and smiled that accordion grin as the coach chugged along.

The athletes noticed an orange glow in the black windows and then heard the sound of music. 'They were celebrating their national holidays and we all wanted to join in,' Dana said. 'So we shouted, "Stop! Stop!" at the driver and so he did. We traipsed out and went to this lovely vineyard and the people there recognised Emil because he was already getting known. He liked singing a lot, even if out of tune.'

'Emil Zátopek will dance a solo,' a man declared and, never one to shirk a challenge, he duly did. Then he danced with the wives of the local dignitaries and even indulged in a race in the darkness. Such behaviour would be deemed reckless nowadays with an Olympic Games looming, but Zátopek had a keen sense of humour and zest for life. Dana felt herself falling. 'When we found out we were born on the same day it seemed like fate.'

A far more serious race took place on 29 May 1948 when Zátopek finally stepped up to the 10,000 metres. The venue was Budapest, away from the glare of publicity at home, and he found it hard to monitor his pace over the longer distance. He started too fast but the time was 30 minutes 28.4 seconds, which was a new Czech record and good enough to put him in the world's top ten.

Encouraged by his beginning at the 10,000 metres, a date was fixed for his home debut at the Strahov Stadium in Prague. This time Zátopek started fast but did not fade. The physical tics that made him such an oddity – 'a man wrestling an octopus on a conveyor belt' would be one of the more memorable descriptions – increased in tandem with the pain. His calves began to tighten as the lactic acid stung. His lungs burnt as the air was dredged for restorative gulps. Yet the announcer told the watching crowd that Zátopek was breaking records with every kilometre travelled. Those aficionados in the crowd passed on their knowledge and it spread into a hum of expectation and then a roar of acclaim. Heino's world record of 29 minutes 35.4 seconds, set four years earlier in Helsinki, the home of distance running, was in danger. Zátopek was closing in on a place in history in only his second race at the distance. František Kožík, who was watching the race, let his romance consume his memories. 'Oh, Emil, if you only knew what was at stake,' he would write. 'Please run, go on running, leave your vest alone. Why do you have to wipe the streaming sweat from your cheeks just at this moment. Run, run, do what you can, perhaps the impossible is possible, after all.'

Not this time. Zátopek crossed the line in 29 minutes and 37 seconds. He was effectively ten yards short of being the best ever. Now the times of those races look less spectacular, but it would be 17 years before Ron Clarke broke the 28-minute barrier and a quarter of a century before the advent of African distance runners, sports science, slow-twitch fibres, fast plastic tracks, genetics and altitude training took the mark below 27 minutes. For his era, Zátopek was heading towards being the best, better even than Nurmi. And now he had the Olympics to look forward to with his girlfriend.

7

Olympian

When Jim Peters had failed to be selected for the 1946 European Championships, his wife Frieda hoped that he might get used to the idea that he should move on. She loved him deeply and wanted to spare him any more hurt, but they also had a family to care for now, with little Robin. Running seemed a secondary pastime. Peters had an innate feeling that he had something better to give to the sport, but when he was soundly beaten by Viljo Heino in front of 50,000 people at White City, he realised he was a big fish in a small pond. He dropped out after three miles. Team-mate Jack Holden also gave up with bad blisters, despite casting off his spikes and attempting to run barefoot. Heino just demolished everybody, driving them into early retirement with his phenomenal pace. Peters ruefully trudged home and considered himself 'well below world class'.

Life changed one night when he attended a talk at a local tennis club given by the former Olympic athlete Johnny Johnston. He had been transformed from a decent club runner to a man who was fourth in the 3000 metres Olympic team-race, behind true greats like Nurmi and Ville Ritola, the Flying feuding Finns. He put this metamorphism down to the coaching alchemy of Bill Thomas and, as he sipped a cup of tea in the tennis club afterwards, Johnston told Peters that he should meet the sage.

However, Peters reasoned that he could neither afford the time nor money to travel from east to south London, so he had a different proposition.

'You know Bill Thomas' methods,' he said. 'Why don't you be my coach?'

They met for the first time on the track in Dagenham, where Johnston said that two AAA titles had been won almost despite Jim's methods. He had a head roll, but Johnston reasoned that Jim's style was fine and that it was wrong to be too obsessed with the aesthetic orthodoxy that prevailed in athletics. 'Your body is like a bank book,' Johnston told him. 'The more money you put in, the greater interest you will draw all the time and the more you can take out when you really need it.'

Then Johnston told him his own methods were all wrong. Hitherto Peters had concentrated on distance. Long runs at steady pace were designed to put strength in his legs, but across the Iron Curtain Zátopek was using alternative thinking and devising his own intervals. Unbeknown to either man, Johnston was of a similar mind and said Jim needed to do speed work. That was the key to winning races. So every week Peters was tasked with doing a trial race where he ran three laps at 65-second pace and then increased that to 60 seconds a lap. Do that and Peters would be used to running faster than he would need to in any race.

The results were not immediate. Peters was still a journeyman by world standards, but by the summer of 1948 he was beginning to show signs of improvement.

The AAA Championship would decide who went to the Olympics. Peters was now capable of running 14 minutes 30 seconds for three miles – still way down on Zátopek and the cream of metric Europe, but when he retained his Essex County Six Mile title in 30 minutes 7 seconds it was proof that the appropriated methods of Bill Thomas were working. Nobody had gone that fast in England for a decade.

Peters spent the day before the AAA race at work before travelling to White City for his Friday-night destiny. His natural pessimism meant he felt his Olympic place depended on this race. He flicked out his legs as if testing for lethargy, but this was it: fail here and he would accede to Frieda's wishes and retire.

The race was tough. Olympic places motivated all, and when Stan Cox made his move in the later stages, Peters could not respond. With three places up for grabs, though, his second place was surely enough. Nevertheless, he fretted throughout the weekend until the announcement on Monday morning, when Cox and Peters were both included in the Great Britain team.

Gordon Pirie was only 17 but had already had a taste of the Olympics. The previous summer some of the young runners from South London Harriers had tested prototype torches on the Farthing Downs. Now the real thing was happening with the Olympic torch relay, an elaborate, symbolic chain in which 1688 torches would be passed between bearers from Greece to the Empire Stadium at Wembley, in London. For some the relay had already been hijacked for political ends, with the mix of fire and brimstone a bit too close to reheating Hitler's pageant of self-glorification. Now the Communist National Liberation Front said it would disrupt the relay in Greece and so the organisers rerouted. In England the torches had been designed with thrift in mind – hexamine wax and naphthalene ensuring the flames burnt longer than in Berlin, architect Ralph Lavers designing a cheap aluminium casing that still looked impressive while fitting with the austerity theme.

Pirie's father, Alick, an impeccably turned-out man with chiselled moustache, was nominated to carry the torch for one leg and he asked his son to go with him. So father and son, clad in pure white, jogged for two miles from Priory Motors in Reigate and lapped up the enthusiasm of the crowd. Nobody there could have guessed that the tall teenager would become one of the most controversial sportsmen of the next decade.

'I was 17 and it was then that my imagination was set on fire and my consuming ambition was born,' Pirie wrote in *Running Wild*, a score-settling biography that would enhance his reputation as sport's *enfant terrible*. 'I ran with my father, an ex-international and Scottish cross-country runner, to help carry the torch to Wembley's Empire Stadium. I shook with excitement. Then, when my father put the torch into my hand, as if symbolically passing on the spirit of a great champion to the next generation, I was surprised to find it was hot. I ran through the cheering crowds and the flame seemed to draw my soul on to the start of a great journey down the years. It was the start, too, of a personal crusade to make British athletics match up to the best in the world.'

Alain Mimoun was also coming to Britain. He had met Zátopek by now and had been roundly defeated by him over 5000 metres in Prague. Yet for Mimoun, a war hero now working on the margins of French society, hunger was a powerful motivator. He remembered how, after his defeat by Zátopek, the Czech had kissed him on the cheek and said, 'Not bad.' Mimoun said that Zátopek knew then that he would be a rival, that he was new and raw and undertrained on that previous meeting. And anyway, he had drunk pink champagne with him too.

There was trouble at home for Zátopek too. He was a pragmatic soul and would bend with the wind if it made for an easier life. Later, he would be held up as a courageous fighter for liberty, but others said that his motives were more expedient. Although his fame would draw him unwillingly into a murky world of

Machiavellian politics, his ambitions were simple and true. He wanted to run, enjoy himself and wanted Czechoslovakia to match his contentment. As someone who had witnessed invasion, and come close to being bombed, he was a proud nationalist, but politics passed him by.

Yet Czechoslovakia was in political turmoil as the Olympics approached. Since the war had ended those in power had been happy to allow a spirit of vengeance to rise in the country. There were executions, mob lynchings and kangaroo courts to deal with those who did not fit in with the prevailing mood. And in 1948 the situation erupted when 12 non-Communist ministers resigned from the cabinet. They expected President Beneš to refuse their resignations, enabling their show of bravado to highlight the problems. They demanded the re-instatement of eight senior police officers but, fatally, Beneš allowed the situation to drift.

Meanwhile, the Soviet Union was fuelling the revolt and wanted an end to the last democracy in Eastern Europe. The police was now a Communist militia and, when two million people took part in a general strike, Beneš bowed to pressure and accepted the resignations. This enabled the Communists to seize power in the bloodless coup of Victorious February. Klement Gottwald was sworn in as prime minister – and would later give his name to a re-branded Zlín. Beneš resigned and Jan Masaryk, son of the President-Liberator, Czechoslovakia's first president, and a non-Communist minister, was found dead on the pavement below his flat. Decades later the suicide verdict would be disproved as Soviet files confirmed he had been thrown to his death.

And so began a decade of show trials and Communist propaganda. The StB became a paranoid police arm and dissenters were now risking their lives. Fear and loathing spread throughout the country. The Czech Communist Party, the KSČ, began screening members for appropriate political views, and if they fitted in then they might be fast-tracked into the StB, regardless of education.

The head of Sokol, Antonín Hřebík, was one man called in for questioning by the StB. Although regarded as an anti-Communist, the thick StB files actually showed that the Auschwitz survivor was happy to let the Communists assume power. As a show of national unity, it was agreed to allow Sokol to host a final *slet*, a mass gathering of gymnasts and athletes, albeit there were scores of StB agents positioned along the route to report on any anti-Communist remarks or behaviour. There were 230 arrests as it turned out. It was also the year that saw the creation of ATK, the army gymnastics club, which enabled athletes to carry on with their careers while undertaking national service. This gave Czech athletes a distinct advantage over their western rivals, who might have arduous jobs and true amateur status. In the east, the importance of sport as a totem for national pride and even political will was growing. Zátopek, and his peers, were becoming pawns without knowing it.

In London there was trouble too. Not everybody wanted the Olympic Games, with many regarding them as an unnecessary extravagance as the nation struggled to recover from the war. Back in September 1947, the *Evening Standard* had tried to capture the zeitgeist by opining, 'The average range of British enthusiasm for the Games stretches from lukewarm to dislike.'

London was still visibly dealing with the Blitz. Rubble remained untouched in streets and houses were still damaged and awaiting builders. Rationing was in place and the idea that athletes would be receiving increased portions, up to 5467 calories a day, equating them with the dockers and miners who were grafting to get the country back on its feet, grated with many. It seemed like unnecessary whimsy and, even in 1948, people in high places wondered if the Olympics would be called off.

Britain, too, could scarcely look to countries like Czechoslovakia and tut at its treatment of sections of society. That May the SS *Empire Windrush*, a former German warship, arrived at Tilbury Docks from the Caribbean. Around 500 black men traipsed off that ship to the horror of a country unused to multiculturalism and fearful of change. Already, the country was in the throes of a post-war housing crisis and the prospect of these visitors, many of them ex-servicemen, taking their jobs and houses created a racial divide that would take generations to bridge.

This was the London that Emil and Dana flew into. They did not know about British rationing and the SS *Windrush*, or even much about the Blitz and the Battle of Britain, but Dana looked at the pink clouds as the plane arrived and felt blessed.

In truth, it had already been quite a journey. At one point, the officials had questioned Dana's participation, pointing out her family connections and wondering if she was a dutiful citizen. When Emil heard that she might be barred, despite having qualified, he let it be known that he would not be travelling to London if she didn't.

The authorities would not risk that because Zátopek was now being heralded as a hero of the new state, but it was still a bold act that might be stored up for later. If Zátopek had any doubt about his role as talisman for the politicians then it was evident from the Army Day meeting at Strahov Stadium two weeks before their departure to London. The idea was to show Zátopek in all his Czech glory.

His friend Roudný explained, 'He had to run 3 kilometres against a relay of three soldiers. I was selected as the second soldier. He had a certain advantage because we ran in thick uniforms and hobnail boots while he had lighter clothing, but he was very angry because he said there was no way one man could beat three.

'Emil and us three soldiers stood in front of the grandstand and listened as his performances were praised. And then came the race. Emil started well against our weakest runner, but by the second he was already fairly exhausted and I managed to get ahead. Then I felt the pain and told him I could not keep up. He snapped, "Get over it," in colloquial terms. I responded and had a small lead after our leg. In the final section Emil struggled to make up the ground and he lost by about 60 metres. We were worried because this was meant to be a show of Emil's strength and beauty, but he had lost. We wondered what the colonel would say. And then, over the loudspeaker, we heard his voice: "The individual is nothing – the collective is decisive."'

At that point, Emil may have realised that, win or lose, he was now being used to promote socialism. 'All of us were frustrated as we left and we felt very sorry for Emil, who did not want any of this,' Roudný said.

It was a small sign of the load being heaped on his shoulders and also of the way he was being manipulated. But, for all the pressure and the problems of home and abroad, the Olympic Games were something that focused every mind.

He had entered both the 5000 metres and the 10,000 metres. The longer distance would come first, on the opening day of the Games, but he would have to run a 5000 metres heat the very next day, and then the final two days after that. It was a daunting schedule.

The 1908 Olympics in London had cost just £15,000, although that did not include the construction of the new stadium at Shepherd's Bush, which cost £60,000 and was built for the Franco-British Exhibition. This time the total cost was £732,000.

The government had backed the Games because it felt that it could make some serious money from them, as well as providing a morale-booster. In the end the receipts were £762,000. Costs included £174,097 spent on food and transport and £78,012 for the use of Wembley Stadium.

Seven athletics facilities were allocated to the various teams. Southall Athletics Ground was preserved for women, while the main centres at Uxbridge and Paddington had separate areas for the field eventers like Dana. Some athletes were billeted in civilian houses, but Zátopek was at West Drayton RAF camp, which was housing 700 athletes and had three kitchens and three dining halls. Dana was over at St Helen's School in Northwood, a women-only base housing 120 athletes. Training took place at Uxbridge. Emil was not a happy figure in those early days, as he played his guitar to pass the time and wondered what Dana was doing. She was musical herself, and played the viola before taking up the accordion. They liked to play chess together and listen to Moravian folk songs on an old gramophone. Now they were isolated in an oppressive atmosphere. The heat in the barracks, covered only in tar paper, was intimidating and, although the Brazilians and Portuguese at Drayton enjoyed the conditions, Emil fell into a slump.

He got out of it, as he often did, by training. His drill now was four sets of 100 metres followed by six sets of 200 metres. With the big day looming he could not afford to resort to his usual, masochistic methods. He needed to keep his body ticking over and rest. And it became an interminable wait. Heino, the 10,000 metres world record holder, and Gaston Reiff, the balding Belgian who drank gallons of milk, loomed large in his mind. Reiff was on his way up. When he won a cross-country run near Brussels when a teenager, a string of Belgian club chiefs had stormed the changing rooms in an attempt to sign him up. Reiff did not like a fuss and climbed out of the back window to make his escape. Emil knew he had promise and he had already lost to Reiff in a Belgium versus Czechoslovakia match the previous year. Heino, though, was already a running icon. This was a man who had been shot in the leg in the Winter War between Finland and the Soviet Union and had taken to carrying a pistol with him on training runs near the border. He was armed and dangerous, hard, resilient and the record holder for four long years.

Although they became known as 'the Austerity Games' these were the global Games too. By the opening day 134 visiting broadcasters had assembled, representing 60 organisations and 28 countries. The BBC alone had a broadcast team of 266. In the Empire Stadium three main cameras were used. The main position was in the back row of the stand almost immediately behind the Royal Box and some 20 yards short of the finishing line. Another camera was set up lower down in the stand, specifically to get a close-up of King George when he declared the Games open. A third was in the commentary box for interviews.

At that time the Radios Industries Council estimated that there were 80,000 television sets, mainly within 50 miles of London, although the research threw up one hardy viewer in the Channel Islands some 180 miles away. The reception there was reported as variable.

In addition the official film of the Games, *XIV Olympiad – The Glory of Sport*, was the first time the record of the Games had been shot in colour.

Although nerves bubbled up inside, Emil could appreciate the mix of nations and the sense of camaraderie. This extended to the National Olympic Committees – the Dutch offered to supply 100 tonnes of fruit and sent bi-weekly consignments; Denmark sent 160,000 eggs; the Czechs delivered 20,000 bottles of mineral water; Iceland weighed in with some carcasses of mutton. Organisations helped out too, with the British Trawlers' Federation providing 3000 stones of fish.

Emil was sharing a room with Václav Čevona and they talked through their races. Emil was anxious, as he had not seen Heino or Reiff in training yet and wondered what shape they were in.

The opening ceremony was held at the Empire Stadium on 29 July, and Zátopek decided that he wanted to go. The official report of the 1948 Olympics would recall it as a perfect day with a blazing sun, but Zátopek was told not to attend. The 10,000 metres was the highlight of the next day's action and standing for hours in such temperature was considered too much of a risk. Zátopek, though, had other ideas. This was the Olympics in all its pomp and glory, even if this was a more monochrome affair with its nod to austerity. The trumpeters of the Household Cavalry and pipers of His Majesty's Brigade of Guards played. Choirs sang and 85,000 people got their first sight of the new 400 metres track, the first time a circuit that length had been installed in Britain in place of the usual 440 yards.

At 2.35 p.m. the King entered the arena accompanied by dignitaries, including the Lord Portal and Lord Burghley, the charismatic chair of the organising committee. Then came the parade of 59 nations.

'Heino has stayed home,' a friend warned Zátopek.

'Well, I'm not only running against Heino,' he replied. 'I'm going.' And he did, sneaking in behind the taller athletes so as not to attract attention from the Czech hierarchy. The parade took 50 minutes. Emil looked around at the fans and then at the track, where he would be running the following day. He almost switched off as Lord Burghley began to speak:

Your Majesty, the hour has struck. A visionary dream has today become a glorious reality. At the end of the world-wide struggle in 1945, many institutions and associations were found to have withered and only the strongest had survived. How, many wondered, had the great Olympic Movement prospered?

Zátopek rubbed his head. People wilted in the furious sun. He saw someone faint. He cast his eyes around looking for athletes he might know, for Heino, Reiff and Mimoun.

In 1946, the clarion call went forth to the athletes of the world, inviting them to gather in London in 1948 to celebrate the XIV Modern Olympiad. Here today, in this vast arena, are assembled 6,000 competitors, the cream of the youth of the world drawn from the 59 nations, who have answered this call.

Emil thought of Nurmi and Ritola and the rest, of those early days with Jan Haluza, of his brother running through the wheat fields in front of their house, pursued by his father with ruler brandished above his head – of Emil the Wimp and Emil the Second, of silicates and soot, dogs and shitty trails in the forest. It was July 1948 and the fastest man ever over 10,000 metres was Viljo Heino. The second was Emil Zátopek.

The eyes of the world today, and for the next 14 days, will be on London. Not only will they be turned towards this ancient city to follow the fortunes of their champions and those of other countries, but also, I believe that in the hearts of millions of men and women in every corner of the earth, that warm flame of hope, for a better understanding in the world which has burned so low, will flare up into a very beacon, pointing a way to the goal through the Fellowship of Sport.

At 4 p.m. the King rose in the Royal Box and declared the Games open. Cheers merged with a brass fanfare. As Zátopek pondered the immense scale of even a supposedly watered-down Olympics, little dramas were taking place all over the stadium and beyond. Roger Bannister, the runner and trainee doctor from Oxford University, had been nominated as a possible for the Great Britain team, but withdrew his interest because 'I held the notion then traditional in Oxford athletics that over-competition too young could produce staleness.' Instead, he became an unpaid assistant and so he had left Uxbridge that day for the ceremony and had the foresight to take with him a raggedy Union Jack that had been discarded. Just in case.

Sure enough, when he and the commandant oversaw the handing out of the flags for the nations' parade, the Union Jack was missing. Bannister was given an official jeep and an army sergeant and told to find his flag at once. There ensued a frenetic dash through crowded streets, Bannister keeping his hand on the horn, and a mad search for the car he had parked earlier. He located it with sweat pouring from his brow. 'Time was perilously short,' he said. 'So I jumped out of the jeep and using the flag as a battering ram, with the brass spike foremost, I charged through the crowd and reached the British team just before they marched into the stadium.'

The parade passed off without problems as far as the crowd was concerned. There was no Soviet Union, barred because it had no Olympic committee and its state-sponsored sporting programmes upset amateur sensibilities at the International Olympic Committee. Neither was there a German team nor a Japanese one. The war hung behind the Games like a stained backdrop.

'I so wanted to see the opening ceremony at Wembley,' Zátopek would write. 'It was only later, in the stadium itself, that our leader saw me and began to complain about the lack of discipline.'

The leader shouted, 'Emil, what are you doing here?'

Emil pointed to the Royal Box and whispered, 'The King is looking at us.'

Much later Zátopek would explain in detail why he had to be there. 'It was a liberation of the spirit to be in London,' he said. 'After all those dark days of the war, the bombing, the killing and the starvation, the revival of the Olympics was as if the sun had come out. Suddenly, there were no more frontiers, no more barriers. Just the people meeting together. It was wonderfully warm to feel. Men and women who had lost five years of their life were back and there were all the young ones too.'

That was later, though. For now Emil was thinking only about Viljo Heino. Emil was woken from his thoughts by a roar. A man in white was carrying the torch. The identity of the last torchbearer had been a closely guarded secret. Most people felt that the perfect choice would be old Sydney Wooderson, that much-loved figure and epitome of Britishness. Now that he had retired, here was a chance to honour him – but instead the organisers had plumped for style rather than substance. Their choice was John Mark, a 22-year-old Cambridge blue. Wooderson, with his wiry physique and bottle-lens glasses, was not deemed to embody Olympic athleticism. For some this had unhealthy overtones of Hitler's Aryan race, but defenders pointed out Mark had the look of a Greek god. The Queen Mother herself is alleged to have said, 'What a shame they didn't get little Sydney to do it.' Mark was the unfortunate object for some of this disdain that bridged the class divide. A good club runner, who had been on the 'possibles' list, he had been picked up by a white Rolls-Royce and shepherded away to train in secret. Now he circled the stadium and lit the flame. The Games were on. Zátopek went home and tried, in vain, to sleep soundly.

8

Seeing Red

The 10,000 metres athletes made their way down to the stadium. Jim Peters was not flushed with confidence, despite his improvement under Johnny Johnston. 'The day was one of those sultry, stifling July ones, and as we drove to the stadium, we felt sticky and almost listless.'

The day had already got off to a muddled start when it turned out that officials had forgotten to mark the points at which the hurdles should be placed. That led to a delay. And when the 10,000 metres runners got to the track, they found that the organisers had been struggling to cope with the metric system for their race. Another lengthy delay ensued.

Jim looked at his opponents and did not recognise many of them. 'But there was one man I did know, only too well: Heino of Finland,' he would write. 'The incredible Heino, who had run the opposition to a complete standstill and was the world record holder for the distance with a time of 29 minutes 35.4 seconds. I knew I couldn't hope to beat him.'

Zátopek looked at Heino on the warm-up track too. It was a sign of how the younger man was progressing that he now felt comfortable in talking to a man he idolised rather than merely touching his arm, like the star-struck fan he'd been back at the European Championships two years earlier.

'It's hot,' Heino complained. 'It wouldn't be good to go fast at the start.'

Zátopek thought about that and told the team trainer, Karel Kněnický.

'Heino is right,' Kněnický told him. 'Don't go too fast or you will fry.'

'Karel, I've done my own calculations,' Zátopek said. 'I need to run 71 seconds a lap. But I need help. Can you make a sign from the stand? If I'm going too fast then wave white shorts. If I'm too slow wave my red shirt and then I'll know to step it up.' Kněnický, a PE and geography teacher by trade, agreed.

Up in the stand Gordon Pirie, now a teenage bank clerk, was watching. 'The Olympics were just another meeting to me,' he said. 'Only more people went to watch. I was not particularly enthusiastic about any race until the 10,000 metres event came on.' It would prove life-changing for the young runner, who liked to be contrary even then and, to the mirth of those around him, talked up the chances of the Czech athlete called Zátopek.

Finally, the moment came. The runners crouched. The gun sounded. Expectant cheers flew from the stands. Flashbulbs. Faces blurred. The soft snare drum of spikes on cinders.

There were all sorts of stories in the race that day. There was Stan Cox, earning a low wage as a storeman with the Standard Telephones and Cables Company, working a five-day week to support his wife and two children. When he was permitted an extra milk ration to help his Olympic ambition, the local paper ran the headline: THE MILKMAN IS LEAVING AN EXTRA PINT AT STAN COX'S.

Harold Nelson, of New Zealand, had drunk neither milk nor water for a day. That was the considered advice of the medics back in 1948, bereft of any understanding of hydration. Nelson had taken a dessert spoon of honey before the race to get rid of any liquid in his stomach, and that would be enough.

Steve McCooke, the third of the British runners, had an injection in his Achilles tendon before leaving Uxbridge. However, the two-hour delay due to the distance mix-up meant the painkiller had worn off. As he tried to flick his feet off the track he felt a raw, scything pain.

Meanwhile, Zátopek was shocked to see Heino start so quickly, given their discussion on the warm-up track. He watched him move ahead, but looked to Kněnický in the stand. He knew precisely where his friend was and saw the white shorts that were the code for 'too fast'. Zátopek shrugged to himself and assumed Heino and others were getting carried away by the occasion. The first lap was completed in just 67 seconds, but the pace dropped after that punishing start. After only two laps McCooke could not bear the pain any longer and he dropped back. Nelson was running towards the back of the field of 27 starters. Zátopek was closer to him than Heino, who went through the first five laps at world record pace.

Evert Heinström, the second Finn, and Bertil Albertsson, the Swede, followed. Jim Peters tried to relax into a rhythm, but found it impossible. 'Stan and myself found the pace very hot indeed.'

The Czech radio commentator watching events unfold was dismayed. Zátopek was their superman and yet he was way off the lead.

In the eighth lap and our Zátopek is still only 17th. Our Zátopek, who we are accustomed to see only in the lead. Why doesn't he go to the front? Someone ought to tell him he must speed up a bit.

That job fell to Kněnický, but had he got the code wrong? Was he waving white shorts instead of a red vest? Zátopek recalled, 'On the seventh lap Heino had an advantage of 80 metres. Could Karel have confused the shorts with shirt?' On the ninth lap Zátopek finally saw red. 'I started to overtake everyone. Only Heino reacted when I went past him. The fact that he found more breath surprised me.'

Nelson was now struggling with stomach cramps and eventually he pulled out: 'Everything was a red haze and I collapsed unconscious on the side of the track.'

Zátopek, head cocked at a 45 degree angle as if trying to rest on his shoulder, lips parted, eyes rolling, arms clawing, began to move. He hit the front at around the four-kilometre mark and began to pound out 71-second laps with metronomic reliability. In the crowd people began to take notice of the man in the crimson vest, No. 203. Pirie said, 'The spectators enthused about the stylish Finns, but I pointed out Zátopek, running at the back of the field, apparently in his death throes. The people around thought I was crazy. Time showed, however, for after some laps the others tired and Zátopek was in the lead. He murdered Heino with a couple of sprints.'

Heino had his own secret woe as he circled Wembley. Not long before he had come to Britain he had been running in a pine forest and slipped and hit his knee on a rock. He had tried to keep the injury a secret, but now it was revealing itself with every step. The pace was too much for a man with a problem. With nine laps left he dropped out and almost collapsed. He was one of numerous runners who failed to finish. A marshal shouted the news at Zátopek: 'Heino is out!'

Just to make sure nobody had any pretensions, Zátopek put in a body-sapping 70-second lap on the 19th lap. He went past runner after runner, lapping Peters and most of the others.

'I was bitterly disappointed, not because I hadn't been placed,' Peters said afterwards 'but because for the first time I'd had the honour of representing my country and I suffered what I considered the humiliation of being lapped.'

He was not alone. The officials were confused by Zátopek's pace and initially declared that he had finished a lap too soon, but Zátopek knew better. When he did come home after 25 laps, finishing off with a 66-second final circuit, he was an unprecedented 300 metres clear and had lapped all but the other medallists. They were Alain Mimoun, the old soldier, and Albertsson. Cox and Peters were seventh and eighth. In the confusion, with runners on different laps, the officials declared Belgium's Robert Everaert as sixth. He pointed out that he had dropped out after only five laps, but the officials refused to be moved until a Belgian official intervened to avoid a farce.

Yet, amid the confusion, something very special had taken place. Zátopek had taken 12 seconds off the Olympic record with his time of 29 minutes 59.6 seconds. Only three other runners were within a minute of his time.

Zátopek jogged lightly off the track, took a towel and smiled broadly into the camera. The impact of his victory was enormous. At home Ivan Ullsperger, a young runner, would watch the delayed coverage in a cinema. 'It was a huge moment for us all,' he said. 'He was our hero.'

It was a huge moment for Gordon Pirie, who had watched Zátopek undermine the rest with his jolting change of pace. 'Heino shook his head and dropped out. I stood in my seat watching Zátopek intently for lap after lap. His forceful style had the crowd on their feet too, and yelling their heads off.' Pirie said this 'tremendous dynamo' sparked something inside him. His friend Keith Whitaker told the writer Dick Booth, in

The Impossible Hero, that Pirie could not stop talking about Zátopek that night. It was as if he saw a life beyond the ledgers and suits of banking. 'I wanted to run every day,' Pirie said. 'Zátopek inspired me to do something different. From that moment I wanted to run like Zátopek – like a machine.'

Jim Peters was less inspired. He would hang around and watch some of the Olympics before travelling home from Wembley on a train with Johnny Johnston, smarting from the humiliation of being lapped. 'Johnny,' he said. 'I'm going to retire.'

His coach was quiet, so Peters filled the void with an explanation: 'I really must give up athletics. I'm getting tired at work and, if I don't work, we don't eat and we still haven't got our own home.'

Johnston considered the words and looked out of the window. Then, slowly and methodically, he turned to Jim and said, 'You'll never run the 10,000 metres at the Olympics again.' There was a pause for effect. 'If you want to run in another Olympic Games, old boy, it will have to be in the marathon.'

That took Jim by surprise. The marathon? The longest, most gruelling, most self-flagellating event of all? He knew that people had died trying to conquer the distance; that it was created in the first place because of an apocryphal myth about a messenger's fatal collapse in Athens in Greece. He was already tired at work so the idea of training almost every day was anathema to his renewed vision. He shook his head, went home and forgot about running for three months.

Zátopek could not forget. The schedule meant that he was back on track the following day for the 5000 metres heats. However, before he returned to the stadium, his girlfriend had her moment, as the javelin took place that afternoon. Dana could feel her pulse quickening as she made her way to the stadium, but she also knew little was expected of her. She was a raw novice and, although the size of the Olympics had both captivated and daunted her, she was free of the burdens faced by Emil. Her best throw that afternoon was 39.64 metres. It was good enough for seventh place, a respectable effort. The winner was Hermine Bauma, an Austrian whose new Olympic record of 45.57 metres would be rendered paltry by Dana in the years ahead.

Zátopek did not see that. He was readying himself for the 5000 metres heats. Since winning Czechoslovakia's first gold medal, he had tried and failed to keep himself focused. He had got back to the RAF camp at West Drayton to be faced by a pile of telegrams from fans at home. Some people lauded him and others tried to appropriate him. He watched his team director tell anyone who was listening about the opening ceremony, rewriting the past to fit events: 'Do you know that Heino was hiding in the shade and then he was hit by the heat? Emil went to the ceremony, got used to the heat and won.' It was a volte-face that amused Zátopek and then irritated him.

When he got to the track, he felt the confidence surging through him. He spoke to Erik Ahldén, the Swedish runner, before their heat, the second of three, and they decided to pace each other. Four men would qualify and it should have been routine. The first heat passed off without major incident, with Evert Nyberg of Sweden and Väinö Koskela of Finland taking the top places and proving that the Scandinavian axis remained strong. Then came the second race, one that would defy logic. The two men headed the dozen runners, but then Ahldén broke clear and upped the pace. Zátopek was comfortable in second place, but later said he was annoyed by the Swede reneging on their agreement. So, instead of shrugging and settling for an easy qualification, he tore after Ahldén. Inspired by a sense of injustice, he surged along the track. The gap narrowed and the crowd roared, surprised by this unexpected entertainment. By the end Zátopek was a yard short and, although he had qualified for a second Olympic final, his annoyance festered. Nevertheless, he was beginning to feel inviolable. 'Everyone saw me as a hero and even I told myself that I was a phenomenon.'

They had the Sunday off. Zátopek played his guitar. At home Ivan Ullsperger wondered if the great Zátopek would win again. He had read about the heats and how certain writers suggested his last-lap sprint may have sapped some of his strength. Ullsperger did not think so. He had qualified, after all. Mimoun, the French-Algerian runner who had been second in the 10,000 metres, had faded in the final heat and drifted to sixth place. The heat had seen all the other big guns qualify – Willy Slijkhuis, Bertil Albertsson and Gaston Reiff.

Zátopek felt that Ahldén would be his threat. And the weather. The heat of the first two days had been replaced by a smudgy grey sky and hard rain. The downpour left the track darker and sodden, pockmarked with puddles. Curtis Stone, an American who would go on to run in two more Olympic Games, looked up and sighed: 'The clouds burst just before we began.'

For many this was their best chance, after having their lives and running ambitions dismantled by the war. So much had happened since the last Olympics 12 years earlier. Lives had been changed and lost, wasted and sacrificed. New heroes had arrived and old ones had started to fade.

***

At 4 p.m. the women lined up for the start of the 100 metres dash. At the time the reigning champion was the now retired Helen Stephens, who had been embroiled in one of the more remarkable of Olympic intrigues in Berlin. Standing 6 feet tall and with a tan and physique honed on the family farm in Missouri, she developed a bitter rivalry with Stella Walsh, a Polish-born runner from Ohio. To get around America's stringent amateur rules, Walsh chose to run for Poland and became Stanisława Walasiewicz. She won the gold medal in Los Angeles in 1932 in a world record, but Stephens beat her in Berlin in 1936 and was then summoned to meet an infatuated Hitler. Stephens recalled, 'Hitler comes in and gives me the Nazi salute. I gave him a good old Missouri handshake. Immediately Hitler goes for the jugular vein. He gets ahold of my fanny and he begins to squeeze and pinch and hug me up, and he said, "You're a true Aryan type. You should be running for Germany." So after he gave me the once-over and a full massage, he asked me if I'd like to spend the weekend in Berchtesgaden.'

She declined, but the strangeness of Berlin was not over. When a Polish journalist accused Stephens of being a man, foreshadowing the case of South African runner Caster Semenya in the same Berlin stadium some 70 years later, the Germans issued a statement saying they had conducted a sex test. Decades later, in 1980, Stella Walsh was shot dead in a parking lot. The post-mortem found no female sex organs and a small penis. The truth was Stephens was certainly a woman but Walsh, according to the Olympic rules, was a man.

Stephens never had the chance to defend her title, and the war saw Walsh settle in the USA and marry a boxer. Their races were run if not their stories, but the new star of the women's programme was unquestionably Francina Blankers-Koen. She was plain old Fanny Koen when she had rubbed shoulders with Stephens and Walsh at the 1936 Games but now, just an hour or so before Emil Zátopek took to the track, she was laying down the foundations of a true Olympic legend. Now the holder of five world records, she was 30 and the wife of her coach, Jan Blankers, with whom she had two children. Many felt she was too old for the Olympic stage, but in the mud of the Empire Stadium, she thought otherwise. The crowd thrilled to the event, with women allowed to wear shorts and sleeveless shirts for the first time. Blankers-Koen had made her orange shorts herself. The papers would soon be talking of how she took her children to meetings, fed them in the changing rooms and let them play in the long-jump pit while she set world records. In the final she was fastest away and her long legs scarcely touched the ground for long enough to mark it with black smudges. She took the tape and the gold medal with Britain's Dorothy Manley, a typist, in second place and Australia's Shirley Strickland, a nuclear physics student, in third. Blankers-Koen would win four of the nine events put on for women in the athletics programme and become the undisputed star of the 1948 Olympics.

The crowd was still humming with the Flying Housewife's win when the men were called for the start of the 5000 metres. In different parts of Czechoslovakia, Ullsperger and Jan Haluza listened to the radio for news. All over Emil's homeland, people waited. The powers that be waited to wallow in his success. This was proof that their decision to amalgamate all sport under one body had worked. This was a way of uniting a nation as the new government got to work. And in London the StB informers merged with the athletes and the crowds and made sure that none of their athletes were badmouthing their homeland or, worse, contemplating defecting.

Harold Abrahams, working as a commentator for the BBC, had his doubts about Zátopek. 'There was much speculation as to whether Zátopek would win the 5000 metres, the double having been accomplished only once before, in 1912,' he said. Abrahams could be a stern figure and lamented the 'unnecessary duel between Zátopek and Ahldén of Sweden'. The scheduling scarcely helped either. In modern times there is a week between the 10,000 and 5000 metres finals. Zátopek had three days. Most of his rivals were fresher. Publicly, he said he had only a small chance.

As Blankers-Koen departed with her gold medal after her ceremony, the runners gathered. The muted colour on the Pathé News footage looked as if it had been tinted with a pastel brown.

Very heavy rain had literally saturated the track by the time the runners from seven nations are called to the start of the 5,000 metres. And it's [Väinö] Mäkelä of Finland, No. 208, who goes into an early lead.

Zátopek's best time for the event was 14 minutes 8.2 seconds. It was the best in the field, but Ahldén's form in the heats was a warning, and Zátopek knew that Reiff, the Belgian, was a gnarly, battle-hardened runner and Slijkhuis, the Dutchman, was silky-smooth and much-loved by those British in thrall to the classic style of the Achilles Club.

Zátopek's thinking was clear. He might have told the journalists that the odds were stacked against him, but he did not believe that. 'I hardly broke into a sweat and I'd won the gold medal [in the 10,000 metres],' he said. 'In the 5000 metres I'd go fast and destroy them.'

He deliberately hit the front with the intention of splashing mud on those behind. The spectators did not seem to mind, as they chanted his name, so he continued to churn up the track in earnest. Later, he would say it would have been a fine plan had Reiff not decided to take revenge and step in the mud himself.

Jack Crump, the British team manager, watched the race unfold. He had suffered his own race to be there. He had collapsed just before the Olympics had started and was taken to a hospital in Manchester. 'I awoke the next morning to find myself in a long ward with patients chattering away,' he said. 'It struck me when I recovered my full consciousness that they were quite a quarrelsome lot. One patient, who seemed far quieter than the rest, told me not to worry, for I was in a psychiatric ward and most of the patients were under observation.' Crump wondered if he was going mad, but a nurse later told him that it was the only bed available. Harold Abrahams came up and freed Crump, and so his Olympics could go ahead. Now Crump looked at the drama unfolding in front of him and reasoned that driving himself to exhaustion had been worth it.

The cry of 'Zát-o-pek, Zát-o-pek' was now unmistakable. The man with the thinning hair and red shirt had already become a favourite. What happened over the next few minutes would make him more loved still.

Four laps to go and Zátopek looks well set to achieve a second great victory.

Reiff's white shorts were now covered in mud. Numbers were blotted out. Yet everyone knew who was who. It was Zátopek versus Reiff, and yet, suddenly, almost subtly, the Belgian began to pull away and Zátopek faded. His legs felt heavy and the track was quicksand. The tell-tale ache of failure gripped his calves. Slijkhuis passed him and went into second place. When a man in a large grey overcoat rang the silver bell, Reiff had the race won. Up in the press box, Lainson Wood jotted down some lines for the *Daily Telegraph*: 'The runners splashed their way through mud with grim tenacity.' He felt it had been a strange race so far, with Zátopek taking the early lead and the Swedes then taking it from him. Wood reasoned they were working together. Zátopek had then taken the lead and Reiff, Slijkhuis and Ahldén had followed him for four laps. And now Reiff had just gone away, thanks to a 67-second lap, and there was daylight. Wood noted that Zátopek was finished.

The Pathé man felt the same.

Three laps from finish and Reiff springs the first surprise of the race when he challenges and passes the Czech. Seen in slow motion Reiff goes on increasing his lead to 40 yards.

The footage from that evening drips with the added emotion of the hindsight. Slijkhuis is second at the start of the last lap but Reiff is well clear. He looks over his shoulder and is delighted by the gap.

Now with amazing suddenness Zátopek, who looked right out of the race, comes after him with an amazing burst over the last 300 yards. Even Reiff cannot believe it!

It was a Lazarus leap. These were the last bitter metres of the 20,000 he had raced over the last few days, and something deep inside stirred and refused to let him settle for anything other than heroism. So he drilled his feet into the track and the distance shrunk. The drenched fans forgot their discomfort and chanted as one, 'Zát-o-pek! Zát-o-pek! Zát-o-pek!' That union dragged Zátopek on as he searched his spirit. And more flashbulbs exploded as time slowed and voices softened. Memories of races and bombs and wheat fields merged in a torrent of consciousness.

Fifty metres became forty and the impossible became feasible. With every step and every pump of those arms, Zátopek got closer. Reiff looked over his shoulder again and now felt only blind panic. He was a fast man, and would go on to set world records in the very near future, but he was considered a better runner against the clock than rivals. Now he was under pressure from a deranged soldier from behind the Iron Curtain, and that was far more threatening than a stopwatch.

Rex Alston, a BBC commentator, was impressed by the narrative.

> Throwing all caution aside, with arms flailing, body swaying, he tore after the other two and quickly passed Slijkhuis. The roars of the cheers from the crowd were almost deafening. Stride by stride he brought Reiff back to him.

Zátopek was running from fear. In *Dana a Emil Zátopkovi vypravují*, he said, 'The idea of a gold medal was disappearing. That was my mistake. I should have realised that they had both gone too early. I only understood it with 200 metres left when I saw Slijkhuis struggling. I passed him in ten metres and then realised that Reiff, too, was cooked. The people shouted so loud that Reiff thought a hammer was about to hit him. When he saw that it was me he calculated and ran. He won by a metre. I offered him my hand because I thought he was a real phenomenon. That's not what I thought of myself, though. Not any more.'

It had been an extraordinary finale to a Bank Holiday Monday and another Olympic record – 14 minutes 17.6 seconds. The final words were put to the Pathé film that would be screened in cinemas across the country.

Reiff has indeed proved a worthy winner in putting up a new Olympic record, but not one of the whole vast crowd will ever forget the all-out effort and indomitable courage of Emil Zátopek.

It was flawed courage. Karel Kněnický, who had waved the shorts and vest in the 10,000 metres, blamed Zátopek. 'It's a shame you didn't start your final progression a bit sooner,' he told him. 'If you had sprinted earlier you would have two golds now.'

Zátopek did not need telling. 'That incredibly stupid race,' was how he would dub his own tactics. 'It was all so silly.' Perhaps the true silliness of his Olympics had come when he had duelled with Ahldén in the heats, expending energy that he needed on those last laps when the pain was rising and the mud sticking. 'London cheered for me,' Zátopek would say, 'but when I got back to Czechoslovakia, they just said, "How could I be so stupid?"'

He went back to the RAF camp and stewed. He tortured himself with the race, thinking about how it might have panned out if he had run differently. He knew Reiff was good, but he had the beating of him. After struggling to sleep, he got up at 5 a.m. and decided he had to see Dana. It was a complicated trip involving various modes of transport, but he had to see her. He picked up his gold medal and slipped out. After all the noise and chaos of the Olympic Games, the morning acted as a mute button.

Dana was lying in bed at the school. She was semi-awake when she heard a familiar Moravian melody. It took a few seconds for her to register that the sound was whistling. This was their signal. 'I was in bed and I heard that song, our song,' she said.

She got up and went to the window. She saw his face in the half-light and whispered, 'I'll be down in a minute. Wait a bit.'

'I went down to see him in the garden. I was nervous because men were not allowed to visit us. I told him to come and sit by the swimming pool. We found a spot and I asked him what was wrong. He told me all about the 5000 metres and how disappointed he was. He said, "I should have sprinted sooner. If I'd done that then I might have caught him." Then he looked at me and said, "I came to show you my gold medal." He got the box out of his pocket and flicked it open. Then he held it up. It was the first medal I'd seen. And then, at that very moment, he dropped it and it fell into the swimming pool.'

They watched it sink out of sight.

'Oh no!' Dana said.

'What are we going to do?' Emil asked.

Dana looked at him. 'I have not got a swimming costume. You are going to have to jump in there.'

'He got undressed down to his shorts and then he went into the pool. It was cold but he was worried. He dived down and came back up with the medal. He got out and said he would have to wring out his shorts, so he went to a tree.' He was squeezing them when the headmistress from the school came along. We were not able to speak much English but she was screaming, "Get out! Get out!" We understood that all right. We were ashamed because she was thinking something very different had been going on. She pointed at Emil and shouted, "Out." He was almost naked and he began running. She was very angry and quite fearsome. The gate was open but there was something hard and metal on the ground and he collided with it and went into a somersault. People were watching by now and we felt terrible. Slowly, he disappeared, hobbling, into the darkness.'

For Emil and Dana the Olympics were over, but they still had time to enjoy themselves. It was while in London that Emil asked

Dana to marry him. They went to Piccadilly and bought two rings. Dana's would chaff and eventually they melted them down and made one which they shared.

The Olympics were deemed a success, although Britain failed to win even a single gold medal in athletics. One of the disappointments came in the marathon in which Jack Holden, one of the great home hopes, dropped out before the end with further badly blistered feet. All those who watched that race never forgot it, as the leader, Étienne Gailly, entered the stadium and then all but collapsed, his body spent and his legs now boneless rubber. He toiled and staggered as Delfo Cabrera, an Argentine fireman, and Tom Richards, a Welsh nurse, overtook him. Gailly was almost walking and somehow made it to the end and a bronze medal. Crump felt a voyeuristic unease at watching Gailly. Those feelings would be intensified when he heard reports that hinted strongly that illegal stimulants had been used by some competitors. Both the collapse of Gailly and the spectre of drug use would feature heavily in athletics in the decades to come. For Jim Peters, now at home, the Olympic marathon would be a warning; for Zátopek, it was another challenge.

Zátopek raced again and again after the Olympics, despite a mounting pain in his hip. He was now a source of national pride and a totem for the Communist regime. He could not say no. He took on Reiff over 5000 metres in Prague and the Belgian won again in a time of 14 minutes 19 seconds. Zátopek could hardly walk due to the pain from his hip, but he kept on running, for Czechoslovakia against Italy, and then under lights where he beat Ahldén in Prague. The time that night was 14 minutes 16 seconds and, really, it was time to stop. He had Olympic gold and silver and even had a momentous defeat behind him.

He married Dana on 24 October 1948, and athletes used javelins to give them a guard of honour afterwards. They had crashed their bicycles on the day of the wedding, but otherwise it passed off peacefully. For Emil, life was on an upward curve, but others were not so lucky. As Zátopek toasted his wife and contemplated married life, his old coach was locked in a tiny, dank cell and was awaiting interrogation by the worst of the StB henchmen. It was now Jan Haluza's time to plot his tactics and be a hero.

9

'Welcome to Hell, White Eagle!'

Jan Haluza was sitting in his office on the fourth floor at Kotva in Zlín. It was 27 September 1948 and his former protégé, Emil Zátopek, was a national hero. He was due to get married the following month but Haluza would not be there. A week earlier his friends had told him they had received a warning that the StB were coming for him. Haluza was a wise man but he knew he had done nothing wrong and so he ignored them. But now, as he looked at the men in suits, standing in the doorway, a look of insouciance on the face of the leader, he knew they were right.

'Did you expect us?' the man said.

Haluza maintained his sanguine demeanour. He was renowned for it at Kotva. 'Why should I expect you?' he asked.

The man shrugged, frustrated that their presence had not induced panic. 'Well, you're under arrest,' he said.

It had been a long journey, even to this point. Orel remained important to him and he was also resistant when the Central National Physical Training Committee decided to unite all physical activities under the Sokol banner. 'Orel's struggle for independence soon turned into a fight for the freedom of every person in this country,' he would say. By the end of the war he became more political. A deeply religious man, he wanted to back those who had fought against fascism, and so he joined the Czechoslovak People's Party. His erudition and calm saw him rise through the ranks and, by the end of 1945, he was elected chairman of the Regional Committee of Youth in Zlín. He helped battle the Communists in the elections and had some success.

There was a grisly form of irony in the net closing around Haluza some three years after the liberation and the end of the Nazis. However, the trouble had been coming once the Communists saw the worth of Haluza. Appreciating his popularity as a runner and how he had risen from a poor working-class family to political office, they asked him to join them. Haluza refused. The Communists did not take that slight well. 'If you do not join us then there will be trouble for you,' one of the leaders told Haluza.

He remained firm. And then, after the 1948 Communist coup, he found himself in a perilous position. Again he was asked to join them and again he refused. One of the Communists tasked with recruiting him was puzzled and assumed Haluza did not believe the coup would last. 'Don't worry,' he told Haluza. 'If there was a revolt then I would first shoot you and then myself.'

As he was taken from his office to the Regional Court in Zlín he realised the StB controlled the whole place. He slept there for one night and then, to his mounting horror, was taken to prison at Uherské Hradiště: 'This is how it all began.'

The prison would become synonymous with political trials in the coming years. Haluza was worried now, for himself but mainly for Věra. He wondered when she would find out where he was and then, alarmingly, whether she, too, had been arrested.

The secret police officers shoved Haluza into a solitary cell. He asked again what his crime was, but he was manacled and locked in darkness below a row of interrogation cells known as 'the 30s'. He knew the stories about the StB and how they forced confessions by torture, drugs and blackmail, and he made himself cling to his Catholic faith. It is safe to assume that had he seen the file the police had already drawn up on him then that faith might have started to crumble. Page 23 of the Ministry of Interior files stated, 'Dr Jan Haluza decided to found his own illegal organisation which wanted to cancel the present government and help the Czechoslovak People's Party.'

It got worse on page 29: 'They helped many people to illegally cross the state border. They also prepared a revolution using weapons to cancel the Communist government.'

In short, the StB was intent on proving that Dr Jan Haluza, once a humble cross-country runner and trainer of Emil Zátopek, the national hero, had been working as a spy, a revolutionary and a leading member of the underground resistance. As the StB officer looked through the bars and told him they would start their questioning tomorrow, Jan Haluza had just cause to be afraid: 'I got the solitary cell where you are alone and really suffer because you are arrested and don't know why. I had expected to be prosecuted, but instead they just put me in the cell. I couldn't believe that what we did – simply gathering together (as a group) – was a crime. I am a lawyer and I could not believe that they would make an issue out of nothing.'

The interrogation started the following day. Haluza had already been denied food and water and made to stand in the corner of his solitary cell, facing the wall, for hours. He was then strapped to a table. The interrogators proceeded to beat his feet until they bled, demanding that he confess to his crimes. Haluza was wearing his Orel top with its eagle motif. 'Welcome to hell, white eagle,' his interrogator grinned as he struck. Haluza cried out in agony but refused to implicate himself. It became a battle between his innate sense of justice and the intense pain from his feet, which dripped blood on to the cold stone floor.

He was dumped back in his cell for several days after that and wondered if his ordeal was over. The answer came in the blackness one morning. 'They came for me and another interrogation started, but it wasn't just a beating this time.' Instead, he watched in horror as these thugs put metal strips into his shoes and wired them up to a generator. They flicked a switch and 220-volt electric shocks paralysed his legs and thighs. His body convulsed, but that only made it worse, as he was strapped down with shackles that were dubbed 'US Bonds'. Whenever Haluza struggled the shackles would tighten and scythe deeper into his skin. Somehow, Haluza managed to shake off his shoes. A man moved into the light of the bulb as Haluza passed in and out of consciousness.

'Don't you worry,' the blurred face said, the light circling it like a halo. 'We have a cure for you.' Haluza wondered, briefly, if he were seeing an angel. Then, suddenly, the light was a blinding one and he realised the man had moved out of sight. He heard some muttering and then was prodded. 'Put these on!' the man shouted and forced a pair of heavy boots on to Haluza's purple feet.

'These already had the metal strips securely fastened and they did the laces up. They were sturdy things and I couldn't shake them off. The interrogation started all over again and it was horrible. My heart felt tight, my brain was affected, my legs were shaking. In the end they left me standing in the boots and they turned the electricity on. This caused my legs to go weak and I collapsed immediately.'

Slowly it dawned on Haluza that these people would do anything to make him confess to crimes he had not committed. It was inhuman but it was real, like the Nazis all over again, twisted people forcing others into a doctrine via the most appalling methods. 'Had they learnt nothing,' he wondered. 'I went through months of cruel, inhuman beatings alternated with psychological terror,' he said. 'More than once my feet were broken. Many times I went through a bestial torture of electric shocks.'

Věra had been arrested and, as she was put in her own cell, she, too, let her mind run riot. Scared and confused, she remembered the wedding day when, on the way to the church of Saint Hostýn, a fallen tree had blocked the road. Her grandmother had crossed herself at the sign and warned that Věra would face a lot of obstacles in her marriage. Her grandmother had been right.

Finally, they learnt the nature of the accusations. Haluza admitted that he had always struggled for freedom and democracy, but always by peaceful means, in accordance with the law and the Ten Commandments. They were the authorities to whom he answered, God and the law. However, when he was accused of being part of a revolutionary group under the leadership of Antonín Huvar he wondered if either of those could save him. In truth Huvar was only a local chaplain, but he had participated in distributing pamphlets mocking the new regime and had even criticised the Communists in his sermons. Věra and Jan were just two of '45 robbers' accused of being part of Huvar's plot.

The secret police files already contained many mentions of Jan Haluza by then. He was listed in relation to anti-Communist activities of an accountant named Kiri Hrubý and then in the file of Vincence Vlack, another member of Orel. The register of arrested people listed:

Dr Jan Haluza, born 12th July 1914 in Šternov, in the county
of Hustopeče, local police station in Újezd, in the county of
Hustopeče, registry office in Šternov, the son of Rudolf and
Julie nee Kalivodová, married, Roman-Catholic, of Czech
nationality. Employed by company Kotva in Zlín. Permanent
address in Zlín, 1st of May Street #2929. Corporal in reserve,
literate, having no property, childless, takes care of his wife.

The bulging file detailed more of his supposed crimes: 'He also
planned with his wife to emigrate and to get in contact with
former members of his party, Dr Procházka or Mr Chudoba,
former Member of Parliament . . .' In addition the files say that,
when he was arrested, Haluza had information about the import
and export of gold reserves from the National Bank. The report
claims Haluza could not explain this and that a missing file made
the writer sure that 'Dr Haluza worked as a spy at this point.'

Haluza was asked to make a statement when he arrived at
Uherské Hradiště. This forms page 48 of the 253 pages in his file,
including all manner of detail about his life, from his 6000
Koruna-a-month salary to his brother the priest and brother the
locksmith. It also shows that Haluza was trying to refute allegations
of links with other alleged subversives:

In June 1939 I was declared the juris doctor at Masaryk
University in Brno. Beginning January 1940 until February
1942 I taught at the gymnasium in Prague, Bubeneč. In
March 1942 I was employed by the Baťa company in Zlín
as clerk of the export school. In Zlín I am employed until
the present time and now I work in administration section
No. 580 – the chief of section is Dr Drábek. I am independent
referent in our section and my work is to check all questions

concerning the prices, rights, economy and to prepare information and explanations.

Concerning my person, I am Roman-Catholic. Sometime in 1942 or 1943, at some religion celebration, I met František Němeček, the clerk of the Baťa company in Zlín. Since that time I met him again and I know that he was also active in the People's Party. I did not try to be in contact with him too often. I had the impression that he is talking too much. I was not happy if he tried to speak with me.

In February of this year Němeček was removed from his job as clerk and he got other, worse work. I do not know the reason why he was moved.

Between February and June of this year I met him only several times. During our meetings we spoke only about common things and our talk did not contain any new ideas or plans for the future of the People's Party.

I am absolutely sure that during our meetings we did never talk about some treasonous illegal leaflets. I also cannot agree that Němeček told me that he had read some illegal leaflet, distributed by university students in Prague. I am sure that I never did hear about such a leaflet.

The date for the trial was set for 5 November, but the interrogations continued. His jailors mocked Jan's religion and told him that Věra was an unfaithful prostitute: 'During the interrogation one of them wanted to use drugs to damage my memory, but he changed his mind. The main tactic was cross-interrogation. They put some warm clothes on me and lit a circle of 5,000-watt lightbulbs that produced a considerable amount of heat. The idea was to make you sweat and hallucinate, but it didn't work with me.'

The trial was a farce, with the court-appointed lawyer having no intention of saving Haluza or refuting the allegations about stealing guns, grenades and explosives. Haluza complained and said that, as a trained lawyer, he would defend himself. The court was not very interested in what he had to say. Nor were the journalists who began to write that the former athlete was now a traitor.

On 9 November the judge delivered his verdict in the case 'II 3/48' of Haluza and the other defendants: Antonín Huvar received ten years of prison; Jan Lednický was sentenced to eight years; Dr Jan Haluza received six years, including three months of sleeping on a hard bed; Věra Haluzová was released.

Věra had been at home wearing an Indian summer dress when they arrived for her. By the time she was released from prison the seasons had changed and there was snow everywhere. She shivered as she walked away and got hypothermia. She fell seriously ill. 'My wife was liberated after months of custody,' Haluza said. 'But she had to live with constant fear, intimidation and spying.'

It would get worse for Haluza. As Věra battled illness and loneliness, he was linked to the crimes of Milada Horáková. In her short life, Horáková had already been arrested and tortured by the Gestapo, freed by the US Army, elected to Parliament and awarded two medals by President Beneš. Then the Communists took over and she resigned. On the same day that Haluza had been arrested, her husband returned home to find the secret police in his garden. He tried to warn her but, like Haluza, she had been seized at work and hauled into custody. Sometime that year two Soviet 'advisors', called Lichachov and Makarov, arrived to train Czech police in methods of interrogation based on the Soviet show trials of the 1930s. The bedrock of this methodology was brainwashing prisoners, whether through torture, drugs or starvation, so that they would sign prepared statements.

'After the trial the prisoners were sent to Pankrác and then to Jáchymov, but I stayed in Uherské Hradiště because I was supposed to be a member of the group of people connected with Milada Horáková. I refused to tell them that I was part of that group and they took their revenge on me with all possible techniques they could think of.'

'Why are you doing this?' Haluza shouted. His defiance only provoked them and so they tied him to an iron bed and slashed his feet once more: 'That was the first thing they did to me because of Milada Horáková. I stayed in Uherské Hradiště and I slept in the central building. It was a beautiful house, a former school, and there were rooms in the attic where we were interrogated. Even the way they called us for interrogation was harsh. They woke you up early in the morning and put you in a room where you were guarded. You had to stand with your face against the wall and you couldn't turn around unless you needed something really urgent. You were left like this until the evening, when the interrogation began. That was the first horrible thing. The second was that in Uherské Hradiště, where I had won the national championship several times, they dragged me in chains through the city. People in the street recognised me and seemed to pity me. That was really humiliating.'

The name Horáková is a guilty blot on Czechoslovakia's past. A champion of democracy who was awarded a medal by the president in another century, back then she was portrayed as the enemy of the state. Zátopek himself, made a public statement against her. Hindsight casts an unfavourable shadow over that act, but it is easy to believe that Zátopek was toeing the party line. His peers claim that he would easily be swayed by political expediency and so he sided against the supposed traitor. This was the first sign that Zátopek was not as politically rigid as later commentators would paint him. It also shows how the state would use him to manipulate public opinion. They asked, or coerced, Zátopek into making public statements, or at least signing pre-written ones, knowing that the people would pay attention to a man like him.

However, many of his peers think he quickly regretted his stance over Horáková. The following year, when Horáková was declared guilty of plotting to overthrow the regime, after a show trial that was scripted by the Soviet directors, her case became an international incident. Albert Einstein and Winston Churchill were among those appealing for clemency. The Czechs did not listen. It took Horáková 15 minutes to die by hanging in Pankrač prison in Prague, a place where the Nazis had previously used a guillotine to execute people. Her reputation would not be fully restored for 50 years. It was clear that Jan Haluza was in a terrible world of trouble.

10

The Pitiless Race of Elimination

Emil Zátopek was initially blissfully unaware of Jan Haluza's plight. They had gone their separate ways and become separated by differences of geography and career. Haluza was a businessman in Zlín, Zátopek a soldier in Prague. The latter went home from the Olympics and found that, for all the niggling admonishment about tactics from on high, he was a hero of the people. For a while he even trained at night to escape the cloying public attention. His biographer, František Kožik, paints a florid picture of him encircled by a group of Czech schoolchildren who quiz him on his methods. If it sounds romantic, there is no doubt that children loved Zátopek and that his answers are still illuminating.

He said that he would prefer a longer stride, that glycogen decomposes when muscles are exerted, that resting was like turning off an energy tap – and led to a build-up of pressure which exploded in a 'a terrific urge'. He didn't have a stopwatch and merely ran as fast as he could in sprints. He spoke of the increase in sporting theories, of athletes who lost half a stone to be lighter and faster only to find they were slower. He was dismissive of critics of his style: 'When I began they used to say,

"It's impossible the way he runs, he isn't a runner at all." Then when I began to break records the grumblers began to change their tune and said, "Yes, you should use Zátopek as an example."' Be economical but be true to yourself, he said. 'A hare runs that way too.'

Zátopek and Kožik were not always entirely truthful and, while he renounced alcohol publicly, Emil certainly liked a glass of beer. And for all his innovations in training methods and his rudimentary grasp of sports science, he was capable of some alarmingly naïve practices.

Zátopek led the athletics programme in ATK, where he was a company commander, with Aleš Poděbrad as his representative. One of the other runners was Jan Mrázek, who remembered the time Zátopek had sprinted to the team dinner. Tired and thirsty he noticed the five-litre bottle from which people plucked pickles to eat. 'He drank the whole bottle,' Mrázek said. 'When we looked at him in horror, wondering if something would happen to him, he just uttered words I cannot forget: "The hare runs through the woods, eats what he finds – and he's fine."'

On another occasion, he noticed some Germans drinking lemonade by the side of the track in Strahov Stadium. Zátopek ran up to them, snatched the lemonade from them, downed it and carried on running.

Poděbrad said Zátopek also drank a whole bottle of the highly alcoholic herbal bitters called Becherovka and still beat the great Hungarian runner, József Kovács, in a duel, and there was an infamous meeting with the Hungarians in Prague which was cancelled because Zátopek and the whole team went down with diarrhoea. Clearly, Zátopek was a mercurial figure, sometimes scientific, sometimes whimsical, sometimes meticulous, sometimes a hedonist. Poděbrad explained: 'He could be specific with food and preferred garlic and onions. He justified that by saying, "The doe that runs fast only eats green food."' This juggling of the almost profound with the playful betrayed a contradictory nature that was again highlighted when he ate three kilos of melons before an interstate match in Bulgaria. 'It had unfavourable consequences,' Poděbrad said, with some understatement.

Yet Emil's every move was now being monitored, both by the public and the StB informers. File No. 310_88_25 states that Zátopek is politically lax. Another entry states: 'He admits he joined the Party because he had to if he wanted to be in the military and that he knows about the existence of political prisoners.'

Fame was something to be mistrusted – and used – in the minds of the Communist regime, and there was no doubt that Zátopek was famous. When Zátopek led a Czech team in Helsinki, most of his peers had not seen the sea before. They went down to the port to look at the boats and came to a large American ship with a guard blocking the gangway. He asked who they were and they said they were Czechs. 'Zátopek?' he said brightly.

Emil wandered to the front and the guard immediately called the captain. The group were invited on to the boat and into the captain's cabin, where Zátopek gave an autograph. They went below deck, where the captain explained that this was a former warship and showed off the guns. A large black man was eyeing them curiously, a novel sight for the Czechs. One of the Americans motioned to him and said, 'Czechoslovaks.'

The black man smiled and said, 'Zátopek?'

Ludvik Liška was third behind Zátopek as he opened his 5000 metres season with a win in 14 minutes 23.6 seconds in Prague in May 1949. Days later Zátopek travelled to Warsaw and improved to 14 minutes 10.2 seconds. That was an impressive time. He was still some way off Gunder Hägg's sub-14 minute world record, but only Sydney Wooderson had run faster.

He had settled into wedded life, although he joked that in southern Moravia they sang 'the troubles start when you get married'. Sure enough, Dana had asked him to run to the shop to get some milk every day for a week. 'Why do I always have to go?' he complained. Dana did not pause for breath as she replied, 'You're a runner. You should go there and back without thinking – and be back in record time too.' He said that she had been so convincing that he ran to the dairy three times a day and ran on the spot while the assistant got his order. 'Hurry up,' he had implored her. 'Or Dana will think I'm out of form.'

***

There was no danger of that when he won the cross-country championships at Jičín, north-east of Prague, where the first prize was a huge portrait of Trotsky in a gilt-edged frame. 'This is our wedding present,' the organisers said beforehand. 'Christ,' thought Zátopek, 'I better win then.'

He started strongly but got so far ahead that when he got to a crossroads he did not know which way to go. When he saw the runners far away on a hill, he realised he had taken the wrong fork. He caught them in 29th place and stumbled over stones and bushes as he battled the final lap around the local cemetery. It was the narrowest of wins. 'My legs were shaking on the podium while the local club president's hands were shaking as he handed over Trotsky. "Thank you, Emil," he said. "We were afraid that your wedding present was going to go to some old man."'

On 11 June Zátopek went to Ostrava, known as the country's steel heart due to its heavy industries. The chimneys expelled choking grey plumes over the annual Army Championships.

He was quite merry too, a happily married man, even if Dana was the boss, and he felt good, natural, like the hare in the forest, as he would say. His glycogen levels were high and he felt them burning, like coals in the engine of the man they had started calling 'the Human Locomotive'. It was one of those easy runs where he felt his body brimming with energy. He felt the hiss of the crowd like coal on fire, expelling steam towards him. 'We want the record,' he heard some boys shout, as a few words tumbled out of the white noise. 'The record?' He had not even thought about Viljo Heino's mark of 29 minutes 35.4 seconds, which had stood for five years. He listened to the split times and realised he was behind schedule and yet, as he relaxed and felt the crowd noise rise from a hum to rumble to roar, he accelerated. 'I thought that if the seventh kilometre was better then I'd have a go,' he said. It was. The announcer shouted, 'Emil Zátopek could threaten the world record!' The boys' chant was taken up by those around them and, before long, the whole crowd was chanting: 'World record! World record! World record!' Zátopek waited for the time after 8000 metres with a tortured expression – '23 minutes 37 seconds! *Better than Heino!*' – and then it was on. 'After I heard that, I was going so fast that people started getting out of the way.' He flicked his legs off the track, knowing that a runner loses speed by remaining earthbound for too long. He ran the ninth kilometre in just under three minutes. If he did the same again then he would have the world record. Ron Clarke, the great runner of the future who would become a fan and friend, would say that world records provided a fleeting sort of glory, a peculiar sense of disappointment in which exhilaration drained away to leave profound weariness – call it the sadness of the spent, or the loneliness of the long-distance runner.

But Zátopek did not feel that. Instead, he felt the warmth of the crowd and the thrill of a mountain being climbed. He felt the nation behind him rather than on his shoulders, and pumped his arms and let his tongue hang over his bottom teeth. 'Faster, higher, stronger.' That was what they had said at the Olympics, but he wanted more. He wanted to be the fastest. He ran and ran and he did not stop until well over the line. The crowd was in a collective delirium, and he wondered at the ability to be so selfless for someone else's achievement. And yet they were part of it too. This was a triumph for the country. Hell, even for the Party.

'*29 minutes 28.2 seconds!*'

He had beaten the old record by seven seconds. Destroyed it. 'The stadium exhaled and next day the world knew,' said Zátopek.

Heino certainly did. His life had derailed since the Olympic Games. The home of distance running, Finland, had turned against him after he dropped out of the 10,000 metres in London. While Zátopek was revered, Heino was reviled and even received hate mail. The defeat and manner of it was at odds with Finnish *sisu*, and yet Heino himself was beginning to doubt the new generation. He was the last of the Flying Finns, and a post-war nation was growing fat on a growing economy. He did not think there would be many successors to his crown. Finland, he deduced, had lost its heart, and he found it horribly ironic that he would have to read letters telling him of *his* failings. Nobody who truly knew Heino could doubt his resolve. Shot in the war, he had nursed himself back to the top, and now he was nursing four children after the sudden death of his wife. It was a tragic Olympic aftermath that was unbeknown to rivals like Zátopek in a world before 24-hour news.

Zátopek's schedule was now relentless as the authorities sought to use him as the face of the new Czechoslovakia. The reorganisation of sport had born fruit at the Olympic Games, where Czechoslovakia had reached eighth in the medal table, well ahead of the hosts, and Zátopek was the trailblazer. Days after taking Heino's world record, he ran in Stockholm and, although he won the 5000 metres race in a time of 14 minutes 14 seconds, he injured a muscle and saw signs of a haematoma. Yet his rest did not last long. The next month he travelled to Helsinki for a match that the Finns were using as proof that they were still the distance kings and that, regardless of what Heino might have felt, *sisu* was alive and well and not coagulated beneath a soft heart.

The Finns stacked the odds in their favour. Zátopek would run twice in two days in the Finland–Czechoslovakia match before taking on another two races in Turku and Pori. The Finns may have been a partisan people, but Emil's fame bridged boundaries and 'Zátopek – the running ace' – was championed in posters and in newspaper advertisements.

The Finnish plan was to get Salomon Könönen to go off at a frenetic pace and draw the energy out of Zátopek's legs, enabling Heino to pass him in the latter stages. They felt Zátopek, still smarting from giving Gaston Reiff too much of a head-start in the Olympic 5000 metres, would be unable to resist chasing him. They guessed wrong. Zátopek was too intelligent to fall into the same trap and allowed Könönen to drive himself onwards 'almost to death', as Kožik put it, before easing past the stricken frame. Heino could not match him either. Zátopek won in 29 minutes 55 seconds. Perhaps the Finnish dissenters were right; maybe Heino had lost heart after his domestic tragedy.

Zátopek just kept on winning after that. He won the 5000 metres for his team and country, and then improved his time two days later in a second fight with Väinö Koskela. The Finn had one last chance when they went to Pori for a 3000 metres, not Zátopek's favoured distance, but as tiredness set in and he felt the cost of winning, he just hung on for a fourth win in six days. Finland had been well and truly beaten. Their newspapers, schooled on Paavo Nurmi and Ville Ritola, gushed over this newcomer. He was now the world's Nurmi and, unlike old Stoneface, he did it with a grin.

Ten days later Zátopek went to Moscow for the first USSR v Czechoslovakia meeting. Things were changing in the mother country. For decades the Soviet Union had ignored the Olympic Games, bristling at the bourgeois nature of its amateur status, which made it a rich man's sport. They had also hamstrung themselves with a series of post-war purges. A security forces colonel from the frontier guards was appointed to chairman of the All-Union Committee, and the famous Starostin brothers were swiftly arrested on charges of plotting to kill Stalin. This was later commuted to 'lauding bourgeois sport' and they were sentenced to between eight and ten years' hard labour. Their only crime had been to tell friends 'about foreign life', and one of the bemused brothers confided that the security police had been most interested in 'sweaters, suits and hats'. Yet, despite losing the Starostin brothers, including the founder of Spartak Moscow, sport assumed unprecedented significance.

Stalin wanted to use sport to promote socialism, and moves were made to join the international fold. This meant publicly renouncing the previous system that had paid up to 25,000 roubles to anyone breaking a world record and up to 15,000 roubles for a national one. Athletes received salaries and bursaries, none of which was allowed by the International Olympic Committee. However, the goal of sport remained the same, even if the means became clouded in doubt. The Party sounded a clarion call to 'raise the level of skill so that Soviet sportsmen might win world supremacy in the major sports in the immediate future'. By 'major' they meant athletics, the heartbeat of the Olympic Games and the greatest stage of all on which to expose American weakness. The suspicion that the Soviets would go to any lengths to show their superiority fomented during the Cold War and was still festering in 2015 when Russia became the first nation to be suspended from all athletics competition due to state-sponsored doping.

One of these supermen primed to undermine the west would be Vladimir Kuts. By the time Zátopek arrived in Moscow, the young Ukrainian with the shock of white hair had lived several lives. Childhood famine had wiped out relatives and friends and then, when he was 14, the Nazis seized control and forced him into slave labour. He was regularly beaten with a club, sometimes with 25 successive blows, but he escaped when he was 16 and joined up with nearby Russian forces that were fighting the Germans. Thor Gotaas, in *Running*, said, 'He lived with a gun in his hand and death at his shoulder in his battle for the Soviet Union.' After the war he made the long walk home only to find his village was no more, razed to the ground and with all familiar faces gone – dead or fled. He had endured five years of hell and had nowhere to go. So he joined the navy and started running towards epoch-defining clashes with Zátopek and Gordon Pirie.

That lay in the future. For now Zátopek was a conduit in relations between the two countries. The Czechs were treated to the airbrushed view of Moscow: visiting the Kremlin and Lenin's tomb, being told that 500 million roubles was spent on physical exercise each year, that there were 100,000 football clubs, and that 350 national records and 25 world records had been broken in all sports that year.

Zátopek won his race and was reported as championing the fantastic lifestyle of those in the Soviet Union, where they had milk, tea, fruit, bacon, eggs and bread and butter for breakfast and then danced until midnight. Kuts knew the truth was far less wholesome and, if he was still only 22 and some way from his peak, the bitterness and coldness froze his face into a death mask that alerted the leading Soviet coaches.

As he made his way to a special concert put on in his honour, Zátopek, of course, had never heard of Kuts. Leading folk artists gathered to tell the tale of a Cossack being visited by a dead runner. The Cossack challenged Death to a drinking contest and Death drank himself into an early grave. As Emil applauded, he had no idea that in his house in Finland, with four children to care for, Viljo Heino was refusing to accept that he, too, was a dead man. And so, on 1 September, at the age of 35, the last of the Flying Finns turned up at a track in Kouvola, a town in south-eastern Finland that would become famous only for its crime rate and brutalist Soviet buildings, and regained the 10,000 metres world record. His time of 29 minutes 27.2 seconds was one second faster than Zátopek had managed. The season was over and so Heino would have the prize until the next year. At least that was Zátopek's reasoning, but others were less patient. The ATK chief, Lieutenant Colonel Sabl, would not let Zátopek rest. 'Don't you want to try to win back the record?' he said to the athlete. 'You know what it would mean to us.'

'Yes, I know, but I hardly train these days,' Zátopek said.

'You must run again and regain the world record for Czechoslovakia this year. How long do you need?'

Zátopek again found himself being ushered in directions that he would rather not go. He was now only partly in control of his own destiny. He did the running, the training, the masochistic 60 x 400-metre repetitions. Yet he only got part of the glory.

Sabl agreed to keep the attempt on 22 October a secret, but Zátopek let the news out himself when he used it as an excuse to get out of writing a newspaper column. The next day the paper carried a different headline: ZÁTOPEK TO WIN BACK THE WORLD RECORD!

Emil sighed. 'Oh well, I better do it now or go to bed without supper.'

His training methods were already a source of huge debate. One of the best summaries would come from Fred Wilt, an intriguing American who had finished 11th in the Olympic 10,000 metres final while juggling his duties as an FBI agent. Wilt was a curious, inquisitive soul, befitting his day job, and began writing to other athletes and coaches from all over the world to find out how they trained. That would bear fruit in his fascinating booklet *How They Train* in which he rightly pointed out that, while much was made of Zátopek's habit of running 60 x 440 metres in a single workout, that in itself would have been a modest accomplishment if he had been running those laps slowly. Wilt knew that pace was crucial to understanding Zátopek's work ethic. He wrote, 'In 1948 his daily training involved 5 x 200m, 20 x 400m, 5 x 200m. Each fast run was followed by 200m brisk jogging for recovery. The speed of the 200m runs was approximately 34 seconds. The 400m runs were each as fast as possible, starting with 56–60 seconds and ending with 70–75 seconds. The 200m recovery runs were done in about 60 seconds each. If Zátopek found it necessary to work for speed he ran more 400m intervals. Prior to the 1948 Olympics he ran 60 x 400m fast followed by 200m slow for ten days in succession.'

Meticulous in his research and study of his peers, Wilt also hinted at the philosophy and personality of his subjects. 'Zátopek's theory was to work as hard as possible so that a race seemed comparatively easy,' he said. 'He felt that strength and energy only increased through continual testing. Zátopek had no fear of becoming burned out through training. His strategy usually involved leading. While leading he sought to wear down his opponents by making countless bursts of speed and changes of pace, and finish with an amazing sprint.

'He was probably the most colourful of all runners. His leg action was perfect, and his upper body with bobbing head, flailing arms, rolling shoulders, screwed-up face, mark him as the most uninhibited runner ever seen. Before Zátopek, nobody realised it was humanly possible to train this hard. Emil is truly the originator of modern intensive training. Zátopek was personally perhaps the most humble, friendly and popular athlete of modern times.'

Emil ran 20 kilometres a day for 14 days in preparation for his record attempt, but the haematoma became visible on his left calf so he cut back on his schedule. He even took two complete days off before the attempt, studying his leg and frowning, trying to will the swelling away. The promoters were anxious and sought confirmation that Zátopek would run. He knew he could not really back out, but also that it would be a crushing anti-climax if he had to drop out of the race once it had started. He gave the go-ahead.

More than 20,000 people had crammed into the stadium in Ostrava by the 4 p.m. start time. Zátopek was given a thunderous reception as he appeared in his old sweats. He removed them to reveal his white ATK top and blue shorts. He slapped his thighs and looked at the swelling on his calf. Perhaps it was the injury that meant he started slowly. He completed the first kilometre two seconds short of Heino's pace. After two kilometres he was four seconds down. Some of the ATK chiefs looked at each other nervously. The crowd just stayed with him. Patriotism and love of the working-class hero outweighed split times.

And then, as Wilt had pointed out, Zátopek changed tactic and surged. He completed the third kilometre in 2 minutes 54 seconds, some seven seconds better than Heino had managed in Finland. Suddenly, Zátopek was not only back on track but he was almost three seconds inside world-record pace. By half-distance his fears about his injury were erased by adrenaline as the announcer shouted that he was six seconds inside the target time.

An official raised a white flag after Zátopek's estimated time for each kilometre had elapsed. The crowd soon became accustomed to cheering as Zátopek crossed those marks ahead of schedule. It went wrong in the eighth kilometre. Now it seemed that fates were conspiring. It had been too late in the season, too soon after his training injury. Each of the last four kilometres were run at a slower pace than Heino had managed. Yet the gap to the man in Finland was not much. In some ways the last kilometre was the easiest. It was flat out. Run as fast as you can, nothing more, nothing less. So he did, and the last kilometre was the fastest by more than three seconds. He completed it in 2 minutes 50.7 seconds. The time was 29 minutes 21.2 seconds. Once again, Zátopek had not just beaten a Heino record, he had dismantled it by a huge margin of six seconds.

It was snowing in Finland and Heino had no opportunity to attempt another record. After so many years of Finnish domination, Zátopek the patriot was happy to know that 'Czechoslovakia' was now in the record books.

11

Get Zátopek

Emil Zátopek's rivals were gathering strength and experience and numbers. Vladimir Kuts was still a young athlete in the Soviet navy, smarting from years of tragedy and trauma. In England, Gordon Pirie had been posted to RAF Watchet in Somerset where he was working as a wireless mechanic at the Gunnery School. He was 18 when Zátopek broke his first world record and he was smitten. Pirie had a picture of the Czech runner on his locker in his billet. Zátopek became an obsession.

Pirie had already been accused of over-training, but after wrestling with the problem one night made a decision that would change his life. 'My training would become harder,' he said. To do that he imagined a ginger-haired irritant who had beaten him in a services race. He was called Christopher Chataway and came from the establishment that Pirie so detested. Pirie would talk of the need for athletics to be free, and hence professional, and despised 'the part-time playboys who shoot up for a few seasons and then fade like a rocket because they won't give up the good life.' He hated the 'To and From Committee' that decided whether he could run abroad. He would be libelled, dubbed a traitor and a Bolshevik, and begin his biography with a chapter titled 'My Critics', but for now the British airman was adamant that he would be at the next Olympic Games and that he would beat

Zátopek. Much of that would stem from his belief that Zátopek's way was better than the British one. 'They suggested I was too young and that I should kill myself in a short time,' he wrote. 'Kill myself be damned. I'll kill the other runners but never myself. I looked forward to the future with great confidence. I [will] beat the world.'

Jim Peters did not have that sort of belief and, by the end of 1949, had done very little to pursue his new goal of becoming a marathon runner. In his diary he reflected on a poor performance over three miles and wrote, 'Felt lousy. No hard training. Too hot and tired of the sport.' He read the words and, not for the first time, thought that was the end of his athletics career. Frieda would have been happy if it were, but Johnny Johnston, his coach, was having none of that. He brought up the 'marathon business' again and told him it would take a couple of years. Jim agreed to at least try, but it had to be a secret operation, as Frieda was fervently against it. So he ran four miles a day for six months and then entered a 20-mile race.

However, Frieda could read her husband well and eyed him suspiciously as he left that day. 'It's not a marathon, is it?' she asked.

'Good lord, Frieda,' he said 'why would I want to run a marathon?'

He was telling a half-truth. The 20-mile distance was six miles short, but the ambition was plain. He won the race in Chelmsford and broke the two-hour barrier, but he was so distraught with the physical exertion that he could not speak for half an hour. His feet hurt and his mind raged. When he got home Frieda got the truth out of him with little trouble.

'I'm surprised at you, Jim Peters,' she said. 'And what did you get out of it?'

He dug a hand in a pocket and pulled out a small Essex county medal. Frieda looked at him with a mix of disappointment and sympathy. 'Is it worth it?' She was placated a little when they finally found their own house. For Jim this meant he could start his training runs from his own front door. He began training harder than ever, but faded out of the public consciousness. 'To the athletic world I was dead.'

Alain Mimoun must have felt something similar as he carried on being a waiter at Racing Club. The Olympics faded quickly. In *The Destiny of Ali Mimoun*, he told the author, Pat Butcher, 'I went to see my boss, but nothing. To make matters worse, I even had to serve a guy who I'd hammered in my first international cross-country victory. There's [Raphaël] Pujazon, sitting there like a film star. I'd kicked his arse and fought seven years of war, while he was a Spaniard who'd simply naturalised.'

Mimoun had encountered this indifference-cum-racism at the Olympics in London. He went to the massage room before the 10,000 metres to get a rub down. Gaston Reiff, a Belgian, was on the table. The France team masseur told Mimoun that he could not help him and was only there for the elite. Even the ensuing silver medal in that race had not seemed to win over France.

However, Mimoun's and Peters' problems paled when compared with those of Jan Haluza, Zátopek's old coach. That June, as Zátopek celebrated breaking the world record in Ostrava, Haluza, already serving his own sentence, testified in the case called 'Meeting in Vinoř'. The case was linked to Milada Horáková, but Haluza stood firm and refused to implicate two friends in a supposed secret expansion of their illegal activities. When the judge asked about his treatment, Haluza said, 'Mr Chairman, if you were interrogated in the same way that I was then you would have signed your own death warrant.'

Haluza helped an old friend get a pardon, but he was still serving his time. That summer he was moved to a prison in Brno and locked in a cell with 20 other people. He passed through another prison before he ended up in Pankrač, where Horáková would be hanged, and which was used as a base from which to transport prisoners to the Jáchymov mining region.

Marie Curie, the Nobel prize winner, had discovered radium in the area in 1898 and the small Bohemian town of Jáchymov, close to the Ore Mountains, had been plundered ever since, and was now the site of vast labour camps.

Haluza was taken to the main camp in Vilémov and, for a while, a guard took pity on the former sportsman and helped him. However, illness was rife in the cramped and unsanitary conditions and Haluza had to be moved to an older prison called Kartouzy. A dozen prisoners were assigned to each room in the former monastery, with one bucket in the corner. All the time Haluza wondered what was happening. How could God be so unfair? Where was Věra? Any concept of time was lost in a depressive rumination in which he tried to escape the present.

When he was fitter he became a *mukl*, shorthand for a man destined for disposal and engaged in the backbreaking, soulless work of extracting uranium. Then, one night, he was on the move again, this time taken to Jáchymov, itself, to meet the Jestřáb, the investigation department of the StB. Along with a friend he was stripped to his shorts, undershirt and socks and locked in a cold dark cell that was just over a metre high. The pair could not stand up straight but were not allowed to sit as the interrogators asked their questions. 'What is your name? Where were you born? Write what you have done here.'

After five long days Haluza refused to confess once more. Baffled by the questioning and severely dehydrated after not drinking for days, he was on the verge of collapse. He wondered if this was what death felt like, whether he had already passed over. 'When the escort was dragging me to an interrogation, I suddenly saw a water pipe,' he said. 'I immediately flung myself at it. The escort pulled out a gun and warned that he would shoot if I did not get back. The water was infected with typhus. He wanted to shoot but he needed me alive. When I got back to the camp the typhus started to have an effect.'

He was taken to a public hospital in Karlovy Vary and chained to his iron bed-frame. An StB man posed as a prisoner in a neighbouring bed, just in case Haluza said anything. However, he was unconscious for 22 days and then . . . 'I opened my eyes. I was looking around myself for two or three days and I was shouting, "Hu, hu, hu . . ." I had lost my memory and everyone thought I was crazy. But then, on the third day, I shouted out the words "human being"!'

***

Emil and Dana gave the Czech public a more sanitised view of the world. They were happily married for more than 50 years, which is an achievement by the standards of any age, but more so given the fame lavished on Zátopek, and his naturally gregarious nature. Dana could be jealous and there were the normal ups and downs of marital life, but the world was not about to get a view of that. When we met in 2015, Dana sat at her table in a flat in a gated block in a nice suburb north of Prague, and explained how the authorities had returned the manuscript she and Emil wrote together with František Kožík. 'It was done under a political supervisor and so we had to change a lot of things,' she said. 'I'd like to tell the truth. About the man I knew, the personality; how he took energy from the trees – he felt the trees actually recognised him; about all the myths – he didn't run in heavy boots all the time like they said [but] yes, he once started running in the bathtub on some dirty clothes, but not all the time. Things get distorted.'

Some things were not allowed to come out. Dana had two cousins in England. One had been a pilot in 311 Squadron, an RAF squadron based in Devon that was manned by Czech exiles and responsible for sinking a German blockade runner, *Alsterufer*, in December 1943. He had died in action and remained lost to the Czech public. 'Another cousin survived the war. He was a paratrooper involved in the invasion. And then there was General Ingr, a friend of my father and the leader of the army in England where the government was in exile. All of these things could not be mentioned. I could only say little things.'

Much of what Kožik managed to produce still gave an insight into their lives. He talks of walking out with the couple and watching them engage in a snowball fight: 'Dana hits each fir tree dead sure every time. She also easily beats Emil at throwing over the tree tops.' They play leap-frog. Emil admits he is eccentric. He tells of sycophants at the academy who would marvel at his times, even as Emil was deliberately misleading them with exaggerated slow ones. Yet much of the conversation does have the air of a bucolic idyll – harsh times seen through the lens of a children's television programme. So Emil takes salt to some rams and then plays at butting heads before giving them a lesson in running.

The truth was hard to find and only now, with a different regime and his surviving peers being so candid and generous, do we get a more rounded impression. So his great friend Ludvík Liška explains life in ATK thus: 'The political training was twice a week. We took it as a necessary evil. Quite often Emil knew more than a lecturer and was making fun of him, downplaying the whole training. He often led political education officers into such *faux pas* that they preferred to just let us be, which is what Emil wanted. But there were also athletes who had been orthodox Communists, and then he was afraid to speak out – they were not always fair and had their own group meetings in the evenings. Emil was in the Party but he was not very active. I think it would have been difficult for him to get away from it, but he just wanted to stay calm. And then, when he was a senior officer, he had to be in the Party, willy-nilly.'

It was impossible to be so famous and popular with the people and not be dragged into politics. 'We did not talk about the Milada Horáková case,' Liška said. 'I know Emil gave a speech on this topic on the radio, but I sincerely doubt he wrote it himself. Already at that time, the system used him as a speaker. Sometimes they even gave him a blank piece of paper to sign and then they wrote what they wanted on it. So he will have just got this speech, read it out, and then gone training. At that time he was in top form and didn't want to let it bother him much.'

Those Czechs who would buy Kožík's book would not hear about that. Instead, Emil and Dana's trip to Sochi at the start of 1950 is painted in romanticised hues. Yet after the cypress alleys and splendid sanatoriums, peopled by good Soviets enjoying well-earned rests, untainted fact intervened. Zátopek's athletic feats are indisputable and, in the summer of 1950, he was an Olympic champion and world record holder, yet he was still a man on the cusp.

He had been planning an assault on the Czech 5000 metres record at the Army Championships in Ostrava. However, an invitation came to visit Finland instead, organised by TUL, the workers' national sports association. No doubt encouraged by his commanders, Zátopek flew to Helsinki with Václav Čevona, his

Zátopek's childhood home in Koprivnice.

The destruction of Lidice was felt across Czechoslovakia. (© Keystone/Stringer/Getty Images)

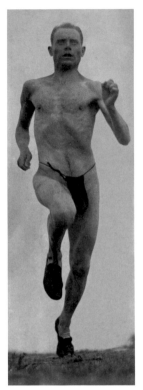

Sisu: the first of the masters, Paavo Nurmi.
(© Ullstein Bild/Getty Images)

A young Emil poses after winning a cross-country race in England. (© Popperfoto/Getty Images)

Rainman: Emil leads Ahldén, Reiff and Slijkhuis at the 1948 Olympics. (© Getty)

The needless duel between Zátopek and Ahldén in the heats in 1948.
(© Keystone-France/Getty Images)

On a pedestal: Emil celebrates the 10,000 metres gold with Mimoun and Albertsson.
(© AFP/Stringer/Getty Images)

The coach:
photographs of
Jan Haluza from
the StB files.

Stanislav Jungwirth leads Roger Bannister at
White City in 1954, two years after Zátopek's
courageous stand. (© Paul Popper/Popperfoto/Getty Images)

Centre of attention: Emil and
Dana pose on a Finnish hill.
(© Ralph Crane/Getty Images)

Born on the same day: Emil
and Dana training for the
1952 Olympics.
(© Ullstein Bild/Getty Images)

Pirie v Chataway.
(© John Chillingworth/Stringer/
Getty Images)

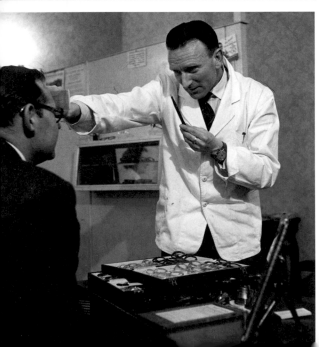

Jim Peters at work
as an optician.
(© Popperfoto/Getty Images)

The epic: Chataway falls as Emil heads for home in the 5000 metres in Helsinki.
(© Ullstein Bild/Getty Images)

Me and my shadow: Emil with Mimoun after that race. (© Keystone-France/Getty Images)

Two down: Zátopek in contemplative mood after completing the second leg of his Olympic treble.
(© Ralph Crane/Getty Images)

The kiss: after the 10,000 metres in Helsinki.
(© Popperfoto/Getty Images)

"Too slow?": Emil leads Jim Peters, the world record holder, in the Olympic marathon.
(© Nat Farbman/Getty Images)

The pitiless race of elimination: the Olympic marathon, 1952. (© Nat Farbman/Getty Images)

Record season: Emil breaks the 5000 metres world record in Paris. (© Ullstein Bild/Getty Images)

The track in the forest: Houstka Spa, site of some of Zátopek's most legendary runs.

Pain: Zátopek would push to the limit like no one before him. (© Ullstein Bild/Getty Images)

"Women wept": Jim Peters' disastrous last steps in the 1954 Commonwealth Games in Vancouver. (© Hulton Archive/Stringer/Getty Images)

Vladimir Kuts hugs Pirie after taking Emil's Olympic 5000 metres title in 1956.
(© Popperfoto/Getty Images)

East meets West: Olga and Harold Connolly wed in 1957 after Emil's help.
(© Ullstein Bild/Getty Images)

Emi with the great
Viljo Heino (left), 1963.
(© Ullstein Bild/Getty Images)

Soldier: Emil in full
uniform as he starts
a race in 1967.
(© Ullstein Bild/Getty Images)

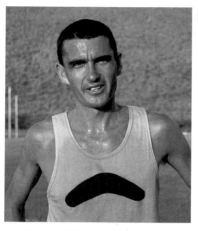

Ron Clarke in 1966, two weeks after Zátopek had given him his gold medal. (© Ed Lacey/Popperfoto/Getty Images)

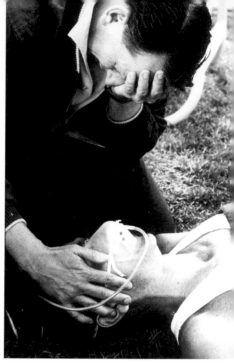

The gulp gap: Ron Clarke collapses after the Olympic 10,000 metres in 1968; Brian Corrigan weeps. (© Popperfoto/Getty Images)

Munich, 1972: Emil and Věra Čáslavská, the champion gymnast who would also be punished by the state. (© Bertram/Getty Images)

Revolution: Prague residents surround Russian trucks after the 1968 invasion. (© Libor Hajsky/Getty Images)

The stand: Zátopek protests during the Prague Spring, 1968. (© Express Newspapers/Stringer/Getty Images)

Before the storm: Emil and
Dana at the 1968 Olympics.
Life would change forever on
their return. (© Getty Images)

A vigil for Jan Palach, whose
suicide would result in political
problems for Zátopek.
(© Gerard Leroux/Getty Images)

Old gold: Zátopek and
Alain Mimoun in 1982.
(© AFP/Getty Images)

The protégé: Ivan Ullsperger, 2015.

Dana at home in Prague, 2015.

old Olympic room-mate. Zátopek clocked 14 minutes 6.2 seconds for the 5000 metres, his best yet. It was a prescient run in a city that would forever be linked with Zátopek, but his greatest feat of that particular trip came when he travelled to Turku, the home of Paavo Nurmi.

Zátopek could almost hear his idol relaying his story: 'I was an errand boy of a wholesale firm and had to deliver goods by pushcart. I shed much sweat in taking merchandise hundreds of times up the steeply rising street to the Turku railway station.'

Emil walked out of the station and was greeted by the Czech ambassador, who told him of the world record vibe. By the time of the race, with some token opposition assembled, the vibe had become a hum of expectation. Zátopek felt no nerves. There had been no promises and, anyway, he felt that perfect storm again of time and circumstance, of physical peak and mental flow. He set off on the 10,000 metres at a sedate pace, and then pressed a button, and the signs of weakness were consigned to the ordinary past. Now he was monotonously fast. Each kilometre was completed in around 2 minutes 55 seconds, until he upped the pace for 2000 lung-frying metres. As usual the eighth kilometre was his worst, but the damage was limited this time. His time of 2 minutes 56 seconds for that kilometre meant he was a staggering 13 seconds inside his own record time. The final 1000 metres were astonishing. The speed increased and increased, hands spilling fleshy blurs on the air – 2 minutes 47 seconds. The overall time was 29 minutes 2.6 seconds.

This time nobody would take the record from him for six years. Heino was now too old. Once coached by Nurmi himself, he now turned to teaching others. He remained firm friends with Zátopek. He noted the new record, some 25 seconds faster than he had managed, and realised it was unattainable. He was another great runner reclaimed by the ordinary and now looked to new generations, both in terms of his motherless children and in athletics.

The Finns called Emil 'Satu-Pekka', a rhyming pun meaning 'Magic Peter', but Dana called him 'Topek', which was a derivation of 'Stopek', the name some Ukrainians had called him. To most he was just Emil, a friendly face fluent in numerous languages, and a quirky figure who had developed his own unique shorthand, effectively his own language.

Those in Britain began to learn more about him in the 1950s thanks to a man named J. Armour Milne. He was a Communist who had written for the *Daily Worker* and now began to give those in Britain a first-hand glimpse of life behind the Iron Curtain. He wrote for *Athletics Weekly*, then a small pamphlet run by Jimmy Green from his back-bedroom office in Kent. Milne's work preceded that of the McWhirter twins, Ross and Norris, two Oxford-educated establishment figures. In the early 1950s they began supplying facts and figures to Fleet Street before setting up *Athletics World* in 1952. Later they would become famous figures, creating *The Guinness Book of Records*, and moving into politics. The latter ended in tragedy when Ross was killed by an IRA assassin, having previously offered a £50,000 reward for information leading to the detection of those behind previous terrorist acts.

Milne was a fan of Zátopek and got to know him in the early 1950s. He would visit him in Prague, monitor his training and send missives to Kent, from where he would be occasionally rebuked for his leftist leanings.

Two weeks after his world record, Zátopek and Milne went to Brussels. The highlight of the year for Zátopek was the 1950 European Championships. Dana, too, had high expectations as her throw of 48.43 metres the previous month in Bratislava had taken her into the world's top five.

Inside the vast Heysel Stadium she failed to reproduce that form. The conditions on the first day scarcely helped. The javelin run-up was flooded and the organisers sought to dry it by pouring spirit on to the track and setting fire to it. Dana finished fifth with a throw of only 41.34 metres, well below her best. It was becoming the age of the Russians in the throwing events. Herma Bauma, the Olympic champion from Austria, did get the silver, but the other two women on the podium were Natalya Smirnitskaya and Galina Zybina. Both epitomised the new Soviet sporting strength. Zybina, in particular, had suffered during the war, losing her mother and brother to starvation during the siege of Leningrad while her father died at the front. Galina survived and would typify the resilience of the Soviets whom Dana would have to beat if she was to achieve her ambition of winning an Olympic medal.

The crowd had already sung 'God Save The King' in honour of Jack Holden's victory in the marathon by the time the runners were called for the start of the 10,000 metres. Zátopek's duel with Gaston Reiff, a re-run of the Olympic 5000 metres, was the most anticipated event, and the 10,000 metres should have been a warm-up breeze for Zátopek. What the likes of Armour Milne could not know was quite how ill Zátopek had been in the build-up, and the role Dana had played in that.

Shortly before the European Championships Dana had prepared Emil some duck for his dinner. A few days later she told him, 'I've found some leftovers of that duck – take it for your lunch.'

Emil always left the cooking and his calorie intake to Dana. She knew best. Hours later he was in Střešovice hospital, suffering from violent stomach cramps, vomiting and diarrhoea. His temperature rose to a dangerous 40°C. Dana arrived and, on seeing the contorted little man rather than her husband, burst into tears. Emil smiled through the pain. 'Don't cry,' he said. 'Just bring me my tracksuit.' It was Friday and the 10,000 metres in Brussels was on the following Wednesday. 'I must train.' However, Emil had lost five kilogrammes and was a cadaver of a champion. Dana knew there was no chance. The doctors admonished him and told him he must stay in bed until Monday, drinking only tea, leaving him to spend that afternoon anxiously watching time tick away and, with it, his prospects of making it to Belgium and beating Reiff.

On Saturday Emil was relieved to find his fever had eased. Most of the doctors were at home and so he got up and started exploring the place, looking to sate a ravenous hunger. 'In the next building I found the canteen and ate two Würstels with mustard and had a drink of beer.' He felt a little better and so he went for a gentle run. 'But I was so weak.' His answer was to eat more Würstels. The following day he was running around the hospital grounds in a frenzy. The nurses were confounded, wondering how a man who had not eaten for days could summon up so much energy. On Monday, the doctors arrived and, when they were told what had transpired, congratulated themselves on their prescription. It had clearly worked. On Tuesday a car arrived to pick Emil up and the doctors told him to stick to the winning diet – just tea.

It was not the ideal preparation for the first of his events, and it was apposite that the race ended up a farce. Zátopek was in a different class to the field and easily ran away from it. He lapped most runners, and that caused confusion for the officials, who erroneously calculated the number of laps left for the also-rans. Jimmy Green had travelled to Brussels from his bungalow in Kent. People had mocked him for trying to set up an athletics magazine. Paper rationing was still in force when he had started out and so, in an attempt to convince the authorities that his was an established operation, the first edition was titled *Volume II*. 'I listened to their advice,' he would say of the expert advice he received, 'and I completely ignored it.' He jotted down some notes which he later turned into a nine-page report for *Volume IV, No. 35*. 'Then came the fiasco,' he wrote. 'The lap recorders got into a fearful muddle and gave the leading runners behind Zátopek the idea that they had only one lap to go instead of two. Alain Mimoun went away and finished strongly – as he thought – only to find he had a further lap to go. The same happened to the next half a dozen runners and many ran off the track to be pushed back to complete the race.'

Green shook his head at the spectacle in front of him. Frank Aaron, a popular runner from Britain, had been going well, sitting second in the closing exchanges, but had lost many places in the chaos. He ran himself to exhaustion and fourth place and duly collapsed. Green sighed and wondered whether Britain would ever be able to challenge the great Zátopek.

He was cheered the next day when Alec Olney qualified for the final of the 5000 metres in a time that was faster than Zátopek's from heat one. Green knew the heats were the phoney war, though, and that the only aim was to survive while conserving energy. Zátopek had learnt that painful lesson at the 1948 Olympics. Now he was older and wiser.

He was also the star of the show wherever he went. Although Belgium rallied behind Reiff before the 5000 metres re-match, the nation was in thrall to Zátopek's peculiar mix of personality and prowess. One Belgian scribe, M. van der Berge, could not contain himself. 'His opponents were, so to speak, not noticeable and yet they were among the best runners in the world,' he opined in his report of the 10,000 metres. 'They were great experts and

screaming at him as Zátopek closed during the denouement of the 5000 metres in London. Emil looked for signs from the stands, as before, but lost view of his friends as the stadium boiled as a cauldron.

On the fifth lap of 12-and-a-half, Reiff began to pull away. This was the race right here. Just like London. Emil had told himself he must not let the gap grow to more than 30 metres. He dug in. The first kilometre had been run at a blistering 2 minutes 48 seconds, but the pace dropped marginally after that. It was still fast but it was not a killing pace, not like London.

'Lap after lap I closed down on him and with 700 metres to go to the finish I got back to him,' Zátopek would say. Reiff did not look around, but he knew where Zátopek was. He could hear the scuff of fleet foot, the breath of renewed effort. He was literally breathing down his neck in the executioner's position. And then they were level and their eyes briefly met. It was the Gorgon stare that froze Reiff as he realised Zátopek was strong; conversely Emil read the tiredness and fear in those fleeting seconds. 'He wasn't expecting it,' he would say. 'He was terrorised by my appearance.' 'You are scraping the barrel,' Emil thought. 'You don't know what I've got in store for you. Not like London.'

That final lap is vividly recalled in *Dana a Emil Zátopkovi vypravují*. 'I went so fast that in the blink of an eye there is daylight between us. A deadly silence fell on the stadium and, thanks to that I heard a few Czech voices. "Emil, Emil." I run like a savage and before people could recover from the shock I was on the finishing straight. Only later I heard some courteous applause, but I was already at the finish. Reiff had 120 metres to go and could hardly stand up.' That was no exaggeration. Seeing London ripped away into the past, Reiff had imploded. His mental fragility translated into physical exhaustion.

Jimmy Green jotted down some notes: 'Reiff, 100 yards ahead of Mimoun, slowed down along the back straight to a crawl, and down the finishing straight the French boy took him unaware when only 12 yards from the finish. Reiff responded too late and was beaten into third place, collapsed immediately and was carried off on a stretcher.'

The time was 14 minutes 3 seconds. Zátopek wryly noted that Reiff's trainer had got the time right but the names wrong. He was 23 seconds ahead of Mimoun, who must have started to believe he had been born in the wrong era. Green noted that Olney was eighth, some 48 seconds adrift. The gulf between Britain and the best still seemed a canyon.

Reiff recovered and was magnanimous. 'I was beaten by Zátopek's strength, by his courage and by his amazing energy,' he admitted. 'Time will show that Emil is capable of running the distance in under 14 minutes. No victory could be clearer.'

The next day Emil returned to the stadium to watch his great friend, Jindřich Roudný, in the 3000 metres steeplechase. Zátopek was now unable to walk freely among the public and so disguised himself in an old suit. Even so he was recognised by a Coca-Cola seller and, as people began to point and comment, he ran again. He hid among a brass band that was playing and then hurdled a barrier before finding a spot to watch the race.

Jimmy Green had high hopes for John Disley, but he was back in the pack and cut adrift by mid-distance. At the bell a Yugoslav runner led, but Green saw the 'newcomer' from Czechoslovakia moving up. Roudný went on to win by 15 metres; Disley was 13th. 'To my mind it was a disadvantage to be here for six days before running,' he would chastise.

It had been an improvement for Britain. Jack Holden, a practising Christian, had produced a God-given run in the marathon, while Roger Bannister had taken the bronze in the 800 metres. Derek Pugh won the 400 metres and then clinched another gold in the relay. For team manager Jack Crump, Pugh's success was the most pleasing of all. He had been there in Antwerp on the day that Pugh had been struck in the head by an errant javelin: 'It appeared that the implement had penetrated the skull, for the athlete ran on several yards with the javelin apparently sticking out of him.' Crump had rushed across the ground and realised that the spear had scored the scalp and become lodged between ear and head. 'Am I bleeding?' Pugh had muttered. Thirty minutes later, after an anti-tetanus injection and a bandage covering the wound, Pugh returned. 'Am I needed for the relay?' he said. Crump reasoned then that the man at least had guts.

For Zátopek another year drew to a close with his status unquestioned. He kept on running, but he damaged a muscle again and, other than a fine run of 14 minutes 5 seconds in a home match against Finland, was going through the motions. He travelled to Germany for the Sports Festivals and visited the memorial to Rudolf Harbig. The German had been coached by a man named Woldemar Gerschler, who would become a key figure in the life of the young Gordon Pirie, and had set a world record for the 800 metres in 1939 only for the war to interrupt his ambitions and ultimately end them, when he was killed while fighting on the eastern front in Ukraine in 1944.

Zátopek discussed the visit to the memorial in Dresden with Kožik, who was keen to exploit the emotion for Communist ends. So the pair contrived the following paragraph for their book: 'When one realises that he was taken from us right in the middle of his most successful years, at the very thought of him we should only shout the louder: may there be no more war.'

12

East v West

The battles never ended for Jan Haluza. His feet bled, his legs were horribly swollen from standing and his mind was scarred. Once awake he was transferred back to Camp Bratrství in Jáchymov, but took solace from a brief meeting with Věra. He did not know that it would be one of only three times he would see her in four years. He took to whistling 'Mozart's Lullaby', their signal, hopeful that he would hear a refrain, but he never did. 'Sleep little one, go to sleep,' he would say in his head.

The camps were brutal, but you got to know the ropes. Don't mention religion, because the worst crime of Communism was atheism. Haluza had seen how the Baptists were made to stand to their waists in snow and minus 30 degree temperatures for up to three days solid. Some of the kinder inmates tried to smuggle sleeping pills to them so they would collapse and be transferred to the infirmary. To do so was to risk your own life. Other prisoners conducted baptisms in rainwater collected in a cooling tower. It felt hopeless.

Don't stand in the front row at roll call either or the commander they nicknamed 'Palecek' would beat you in the face with his keys. Palecek was a vicious man who seemed to delight in having the power of life. He was well known for shooting people on a whim. Sometimes he would ask prisoners to go for a walk and then return alone.

The prisoners had little but some blind faith in divine justice. When they worked the uranium mines each blast brought the risk of injury or worse. Every explosion would leave a tantalising bounty of gold and red crystals, but it was radioactive. As were the thin clothes that the men were forced to wear day and night. Cancer would be the aftershock of Jáchymov for many who survived.

In those years Haluza was often on the move. This was to prevent political prisoners from having prolonged contact with each other. They also wanted to tire out the prisoners so that they could not complete their work to a high standard and, thus, qualify for their full food ration. Often they survived on a diet of flour and water. Hunger strikes were common. For the main part, resistance was not only futile, but often fatal.

At another camp called Mariánská, Haluza was placed in a building surrounded by double barbed wire. From there he would join what was known as the 'Jáchymov bus' or 'March of the Faggots', a procession of prisoners standing five abreast and bound by iron chains. Somehow hundreds of men had to synchronise their movements while holding each other by their arms. It meant a journey of around 800 metres could take two hours, and far longer in the mud and ice of deep winter.

Helping each other was frowned upon. When a prisoner named Eduard Marek caught a friend who had fainted, he incurred the wrath of a commander named Vašiček who had worked as a waiter in another life. Returning from work, Eduard heard the announcement: 'Convict 07844 immediately report to the chief of camp.' He shuffled to Vašiček's cabin where he was made to wait for several hours.

'So you are the merciful Samaritan,' the commander said, finally, to the shivering cadaver in front of him.

Marek replied in staccato breaths, 'It is normal to help a friend.'

Vašiček was unimpressed. 'He was on hunger strike. You should have let him go.'

For his kindness, Marek spent 14 days in isolation in a freezing correction unit, a barren room with a concrete floor and no furniture. 'You had to exercise all night or freeze to death,' he said.

The lexicon of the camp mystified Haluza. The guards suspected him of espionage in the mines and threatened him with 'the tailcoat'. Haluza said it could not be that bad and that he could even cope with a life sentence. The interrogator laughed. 'It's not a life sentence,' he said. Haluza quickly learnt that tailcoat meant execution.

One day, Haluza saw a withered face that he recognised. 'Ivan,' he said, slowly, and the two prisoners tried to find the power to charge a smile from cracked lips and sunken faces. Ivan confided in Haluza and told him that he and some other prisoners were planning an escape. Haluza wanted to join; thinking of Věra and Vašiček and tailcoats. He had his faith in God and believed his purpose could not lie in these death camps.

On the night of the escape Haluza went to the appointed place but sensed something was wrong. There was nobody around. He looked for Ivan but he had disappeared. It dawned on him that the plotters had gone without him. Perhaps they did not trust him. His body sagged.

It would not take long before he was glad he had been left out. All of the escapees were caught and shot. Their bodies were brought back to the camp and thrown into their cells. The prisoners existed alongside the ghastly reminders of what would befall them if they tried the same. Haluza looked at Ivan's lifeless form and wondered if things could get worse.

A question arising from Haluza's plight is: could Zátopek have done more to help? It is a simplistic query when framed in hindsight. Božetěch Kostelka, a good friend of Haluza, said Věra visited Zátopek when her husband was arrested and tortured. 'He promised her that he would do as much as he could and he went to see his commander, Major Příhoda, but Příhoda was very political. In my opinion I think Emil would have done more, but the people around him refused. Even if he had wanted to talk to the president, Gottwald, the people around him would not let him get there. I know that Haluza felt no malice towards Zátopek.'

Karel Engel, an Olympian who would become a firm friend of the Zátopeks, said it was hard for Emil to lead a successful military life and stand up to the authorities. In his heart he wanted to help people, but he was also a Bolshevik and believed in the state. That was his working-class background. The juggling of his personal and public lives was becoming increasingly complex. At heart he was unquestionably a philanthropist who wanted to make people happy. Engel said: 'If I was at his house and I said, "Emil, I like that," he would take it down off the wall and give it to me.' On one occasion a tourist bus came to the Zátopeks' street in Prague. Emil was home alone and the driver knocked on the door and asked how to get to a certain street. Emil told them to forget about the hotel they were trying to find. Ludvík Liška, his friend and team-mate, said, 'It did not matter to him if someone stole something; the most important thing for him was that people were happy. When Dana returned home unexpectedly from the mountains she had to tread over sleeping tourists. When she asked what was going on, Emil said, "What could I do? They had nowhere to go.'"

Milan Svajgr, who had got to know Zátopek while the pair trained together at Strahov Stadium, says Zátopek was more complicated than often painted. 'He was a controversial man,' he told me in 2015. 'Before the 1950 European Championships, we were in the gym at the military stadium and he said, "It bothers me here. If I go to Brussels with Dana then I'll stay there." Much later I reminded him of what he had said and he replied, "I was just testing you."'

The Zátopeks certainly had numerous opportunities to defect, but in 1951 they holidayed in the High Tatra mountains in Slovakia. It was a troublesome trip. The couple loved to ski but, on one run, Emil lost control on the slopes and careered into a fir tree. He winced in pain as he came to a soft stop and knew he had damaged his leg. He was taken to hospital where he was told he had torn ligaments and was put in plaster.

Armour Milne had arranged to visit Zátopek. Jimmy Green had promised him good space in *Athletics Weekly* and planned to run his interview over two issues. While waiting for Emil to return from the mountain, Milne watched some footage produced by the Czechoslovak People Republic's documentary film department. He noted that the slow-motion clips belied the notion that Zátopek was an uneconomical runner. Milne noticed that the way his foot struck the ground naturally powered his body forward. As he waited for Zátopek, he spent his time usefully. He visited Dr Zdeněk Hornof, a physician from the University of Prague. Milne would write that Hornof 'turned Emil outside in for my benefit'. He said, 'I saw his medical examination card, records of the various tests he had undergone, even X-ray photographs of the heart and lungs.'

Hornof and his boss at the Department of Sports Medicine, Professor Jiří Král, said there was nothing physically abnormal about Zátopek. 'They explained that Zátopek's heart is no bigger, no stronger than that of any first-class athlete, that his lungs are no bigger, his vital capacity no greater than that of many another outstanding distance runner. They say that his success can only be put down to his tremendous will to succeed, his iron determination that keeps him going.'

It seemed deeply unsatisfactory and unscientific for a journalist seeking a secret. Milne tried to dig deeper. He said Zátopek could hold his breath for 127.6 seconds – after intaking oxygen, that could be increased to 168 seconds. His normal pulse rate was 68.

Milne then penned an aside about Sokol: 'Every athlete joining the million and more strong Sokol organisation is now compelled to undergo a medical check on joining and at intervals afterwards. If there is any doubt about his condition following a check-up by local Sokol doctor, he is sent to the Department of Sports Medicine for further examination. There are now 30 consulting stations throughout Czechoslovakia, working under the central direction of the Department of Sports Medicine of the Charles University.

'Records are kept of the individual's weight, height, vital capacity, information on the condition of the throat, teeth, lungs, heart, blood pressure (tested by means of deep knee bends), urine, and, finally, an X-ray of the chest.'

Not everyone found Milne's reports enlightening. In a letter to *Athletics Weekly*, B. M. O'Regan, of Shaftesbury Harriers, expressed his horror: 'Dear Sir, I was dismayed, even disgusted, at Mr Milne's article; though it contained many facts and figures these only served to cover the author's evident admiration for the rampant Communism in Czechoslovakia. May I appeal for less of this blatant sectarian propaganda, with a hope that *Athletics Weekly* will not degenerate into a political tit-for-tat under the guise of being an athletics magazine.'

Jimmy Green responded to that criticism: 'Though I may disagree strongly with Armour Milne's politics, I recognise him as a keen and knowledgeable athletics writer. There was only one paragraph which could possibly be taken as propaganda and this was such that no reasonable person could object. The Sokol organisation to which Mr O'Regan undoubtedly refers has many excellent features, despite its connection with a political regime which is in direct contrast to that of this country.'

You could almost sense Green's irritation as he concluded, 'Let us have none of this hysterical nonsense. Keep politics out of it.' It was a pay-off that Zátopek himself would have liked to have subscribed to, but which he found increasingly hard to do.

Milne was enjoying himself. He actually ran with Zátopek as he trained at the Masaryk Stadium in the hills overlooking Prague. Emil was a chatty companion, even when running around the grass that circled the track, so as not to get in the way of the lesser runners inside him. Throughout his career some of his peers would voice their disgruntlement at Emil's eagerness to strike up conversation during races. They wondered whether it was gamesmanship, or a form of showing-off, as they rationed breaths and could not waste words. Now Emil told Milne that the only reason he ran so hard at major championships was because he had been brought up in a country with few peers and so he had no gauge. 'I was out on my own in all my fast races,' he told Milne. 'I determined to break as many Czechoslovak records as possible, but to do that I had to forget about the other runners because none of them were capable of helping me or keeping pace with me.' He learnt to race by feel until he found the elite in international competition, notably in the 1948 Olympic 5000 metres final. Milne recounted what had happened to Zátopek in that race. 'I am useless when it comes to tactics,' Emil had grinned. Milne was confused, struggling to analyse such a complex, contradictory character in a few thousand words. 'He is one of athletics' problem children,' he wrote. 'He appears to defy all the rules and yet meets with success.'

Zátopek bemoaned the Finnish fetish for strict diets, pointing out this backfired when they ran abroad and could not get the same food. He ate when he liked and if he liked. He regularly skipped breakfast, but would buy rolls, butter and a quart of milk on the two-mile walk from his city-centre flat to the army PT office.

He told Milne that he had overeaten for much of his early career on the advice of his father, who wanted him to make up for the lost energy wasted in athletics. He broke the national 2000 metres record after gorging on knedlíky, a sort of suet pudding, with friends.

Two months after Milne's articles appeared, Zátopek lost a race. The winner was Václav Čevona and, although the distance was Zátopek's unfavoured 3000 metres, the impact was telling. Immediately, filming of the documentary about him was suspended as it was deemed to have affected Zátopek's routine. It was the first time Zátopek had lost a race over 3000 metres since 1948. He had never lost over 10,000 metres in 23 races spanning three years. When he beat Svajgr into a distant second place over 5000 metres in Ostrava, three days after losing to Čevona, it was his 41st successive win at that distance. Defeats were rare and a reason for panic among those who looked to Zátopek as a constant in a changing society.

It is debatable whether Zátopek wanted to break world records as much as his paymasters wanted him to. However, in the wake of the defeat by Čevona, he sought new challenges. He knew that his late start to the season after his skiing injury reduced his chances of breaking the records he most coveted – the 5000 and 10,000 metres – but he perused a list of world bests and came upon two more.

Milne got to hear about the record attempt and made sure he was at the Strahov Stadium in Prague on 15 September where Zátopek would attempt to break Heino's six-year-old records for most metres run in one hour and the 20,000 metres. Heino had managed 19,339 metres, taking the record from Paavo Nurmi, who had set the benchmark in 1928. For Zátopek it was a record that gave him a direct link to his hero, just one step removed from two decades earlier.

Heino's mark for the 20,000 metres was 1 hour 2 minutes 40 seconds, set two years earlier. The first 5000 metres would comprise the Army Championships but Zátopek was soon clear of the field and rendered that an irrelevance. He then pressed on towards his target of 50 laps at 75-second pace. He tried to make himself go slow at the start, reasoning that it was far easier to accelerate towards a goal than hang on. Milne sat in the stand on the hill and breathed in the excitement. He had a journalist's sensibility and felt he was an insider on something historic. It was trite, he knew, but he felt like he was the eyes of the west, debunking myth and nonsense about the east. 'He ran as only Zátopek could run such a distance,' he wrote. 'One moment he was looking like a super-tuned machine, the next like a fugitive from justice; grimacing painfully in one lap, smiling contentedly in the next, and finally winding up with a last lap that would have done credit to a first-class miler. This was the Zátopek the world knows, biting at the distance in snatches, a man of flying feet one moment, dragging limbs the next. There were times when he really looked like he would provide a real sensation before retiring. Then a deep breath that seemed to lift him six inches taller sent him on his way again.'

Zátopek himself claimed that he dawdled through the first ten kilometres, which he covered in 31 minutes 5 seconds. However, he had been aiming for 31 minutes 45 seconds and so was well on course, with much to spare. At 59 minutes the gun sounded and he knew that the hour record was his. He then gripped the air for leverage and became that octopus on the conveyor belt. He ran and ran, exhorting himself to go faster and completed the hour with 19 kilometres 558 metres covered, some 219 metres better than Heino. Of course, he had to keep going to reach 20,000 metres, and finished in a time of 1 hour 1 minute 15.8 seconds, a huge 84 seconds inside Heino's mark. He had added another three world records, including the ten mile mark, and, as was Zátopek's way, he wanted more.

Heino sent his congratulations, disappointing newspapermen seeking a rift across nations. 'Believe me,' he told journalists, 'Zátopek could run 20 kilometres in one hour.'

It was a remark that got Zátopek thinking, and his pondering intensified when Lieutenant Colonel Sabl talked about the following year's Olympic Games and said, 'The best thing would be to enter all the long distance races – and win them all.' It was the first time Zátopek had contemplated the 5000, 10,000 and marathon treble. 'I was left to reflect open-mouthed,' he said, but the seed had been sown. Breaking Heino's records had been a landmark on the way to Helsinki.

Go to Houštka now and you can get lost in the fields and the past. It is a pleasant drive, 20 miles or so out of Prague, past a supermarket, the brickworks, a strawberry seller and a petrol station – the old and new bound up in swaying green. Finally you go through a small town with an ornate church and fading bistro, get to a road that snakes between towering trees, and finally come to a stadium enclosed by a green gate and a yellow fence. There is a tiny stand, five rows deep, and a bright terracotta track – the most idyllic of settings. Children run up and down as I look at the marble plaque depicting Emil Zátopek and his feats. I see photographs of Ludvík Liška, who has been so kind with his memories, in a relay team with Zátopek and Stanislav Jungwirth, a figure who would come to play a significant part in the Zátopek story. There is another of a thin, dark-haired man named Josef Odložil, who would set the final record on this track in 1965, a year after winning Olympic silver in the 1500 metres in Tokyo. Some 18 years later Odložil was killed by his son, Martin, who struck him on the head in a bar. Martin was sentenced to four years' imprisonment, but was granted a pardon by Václav Havel in 1997 after Emil had signed a petition. Martin's mother was Věra Čáslavská, the 1968 Olympic gymnastics champion and another national icon, but she would also fall victim to political upheaval in that year of Mexico, falling into a deep depression from which she only emerged decades later to take a role in Havel's government. Off the beaten track and on the noticeboard in a relic of a stadium, extraordinary lives are bound together and reduced to names and times. And so I squint and try to rewind some 64 years to 29 September 1951, when they were all alive and kicking up storms.

It was only two weeks since Zátopek had broken his records. Now he was going to try to see whether Heino was right. He publicly set himself a target of 1 hour 24 seconds, but his friends scoffed at that and, inwardly, he had bolder goals.

He ate a large meal and then went into the changing rooms where he found an assortment of people doing calculations and predicting his latest record. A man named Spiroch said, boldly, 'I will be hanged if he does not run under the hour.' Zátopek smiled and joked that it would be funny if he could do it in exactly one hour and then two records would be identical – the one-hour record and the 20,000 metres. He walked out of the changing room and went to the start. There were 17 runners there, but they would be in a different race soon enough. Emil wore the No. 1 and started fast. The first kilometre was covered in 2 minutes 58 seconds, far faster than he had managed a fortnight earlier. Kožik put it colourfully: 'Emil Zátopek of September 29 was fighting Emil Zátopek of September 15.' It was not much of a fight. The first 5000 metres took just 14 minutes 57.4 seconds; the first 10,000 metres 29 minutes 53.4 seconds. A stadium announcer was calling out times and keeping the increasingly excitable crowd informed. Zátopek went through 15,000 metres in 44 minutes 54.6 seconds, a token world record as nobody had bothered to record times over the distance before. Soon afterwards, he did have a world record for ten miles.

'Then I felt a pain in my side,' Zátopek would recall. 'I cursed the substantial meal I had had only three hours earlier.' He began to lose time and completed the third quarter in only 15 minutes 1.2 seconds. The pain grew and grew until it became so intense that it was like white noise, so searing that he could not tell if it was there at all; and then he was out the other side, beyond pain and into a new comfort zone. 'I felt no tiredness, at that moment,' he wrote in *Dana a Emil Zátopkovi vypravují*. 'Like an automaton I ran lap after lap until I heard the gun signalling the last minute of the hour mark.' That gunshot meant he had just 60 seconds left. Momentarily discombobulated, the wind dropped and he began to pick out voices. He did instant calculations in his head. He began his final sprint with 50 metres left of the 20,000. There was no second gunshot and, from that, he knew he had done it. The 20,000 metres had been completed in under an hour. He carried on running. Each step felt like a stay of execution. Ten metres passed. Then another ten. He heard the crowd chanting, 'Run! Run! Run!' When the adulation was cut by a second shot, he stopped. He had completed another 52 metres. The record of 59 minutes 51.8 seconds for the 20,000 metres stood for 12 years. It is still there on the board. 'That was 1951,' Zátopek would recall. 'The year when nothing was supposed to happen.'

Athletic achievement is so intoxicating because it is so quantifiable. A world record means you are the greatest of all time at that distance. Comparisons between the ages are slaughtered on the altar of cold, hard fact. Nurmi and Heino had held the four records (10,000 metres, ten miles, one hour and 20,000 metres) simultaneously, but Zátopek's haul was in a different league and era. He had run more than 800 metres further than Nurmi in their respective golden hours. His 10,000-metres mark was more than a minute faster.

Armour Milne sought current comparisons but was in no doubt that he was witnessing something incredible. 'His first and second 10,000 metres were done in times that no other runner in the world can touch for a single 10,000 metres,' he wrote in *Volume 5, No. 42* under a headline ZÁTOPEK AGAIN. British runners still competed over six miles rather than 10,000 metres, so Milne decided to bridge both the conversion table and the east–west divide for proof of his man's prowess. 'In cold figures this means Zátopek, had he run against the two best six-milers Britain has ever had, would have been 130 yards ahead of Walter Hesketh and 230 yards ahead of Gordon Pirie at six miles. And, with these two retiring, he would have gone on to reel off another six miles at almost the same pace.' Milne added a postscript: 'One would doubt the whole thing, but for the fact that all of us know Zátopek for the great runner that he is, and but for the fact I had the good fortune to see him do it.'

As Milne had pointed out, Gordon Pirie was developing, both as an athlete and an individualist. Pirie bemoaned the old 'cork grips' athletes held in their clenched fists when running (in the belief this would relieve tension); the inexpertly administered massages; the stinking embrocation 'as if the more it stank the more good it did them'. He believed he knew better because he was looking to what Zátopek did. He read Milne's words and wanted to punish himself. He believed the greatest athletes run themselves blind. 'The body is plunged into the depths of exhaustion and the mind into depths of despair. You must be a killer,' he reasoned. 'The athlete has to torture the body.'

He tortured his mind too. Zátopek was his goal and inspiration, but Christopher Chataway was the ghost 'haunting [his] thoughts' and beating him in an inter-services meeting. The classic Oxford style of running bothered Pirie, and he loathed the repression of British runners: 'It is admired as graceful but to me it is clumsy compared with the liberated grace of a man like Zátopek. British runners have been admired because they keep a sort of stiff upper lip even in the agony of the race.' Style, Pirie proclaimed, was a delusion.

Pirie wore out a pair of shoes fortnightly and fastened them around his ankles with cords so he would not lose them in the mud. The cords tightened and gouged out wounds. 'There was terrible conflict between me and my body's exhaustion and the pain in my ankles.'

It started to pay dividends in earnest in 1951 when he forged a rivalry with Walter Hesketh, a teak-tough northerner who had left school at 14 and worked as a shoe-shiner in Manchester.

And Pirie was at last starting to get noticed. A British vest came through the post and he slipped it on and studied himself in his bedroom mirror. His habit of blowing out his cheeks repeatedly, originally to get rid of insects on the Downs, saw him become known as 'Puff-Puff' Pirie. The peacock pride in that bedroom made it a suitable tag.

There were foreign trips now. On one flight the veteran athletics correspondent of the *News of the World*, Joe Binks, joined the chorus of disapproval. 'You won't last out a year as champions,' he said to Pirie and others at the terminal. 'You'll be burnt out and finished by the Olympics in Helsinki. Just you wait and see.'

The trips were illuminating. Pirie had changed jobs, switching roles with Lloyds Bank to move to Croydon so he did not have to join the other 'slaves' in the City, where he felt the pollution was bad for his health. Pirie would get home from his days in the City and cough up thick lumps of black soot.

That seemed like a small grievance when he went to Yugoslavia. He saw wrecked German planes and 'besmocked soldiers with tommy guns'. Pirie said there was a kind of quiet and an 'uncertain deathliness' that he came to associate with Communist countries.

Hesketh went to pieces and dropped out of the 10,000 metres in the heat of Yugoslavia. Pirie kept going, finding that zone of pain and consequence that he so loved and hated. His senses swirled. Kill or be damned. He won in a time of 31 minutes 11.2 seconds; it was hot and he was unacclimatised but, even so, Zátopek was already running sub-30 minutes and the Olympics were coming. Soon after, in Istanbul, he clocked 14 minutes 59 seconds for the 5000 metres in a race won by Chataway. Zátopek's best that year was 14 minutes 11.6 seconds. The gap still seemed a gulf, despite the *News of the World*'s optimistic claim that Britain had found 'its own Emil Zátopek'.

Jim Peters had disappeared and been dead to the athletics world for some time, but he was exhumed in the summer of 1951.

Frieda had settled into her new suburban life in Chadwell Heath and was more sympathetic to his now-stated ambition of running a marathon. Jim knew that it was the ultimate test of mind and body. The myth went that Philippides, a messenger, had run from the Plain of Marathon to deliver news of the Athenians' victory over the Persians. On delivering his missive, he dropped down dead. That was 490 BC. In 1896, the marathon developed a new mystique when a poor farmhand named Spyridon Louis won the Olympic marathon in Greece, despite minimal training and a pre-race meal including three beers. The 1904 Olympic version was also full of intrigue. Felix Carvajal was a Cuban mail worker who raised money for his trip by staging exhibitions in Havana, only to lose most of it in a card game in New Orleans. He hitchhiked to St Louis in his civilian clothes, whereupon a friendly discus thrower cut off his trousers at the knee on the start line to make him look more athletic. The winner that year was Thomas Hicks, who received several doses of strychnine and brandy along the way. However, the most celebrated race was the 1908 marathon at the London Olympics. The records show Johnny Hayes of the USA won the gold medal, but the first man across the line was Dorando Pietri, a shop-worker from Carpi. Unfortunately, Pietri had collapsed and been helped to his feet on numerous occasions, and was finally led across the line by Jack Andrew, the race organiser. The official report remarked: 'It was impossible to leave him there for it looked as if he might die in the very presence of the Queen.' Pietri was disqualified but became an international celebrity. Arthur Conan Doyle, author of the Sherlock Holmes novels, started a campaign to raise enough money for the diminutive Italian to open a bakery at home. Ultimately, he opened a hotel, which went bankrupt and he died of a heart attack aged just 56.

Others followed in his wake. The great Hannes Kolehmainen won for Finland in Antwerp in 1920; Paavo Nurmi was banned a week before the 1932 Olympic marathon due to his expense account. And then in 1948, in London, Étienne Gailly produced his ugly, Pietri-like last lap, staggering every which way and surrendering the lead as he suffered from chronic dehydration. This was the test to which Jim Peters, still occasionally referred to as Johnny by an unconvinced athletics press, had committed: a race in which suffering had spanned centuries.

The first big test on the road to Helsinki was the Finchley 20 in which he would take on the great Jack Holden, the British, Empire and European champion. Holden won.

The Essex Twenty Miles Championship followed a month later. This time Peters clocked 1 hour 47 minutes 8 seconds. It would have been a world record apart from the unfortunate fact that the course was measured and deemed to be 620 yards short. Peters, though, was suddenly back in the limelight. 'Watch your step, Jack Holden,' wrote Stan Tomlin in *The People*. 'Jim's immediate target is to meet Jack Holden – and beat him. His long-range target is the Olympic marathon even though he hasn't run a full marathon course.'

That changed on 20 June 1951. The Polytechnic Marathon had been created after Britain's dismal showing in the 1908 Olympic marathon. The Polytechnic Harriers club, of Regent Street, devised a route from the royal apartments at Windsor Castle to the White City stadium. Significantly, the distance of 26 miles 385 yards became established as the official distance of all marathons.

Peters and Holden again ran together for a few miles. The older man tried his trademark 'jumping' tactic, varying the pace to dismantle his rival, only this time he started it much earlier. By mid-distance Jim was in the throes of a mental torment. 'I began to think what a fool I was ever to have attempted this marathon distance and how pleasant it would be to just give up and lie down in the road.' The gap was 200 yards, but at the point in the course where the road suddenly turned sharply south, Peters saw Holden look around. It was a small thing, unnoticed by most. For Jim Peters it was evidence that the great Jack Holden was still worried about him. He still wanted to monitor his progress and, if he did that with a lead of 200 yards, it could mean only one thing. Holden was feeling the pace.

Peters caught Holden with seven miles to go. These are the killing miles of any marathon, where runners wrestle with their minds. Every sinew, muscle and thought is demanding you stop. The brain begins to fry. Thoughts are starved of oxygen and are submerged in an inner fog. But then, a cyclist rode up alongside Peters. From the periphery he saw a blur of wheel and heard the words: 'Jack is out! He's given up. Can you hear me? He's out!' Then he heard more voices as the crowd swelled and the finish neared. At another point he felt someone running alongside him and heard a familiar voice. 'How are you feeling, Jim?' puffed Johnny Johnston, once an Olympian and now a middle-aged coach.

Jim let the words flow out on each exhalation: 'I'm . . . very . . . tired.'

'Only another quarter of an hour,' Johnston panted before disappearing.

Peters crossed the line at Chiswick and the loud speaker quickly announced his time as 2 hours 29 minutes 24 seconds. No British man, not even Jack Holden, had ever broken the 2 hours 30 minutes mark. He was only four seconds outside the Olympic record.

Alan Holby, a journalist for the *Sunday Express*, decided this was a changing of the guard. He wrote, 'He had beaten the famous Jack Holden, Britain's "Old Fox" of sport, the long-distance marvel, the runner with a stopwatch in place of a heart. You would not have thought it possible for any British runner to beat Holden, but yesterday he found himself up against a steel wire, a pale little man who went on as remorselessly and ruthlessly as a Crusader tank.'

Jim Peters would blush at such analogies. He did not feel ruthless or tank-like as he pushed his son, Robin, in his pram for seven miles on a Sunday evening.

Holden, though, had been badly hurt by Peters. Holby had found him after he had dropped out of the Poly and he told the writer, 'This is the red light for me. I don't intend to run until my funeral.' Jim Peters did not know it but he had run Jack Holden into retirement. 'Nothing can stop this man,' Holby gushed. 'Here is a real Olympic hope.'

13

The Stand

The world was changing in 1952 and Emil Zátopek was acutely aware of it. He was so attuned to the shift in power in sport that he fell into a depression. His mood was not helped by knowing the Russians were going to take part in the Olympic Games for the first time for decades.

Zátopek had taken some time off in the mountains. This time he refrained from skiing but did train by wading through chest-high snow, to the amusement of onlookers. He met with members of 'the select team' to discuss his aims and plans. Zátopek said that, if he was fully fit, then he thought he could win two gold medals for his country at the Olympics in Helsinki.

That satisfied the suits, but problems lay ahead. One of Zátopek's whims was to ignore the masseur in the army's central quarters. He reasoned that his muscles seemed to work well enough without the help of others. The masseur, though, was persistent. 'Let me set you straight,' he told Emil. 'You'll see how good it is for you. And for me too; it will impress people if I say I massage Zátopek.'

Eventually, Zátopek capitulated. Just before the Czech cross-country championships he went to the masseur's cold quarters. For half an hour the masseur covered Emil in soap and iced water. Afterwards, he found that other athletes had exhausted the hot water supplies and so he was forced to rinse off in cold water too. The following day he had a temperature and a sore throat. The doctor told him to stay in bed for a week but Zátopek had promised to run and told the doctor that the posters were already advertising his appearance in Prešov. He could not simply lie in bed and let the event pass. The doctor took some convincing, but eventually travelled to the course with Zátopek. 'One way or another I'll run,' he said, but he suffered terribly. The rivals stayed close to him for the whole ten kilometres and, although he did win, it was by a slender margin and a post-race examination found that the illness had got to his heart. Again confined to bed, Zátopek defied his doctors and got out of bed to do some basic exercises. He put on two tracksuits to force himself to sweat. He ran more and more and always dressed warmly, believing that he would drip away the illness.

He was suffering from debilitating headaches and the Olympics were just two months away when he went to Kiev to compete in a USSR–Czechoslovakia meeting. To the dismay of his handlers, he was beaten over 5000 metres by both Vladimir Kazantsev and Nikifor Popov. Zátopek had not lost a race over 5000 metres since Reiff had beaten him in Prague in September, 1948. In the preamble to the next Olympics, he had started to show untimely intimations of mortality. Kazantsev's time of 14 minutes 13.2 seconds was a Soviet record. The 10,000 metres offered only the slightest solace as Aleksandr Anufriyev, dubbed by writers as a Siberian bear-hunter, took half a minute off his best to finish a close second to Zátopek in another national record. Clearly, Russia's commitment to sport was paying dividends.

At the Czech Championships, the supporters actually cheered for Milan Svajgr; it was as if they were inured to Zátopek's success and craved more drama. Svajgr was fast and battled well in the early throes, but by the end he had wilted. Zátopek's time for 5000 metres was 14 minutes 17.6 seconds, decent but some way off the mark set by Kazantsev or the jaw-dropping time of 14 minutes 6.6 seconds set by a German named Herbert Schade. It was, however, a hugely significant time. Zátopek was still concerned both about his health and his ability to be anywhere near his best on the greatest stage of all, so he told himself that if he did not run 14 minutes 20 seconds then he would not go to the Olympics. He was three seconds away from depriving sport of one of its wonders. Meanwhile, over in France, Alain Mimoun was also celebrating setting a national record in the 10,000 metres. It felt like the world was shrinking and a noose was indeed tightening around Zátopek's neck.

Two contrasting stories from the build-up to the Olympics hint at the complexity of Zátopek's character. The first centred on Milan Svajgr, who claims that Zátopek was partly responsible for him not making the Olympic team for Helsinki.

'We were on a training camp, made the Olympic oath, even got some souvenirs, but I was not in favour of the regime politically, and that cost me,' Svajgr said. 'Everyone knew that and it made it hard. I was even excluded from a camp because I'd missed the May 1st parade. But everything seemed prepared for the Olympics and then the cadre-men from the Central Committee came. They asked about different things, and Zátopek said of me, "I would not let him go to Helsinki because he will stay there." I said, "Emil, how do you figure that? I've competed in Belgium, France, Germany, Helsinki and never stayed."'

Zátopek relented but Svajgr says the damage was done. He did not make the team. Some time later they raced together and the officials took them to a wine cellar. They got drunk and Svajgr said, 'You rascal! You criminal!' He started pulling what little hair Zátopek had left. Svajgr claims Zátopek said, 'Pull, pull, I deserve it.' He says that Reiff and Schade later asked him why he was not at the Olympics and that they had been told he was sick. 'They told them (the Czech athletes) what to answer,' Svajgr said. 'I was targeted.'

It seems Emil could sometimes speak without too much thought, but Svajgr said Emil regretted his remark. He also thinks it may have informed his behaviour in the second story.

Stanislav Jungwirth, known as Standa to his friends, was a very promising runner. Indeed, he would one day break the world record for the 1500 metres. Liška, a friend of both Jungwirth and Zátopek, said, 'I remember Stanislav as an abnormally polite and shy man. His father was a postman, and one day they arrested him for delivering anti-regime leaflets. Stanislav then suffered a lot. His father was thrown in jail and Stanislav was not allowed to travel to the west.'

Suddenly, one of the bright hopes of the team was *persona non grata*. He was excluded from the Olympics, which is when Zátopek made a courageous stand. Dana explained: 'Emil supported him. He was very upset. Emil said, "This is not fair." He said, "If you don't let Standa go to the Olympic Games, when he has got the standard, then I won't go either." It was the 1950s and if you did not have political clearance you were finished. Emil had a huge showdown with the Communist chiefs. He put his foot down and said, "If he's not going, then neither am I."'

Even for a man like Zátopek, standing up to the regime on matters of politics was a risky business. Liška said, 'They wanted to send Jungwirth on a second plane, but Emil did not believe them. He thought if he went on the first plane then they would simply refuse to send Standa afterwards. So Emil said, "Bind our hands or I will not fly."'

Dana was distraught. She was now one of the world's best javelin throwers and was looking forward to the chance to pit her strength against the best in the world, including the mighty Russians. Now it seemed her husband would not be joining her. 'He called their bluff and it was horrible,' she said over a glass of brandy in 2015. 'The political leaders were crazy. We were all staring up at Emil because he was the man that we expected to get medals for the team. I was infected by the myth of Emil. Now he was not going. There were two planes – one at 5 a.m. and one at 11 a.m. – and Emil looked down the lists and noted that Standa's name was not on there.'

As Dana got on the coach to go to the airport with her team-mates, Emil stood outside. She watched him through the window. She loved and admired him, but more than anything at that moment she feared for him. 'We were going to the plane and they were going nowhere. I was left alone. I was crying all the way on the plane. I thought they will be in prison. I was terrified. These were real, big political problems. It was a very brave thing to do.'

Brave, but disappointing for the Finns, who knew all about his ability. František Brož, one of the relay team, said, 'I remember getting off the plane in Helsinki. There were 10,000 Finns waiting for Zátopek, but he wasn't with us.'

Emil refused to back down. He was the biggest name in the team and hoped that would force the Communist hierarchy into a rethink, but it was dangerous. As Dana flew to Finland, he stayed at home and waited anxiously. He went training with Jungwirth. Then he received a call: 'Come to the Ministry of Defence immediately.' Zátopek dutifully obeyed. 'He ran there,'

Dana said. 'And then, with a very solemn face, a man gave him two passports and two tickets. When I saw him I said, "I'm so happy you're not in prison." I knew back then that you simply did not stand up to the Communists. I knew what that meant. I knew how families suffered afterwards. It was the worst.'

Zátopek arrived late and, according to Dana, people were initially wary of speaking to the couple after the drama. Soon, though, any political posturing gave way to the thrill of commonality that comes from a global multi-sport event. Jungwirth owed Zátopek a huge debt, but others were not so lucky. Jan Mrázek was a talented hurdler who was told he would be on the team if he won the qualifying race. 'I won but then they decided they wanted only 20 people and I was the 22nd, so I didn't go.'

For the 1940 Games the municipality of Helsinki had implemented an impressive social housing policy. They had built 23 brick dwellings in the northern suburb of Käpylä. The Games were cancelled but the houses remained and were sold on to 500 families. The area was still known as the Olympic Village, so a new one for the Games was built nearby, designed as a garden suburb.

Emil and Dana were elsewhere. The eastern bloc nations were housed in the University Village in Otaniemi, a lush locale some five miles from the centre of Helsinki. There were nine brick buildings, two restaurants, a canteen, a Finnish sauna and a brand new athletics field with a 400 metres track. With the sea and forest bookending the village, it was a fine place from which to plot world domination.

The stadium itself had been given a makeover. It had been completed in 1938 and was supposed to be used for the 1940 Olympic Games, only for Hitler to get in the way. Many in

Helsinki felt aggrieved that London had got the post-war Games; that a promise had been broken. Now they had their chance, and frantic building work raised the capacity from 50,000 to 62,000 with the aid of vast temporary stands that would be demolished the following year. A huge 72-metre-tall white tower gleamed like a candle when it pierced the sun. Ten dressing-rooms were built. Two tents were erected for the press. There was a marvellously complex electric scoreboard, featuring eight rows of 25-letter spaces, with each space containing 35 incandescent bulbs. In total there were 7000 lamps behind 35,000 holes bored into the copper plate. In a room behind the scoreboard was a telephone exchange with 7500 relays and 100 selectors and 350,000 wires. All this was attached to a simple typewriter that would tap out the names of those changing lives on the brick-dust surface of the seven-lane track.

The numbers continued to add up to an epic occasion. Around 2500 pigeons had been brought to Finland by sea from Sweden and Denmark. They were housed under the north stand of the stadium awaiting their release at the opening ceremony. And how that opening ceremony resonated with Emil Zátopek. It was not the 2500 pigeons or the 35,000 boreholes or the 500 members of the Olympic choir, but the squat, balding man circling the track with the Olympic flame. Four years earlier London had pandered to PR whims and ignored the obvious claim of Sydney Wooderson to light the flame. Helsinki made no such mistake.

Some of the 7500 lamps turned gold to proclaim: 'The Olympic Torch is being brought into the Stadium by Paavo Nurmi.'

The official report of the Games stated: 'The effect of this announcement was electrical. The public cheered ecstatically, the ranks on the field dissolved as thousands of athletes rushed to the track-side to catch a glimpse of this legendary hero of the running track. The progress of the 55-year-old veteran and former king of runners, who ran swiftly and in fine style, was one long triumph. He lit the Bowl in the arena and then, light-footed, bore the Torch onward to the foot of the tower to enable his juniors to speed it to the summit, where another famous Finnish runner, 63-year-old Hannes Kolehmainen, kindled the Flame.'

Nurmi and Kolehmainen, the embodiment of *sisu*; if Zátopek needed any extra motivation then he got it from that nostalgic cameo. Four years on and the Olympics were back where they belonged and, now that Heino had been proved accurate in predicting a lack of heart in future generations, Zátopek was the appropriated hero.

An Archbishop read a Latin prayer. A woman bounced over the barrier and ran onto the rostrum. She was escorted away, her aim unclear. The Archbishop continued:

Almighty, eternal God,

Thou seest men and women in the eagerness and strength
of their youth preparing to strive for the laurel of victory.
Help them to strive also to preserve a pure life and gain the
everlasting crown of Eternity.

In the name of the Father, the Son and the Holy Ghost,
Amen.

Gordon Pirie was in the stadium too. And the man Jack Crump described as 'abnormally confident' was living up to the billing despite a troubled build-up. That February he'd tripped over an anthill when running on the Downs, enabling Walter Hesketh to score another victory over his rival. 'I was carried off in an ambulance. The foot was causing me agony and I had to be carried to and from trains and taxis to get home.'

He had started training again only at the end of March, but the rest had done him good. On 31 May he ran three miles at White City and broke Sydney Wooderson's six-year-old British record. The *News of the World* had made up its mind. 'There seems no question that Pirie is no. 2 to Zátopek in the world over 5000 and 10,000 metres.'

On 28 June he underlined the billing in typically controversial manner. He and Hesketh took on each other over six miles at the AAA Championships and both used their elbows in such an aggressive manner that the track referee had marched into the track mid-race and warned them that if they did not calm down they would be hauled off. And yet, amid the elbows and cold shoulders, Pirie clocked 28 minutes 55.6 seconds, beating Hesketh and taking his British record. When Hesketh was then left off the Olympic team it led to allegations of southern snobbery towards the Manchester shoe-shiner. Pirie scarcely cared. He had been picked for both the 5000 and 10,000 metres and so would have two duels with his hero.

Jim Peters had even more cause to be confident. The previous month he had returned to marathon action for the Poly. It was an eventful race. He very nearly got run over by a car, then found himself wedged between two more going in opposite directions and had to stop. He grew 'mentally despondent' as his legs began to ache prematurely, and would recall that his interior monologue played havoc with him: 'Why are you doing it? You'll kill yourself. There's no money in it.' Others agreed. Percy Cerutty, a maverick Australian coach who had been given two years to live 15 years earlier and had since pioneered 'Stotan' living (a hybrid of Stoic and Spartan beliefs), ran alongside Peters for a while. Cerutty's regime included no cigarettes, no alcohol or socialising after midnight and, more curiously, no white flour. 'You can't do it,' he screamed. 'You'll kill yourself.'

It carried on like this until he got to the stadium. His aim had been to break 2 hours 30 minutes. Instead, he had clocked 2 hours 20 minutes 42.2 seconds. In a sea of ambivalence and pessimism, he had set a new world record and taken almost five minutes off the previous best.

The papers went mad after that: THE GREATEST EFFORT OF THE CENTURY said one headline; PETERS' RUN MADE THE WORLD GAPE opined another. Frieda, for so long the voice of leaden reason to any floating dreams, was now interviewed by the press. Harold Abrahams, the *Chariots of Fire* hero turned journalist, assumed the role of naysayer, pointing out that the Olympics were alarmingly close for a man running so fast and that he may have exhausted his energy bank. Another journalist, in *The Star*, said he had heard that Zátopek was going to run both the 10,000 metres and the marathon.

Peters tried to stifle his optimism. Johnny Johnston reasoned he should fly in late and so he made his trip to Helsinki on a freight plane along with Gordon Pirie.

The front of the plane was so hot that Pirie wore only short sleeves. At the rear, though, Peters and Cox were freezing. Athletes were told to stop exercising cramping legs by walking up the gangway as they were tipping the balance. Then lightning struck the plane and it fell to 3000 feet. It was a baptism of fire for Pirie the Olympic novice, but it was Peters who shivered and suffered the most.

Many of the British writers predicted that Pirie and Chataway would duel for the 5000 metres. Reiff and Schade had their champions, while the McWhirter twins opted for Zátopek. Intriguingly, Armour Milne, the writer who knew him best, predicted that he would not be as good as he was in London. 'I didn't like the way he ran in the Czechoslovak Championships,' he wrote in *Athletics Weekly*. In the same article he lauded Stanislav Jungwirth as 'exceptionally gifted', with caveats about style and bad shoulder rotation. As for the Czech women, only Dana Zátopková could be considered a prospect.

In the *News of the World*, Joe Binks, former holder of the British mile record, suggested Pirie might eclipse the famous Zátopek. On the eve of the 10,000 metres, he began his article with the words, 'Emil Zátopek – sensation or flop?' It was an eye-catching intro, and he went on to explain: 'The atmosphere in Zátopek's camp is dismal, and there was no ring of confidence in his words as he told me that he had not done the whole marathon distance but had hopes of proving himself.

'I feel that the 5000 and 10,000 metres offer our Gordon Pirie the chance of a lifetime and that the same applies to Great Britain's Jim Peters in the marathon.' Binks said that, by contrast, Pirie was 'bubbling over with assurance'. He told the runner that Zátopek was not confident of winning the 5000 metres. Pirie replied, 'He will be thinking again in the 10,000 metres too when I have finished with him.'

Herbert Schade pulled out of the 10,000 metres to focus on the 5000 metres. He had the best time in the world that year in the latter and decided to put all his eggs in the same basket. It was a gamble either way. Binks, sounding a patriotic rallying cry, concluded that, 'The British team are generally feared.'

The 10,000 metres was due to be held on the first day of competition. The weather had turned overnight. The track manager had poured petrol on to the track and throwing sites and burnt off the surface water. The march of the nations during the opening ceremony had badly churned up the track. By 6 p.m., though, the track was fine. So was Zátopek. 'I have to smile as I remember the respect I got off the other runners,' he said. 'When I went to the start the other runners asked where Zátopek would like to stand.'

Pirie had already met Zátopek. The east–west divide was obvious from village geography and Pirie had noted the Russian coaches spying on the top international stars and making movie films. Zátopek was different. Pirie saw him on the training field and approached him. They said hello and ran together. Zátopek saw Pirie had bare ankles and, before the British man could stop him, was removing a pair of socks. He handed them over. Soon afterwards he handed Pirie his Czech running vest; it would be a treasured item until someone stole it from Pirie in Dublin the following year.

As they warmed up before the 10,000 metres, Pirie caught Zátopek's attention and wished him the best of luck. He was surprised when Zátopek told him that he 'hoped' Anufriyev would win.

The tension was palpable. Four years were distilled to these few minutes, the meandering paths suddenly merging. Emil slapped his thighs. Pirie breathed deeply. Up in the stand the great Paavo Nurmi watched with interest. In homes all around Czechoslovakia families gathered around radios as if listening to a wartime announcement. The KSC top brass licked their lips at the prospect of more propaganda. Dana sighed, riddled with nerves and remembering Emil's debilitating illness just a few months earlier.

The clock ticked round to 6.13 p.m. The 100 metres heats had already taken place; so had the 400 metres hurdles. Nina Romashkova was on her way to proving the worth of the Russian system as she led a clean sweep in the discus final. They all paled away to sideshows as the great Zátopek stepped up in an attempt to fend off a new era. The gun. The collective cheer. The mad dash. There were 33 starters, which meant the runners had to form three rows. Mindful of the capacity for mayhem in those early stages when the runners were cramped together, Zátopek darted to the lead. Then, comfortable that he would not be tripped, he drifted back and let others take over. Les Perry, of Australia, was happy to assume that role and, thrilled by the occasion and the noise, cantered into a 40-yard lead after only two laps.

Pirie had started last. Jack Crump bristled at his cockiness, but Pirie wanted to let the field string itself out and then tie itself in knots before he made his move. With his long legs and elegant style he ate up the cinders and settled in behind Zátopek.

As Zátopek had feared, rather than hoped, Anufriyev took over at the front, his Teddy boy sideburns giving him a lupine mien. On the sixth lap Pirie hit the front. All those merciless training sessions had driven him there, all that long-distance shadowing of Zátopek. Kill or be killed. He would show the suits and the Oxbridge cads and the dewy-eyed slobs of Empire Britain that you won by flogging yourself on a daily basis. The idea that you could compete with Zátopek by merely doing endless slow and steady training runs was risible. So he grimaced and bore his pride with a simmering anger.

Peter Lovesey was a 16-year-old schoolboy who would become as passionate about writing as he was about athletics. Many years later, before he became a celebrated crime novelist, he would write a seminal book on running called *The Kings of Distance*, where he would put his memories of 1952 on to the page: 'Seconds after Zátopek showed ahead, the British runner, Gordon Pirie, with characteristic temerity, repeatedly challenged the leadership. Insubordination from a young runner who professed to be a disciple could not be countenanced. With all the dignity of his rank, Staff Captain Zátopek firmly established his intention to lead the field and the Englishman reverted to third position.'

Frank Sando, the Maidstone Mudlark, was trying to overcome raw panic. In the frenetic early exchanges his shoe had come loose. Now he had flicked it clean off. Zátopek was pounding out 71-second laps, deceptively keeping a metronomic pace while varying the speed with little surges. At half-distance Anufriyev had dropped some 50 yards behind Zátopek, Pirie and Mimoun. But Gordon Pirie was hanging on: 'I led briefly but Emil was unwilling to let my pace prevail.'

Pirie's first three miles had been covered in 14 minutes 10 seconds, which was no mean feat, but it came at a cost. When he saw Sando, his room-mate back at the village, move past him with only one shoe, he knew in his head, if not his heart, that it was done. He drifted backwards. Zátopek just kept going, clocking laps at the same pace, dropping runners as if gently shaking autumn leaves from a tree. The French journalist, Gaston Meyer, watched this from one of more than 300 press seats, describing it as, 'The pitiless race of elimination.' The casual cruelty with which runners had their dreams eviscerated one by one was breathtaking.

With four laps to go only Mimoun was staying with Zátopek. Lovesey wrote, 'Mimoun had developed his innate facility for running by training to Zátopek's formula, and his untroubled stride suggested that he was the likeliest adversary to survive the murderous bursts of speed which the Czech could now be expected to introduce. But, perversely, Zátopek ran with the evenness of a clock, just fractionally faster than the earlier laps. His challengers successively slipped away until only the Frenchman had not conceded defeat.'

The concession came in the last four laps. Quickly and yet almost imperceptibly, Zátopek edged away from the blue-shirted Frenchman. The crowd roared. Families around radios did likewise. KSC leaders beat more desks. Peter Pirie, Gordon's brother, raised his eyebrows and knew he had been right in questioning why they had entered Gordon for so many races. Walter Hesketh no doubt raised his hands.

Zátopek finished with a flourish and a 64-second sprint. 'Zát-o-pek! Zát-o-pek! Zát-o-pek!' cried the crowd. He crossed the line and a trainer darted over at pace to embrace him. They collided. In truth, it was the most serious challenge to his ascendancy he had faced all day. His time was 29 minutes 17 seconds. That was faster than his first world record in 1949 but slower than the time with which he won the European Championships in 1950. Yet the pace of change was evinced by him running some 42 seconds faster than he had managed when winning the same title at the Olympics in London four years earlier. It was a huge Olympic record. Nurmi, old Stoneface, now ravaged with age as well as temper, applauded.

Mimoun crossed the line 15 seconds later. Anufriyev was the same distance behind again for third. Sando, who like Pirie had been kept awake by the late-night habits of the other athletes sharing their room, was fifth. He was three seconds from a medal, without a shoe. It was the sort of ill luck that could lead to an Olympiad of what-ifs. As for Pirie, 'I staggered on in an oblivion of fatigue to finish seventh.' He failed to break 30 minutes. Something had gone horribly wrong. The *Daily Telegraph* was one of those unimpressed: 'Whatever made us think that Pirie would beat this superb distance runner?'

In *Dana a Emil Zátopkovi vypravují*, Zátopek would give his own take on events and suggested he had gained a psychological hold over his rivals at the start when they deferred to him and dared not overtake him: 'The papers portrayed us like a train, with me first as a locomotive, puffing and blowing out vapour, and the others as carriages, Mimoun with a beret and the French flag, Sasa Anufriyev with the Russian one, the three British, the Swedish and the rest. I accelerated with ease on the straight and three carriages detached themselves. I did that again and again until the last kilometre when only Mimoun was left.'

In terms of times it was the greatest 10,000 metres ever run, with six men breaking 30 minutes; previously only eight had done so in history.

Zátopek tried to keep his focus. He went walking with Dana in the woods by the training camp. There were telegrams and phone calls, journalists and dignitaries. He had become a hero in London; now he was an international treasure. The Finns took him to a large folk banquet on the night of his triumph. The Hungarians brought him a giant cake. He reminded himself that he must not allow himself to waver as he had four years earlier.

There was only one day for recuperation before the heats of the 5000 metres. The second day of the Games was notable for the closest 100 metres in history. The first four runners clocked 10.4 seconds; the second two 10.5 seconds. Britain hoped that its Trinidadian, McDonald Bailey, would prevail, but most onlookers felt that Herb McKenley had just edged past Lindy Remigino, of the USA. Even Remigino was moved to walk up to the Jamaican to offer his congratulations, only for him to be revealed as the winner by some of the 7500 bulbs up above. 'Gosh, Herb,' he said, 'it looks as though I won the darn thing.' Remigino had come from nowhere, barely qualifying for the USA team, and would return hence, failing to make it to the 1956 Olympics. It was a vivid reminder that upsets could happen.

On the third day there had already been drama before the 5000 metres heats. In 1948 Mal Whitfield, of the USA, had beaten Arthur Wint, of Jamaica, in the 800 metres final by three-tenths of a second to set an Olympic record. In the interim Whitfield had flown 27 missions as a tail-gunner in the Korean War. Now he was back and, once more, he beat Wint to the gold in an Olympic record. The only difference was this time the margin was two-tenths of a second.

The first heat of the 5000 metres was loaded. Pirie lined up alongside Mimoun, Gaston Reiff and Ake Andersson, as well as John Landy, the Australian who would soon be fighting Roger Bannister for the honour of breaking the four-minute mile barrier. Also in the opening heat was Ilmari Taipale, a Finnish runner who had shown no little grit in fighting his way to the Olympics after breaking his back in a skiing accident during the winter.

The pace was fast. Too fast. Pirie watched with irritation as Reiff, Mimoun, Andersson and Taipale indulged in a febrile final sprint. Pirie, who had led for most of the race, settled for the fifth and last qualifying place, edging out Nikifor Popov of Russia. Remarkably, Mimoun had broken the French record.

It got faster. In the second heat Herbert Schade, the great German hope who had sat out the 10,000 metres to keep himself fresh, broke the Olympic record, while British atomic worker Alan Parker was second and close to it himself.

Zátopek knew that there were plenty of threats in the third heat too. There was Chataway, the flamboyant Englishman, and Anufriyev, one of the Russians he had got to know during his travels. Les Perry, of Australia, and Albertsson, of Sweden, made for a deep field. However, the pace was slow enough for Zátopek to indulge in plenty of conversation. He jogged with Anufriyev and said, 'Sasha, come on, we must get a move on.'

They took it in turns to up the pace and stretch the field. Remarkably, Zátopek then slowed to a near walk and waited for Curtis Stone, another friend from the USA. Beforehand Zátopek had spoken about the risks in the line-up and Stone had cheerily told him, 'You're much better than you think you are.' Now Zátopek waited for Stone, toiling in eighth place, and urged him on. Then, niceties dispensed with, he tore back to the leaders. He held up five fingers to remind the others that they would all qualify and there was no need for a finale that could ruin all their medal chances. He even urged Anufriyev ahead of him. The Russian took advantage and came home in front. Albertsson, Zátopek, Perry and Chataway were the other qualifiers. It had been both theatrical and practical, and Zátopek suddenly realised that his antics might have been deemed offensive or arrogant. He sought out the sixth-place man, a Dane, who told him not to worry. He was spent and would not have made it.

Emil remained in the village the following day. He had the option to go to the track to watch events, but instead stayed in the shade of the lush pine trees. He was there when Dana came running up to him, clearly distressed.

'Have you seen tomorrow's programme?' she cried. 'It's terrible. I have the javelin when you run the 5000!'

Emil mulled it over briefly and then smiled. 'That's not terrible,' he said. 'We train together and so we'll compete together.'

Dana tried to explain. 'I can't concentrate if you are racing.'

'That's right,' Emil said. 'A wife must think of her husband, after all.'

Dana turned in a huff and stormed off. Emil sighed and went after her. He caught her and walked her through the woods, picking a wild strawberry plant and handing it to her as an apology.

The 5000 metres was due to start at 4.40 p.m. The javelin final would commence five minutes later. They were a married couple whose crowning moments could be separated by mere minutes. It was an extraordinary coincidence of love and scheduling.

14

Marathon

Sunday 27 July 1952. Emil did not want to go to the stadium too early, with the rest of the squad, and so bided his time. Then he asked a driver to take him the six miles to the stadium. It was a decision that nearly cost him. The trams had been full all morning, with fans clinging to the outside like bees around a hive, and the roads were now blocked. More than 66,000 people were making their way to the stadium. The driver wound down his window and attracted a policeman's attention. 'Zátopek!' he said, as he cocked a thumb to the back seat. The policeman saluted and cleared a path for them.

Zátopek got to the warm-up field just in time to survey his rivals. It was a stellar line-up with stories and threats coming from every quarter. 'Chataway, the Englishman, showed perfect posture of chest; Pirie, his mate, had long, spidery legs. Mimoun had his nervous, stiff style. A little further along Gaston Reiff was jogging on his quick legs, all spruced up and pink in the face and concentrated on his tactic based on unexpectedly reviving a dead moment of the race. The only "sad" man was the favourite, Herbert Schade.'

If he was sad it was because, with each German failure that week, the pressure had mounted on his shoulders. Schade had a haunted expression beneath his bookish glasses and brown quiff.

And that scarcely improved when he gave a thin pencil smile to Zátopek and asked him who he thought was his most dangerous rival. 'Reiff,' Zátopek replied, bluntly but honestly. 'But, still, *you* are the favourite.'

Not for the first time, the papers had billed it as 'the Race of the Century' but, for once, they were not far off the mark. Pirie bounced up and down on his spider's legs and told himself this was his moment, even as the crowd chanted, 'Gaston, Gaston,' and the defending champion turned to him and said, 'This is for me, Gordon.' Puff-Puff Pirie inflated his cheeks. His plan was to go with three laps left and prove all the dissenters wrong. Already, after the 10,000 metres, the sofa sages were sharpening knives at home.

Mimoun already had two Olympic silver medals. The only thing standing between him and legend was Emil Zátopek. Beforehand he made a remarkable admission of futility. 'I trust Emil's ability,' he said. 'Nowadays one simply has got no hope against him.' Others were less convinced, with the majority of pundits favouring Schade and Reiff, the fastest man in the world that year and the defending champion.

On the infield there was a dramatic preamble. A world record was set in the men's hammer throw and so that delayed proceedings as the distance was measured and re-measured. In the wings Dana waited.

The 15 runners set off to a cacophony of noise and hat-throwing. Chataway, his red hair bouncing with each jaunty stride, moved into the lead. Schade, who had been warned by Zátopek not to expend too much energy by leading all the way, ignored the advice and overhauled Chataway. Pirie dug in behind Zátopek. Having followed his career, he now followed his calves. After a few of the 12-and-a-half laps, Pirie was behind Zátopek in sixth place.

A crowd gathered around the white tower began chanting, 'Zát-o-pek! Zát-o-pek! Zát-o-pek!' The lap times were fast – a series of 67- and 68-second circuits – and then Zátopek decided to relieve Schade of his front-running duties. He would claim it was an act of sportsmanship and generosity, but Schade bristled at the altruism and immediately regained the lead. Zátopek edged to his shoulder to explain. 'Herbert, do two laps with me,' he said. The added burden of trying to fathom Zátopek's tactics confused Schade, who breezed to the front after 3000 metres. Zátopek was his usual contorted self. His upper body gained most of the attention due to its constant struggle, but the legs skipped along the track. Those deceptive limbs were nearly vertical as feet hit the floor and it gave the appearance of high-class shuffling. Sometimes, the momentum was such that it seemed Zátopek must fall over. The order now was Schade, Zátopek, Reiff, Chataway and Mimoun. There was a small gap to Pirie. His watching brother, Peter, wondered if he was spent.

His answer came in a cameo that defined Gordon Pirie's Olympic Games and, arguably, his career. With three laps left and the noise ratcheting up with each salvo, he closed the gap and then passed the front five, one after another. It must have felt like fleeting gold. He was leading the great Zátopek and the rest of the world in an Olympic final. And then it was over. No sooner had he hit the front than the others responded. As they passed him Pirie knew there was no way back. And when the feeling of omnipotence is pierced in a runner it cannot be regained, even in the abnormally confident. Five heads moved away from him. He was falling.

Reiff, too, was suffering. He dropped out with 500 metres left, leaving his supporters to join the legions cheering for Zátopek. By the bell Pirie had lost more ground and Schade led, followed by Chataway, Pirie's nemesis since their fledgling National Service days. Chataway might even win. Then came Mimoun and Zátopek. 'The finish was approaching,' Zátopek said, 'the medals were near and we started to feel annoyed at how close we were.'

The bell. There was a minute left, just 400 metres, but it felt like an age. Zátopek led with 350 metres to go. Then it changed: 'To my horror Chataway, Mimoun and Schade overtook me. They had gone past me as if they had agreed the medals and I might as well go home.' Zátopek was at the rear of the foursome. In his head he briefly wondered whether they had gone too fast too soon. At 200 metres he sensed he was right. He eased past all of them. Mimoun dragged Schade with him. Chataway had gone from first to fourth in an instant and was beaten. On the crest of the final bend, he touched the ridge of the track with his left foot and stumbled to the floor. He roused himself and started running again, but now he had lost hope and rhythm and any chance of a medal. Zátopek was now clear of Mimoun. His head rolled as if the hinges were loose, his arms grasped at imaginary aids and his legs pumped. Mimoun's own shuffling gait propelled him ahead of Schade. The crowd went wild. Prague radios were drowned out by cheers. Zátopek crossed the line in a time of 14 minutes 6.6 seconds. It was another Olympic record and 11 seconds faster than his best of the year. The final kilometre had been run in an incredible 2 minutes 41 seconds. Zátopek's last lap had been completed in a stunning 57.9 seconds. Gunder Hägg had run his last kilometre some 13 seconds slower when he set his record. Mimoun was barely a second adrift but it was a chasm. Schade finished third and veered off track.

Zátopek found Mimoun and hugged him. Then he planted a kiss on his cheek. A third silver. The moniker 'Zátopek's shadow' was now irreversible. On the line Pirie just got past the stricken Chataway. That act would cement his reputation as a self-centred troublemaker, and the British press were quick to come down on men they had invested so much ink and optimism in. Maurice Smith, of *The People*, was already formulating a piece which would hit harder than most: 'The British contingent is too big and cumbersome, cluttered up with just flash athletes who never had a celluloid cat's chance in this flame-seared festival. I'm sick and tired of these tomorrows. Right now I feel like suing British athletes for breach of promise.'

Zátopek approached Schade, who looked distraught as realisation of failure gripped every thought. Emil sympathised and offered a few words of advice. He knew what it felt like to have blown a 5000 metres Olympic final and be faced by a four-year wait.

He also knew that his wife was in the throes of her biggest test yet. Or at least she should have been. The delay in the hammer final meant she was on her way into the stadium when it erupted into frenzy for her husband. She wondered who had won. A Russian trainer whom she knew walked past. She asked him what had happened. 'Ah, that Emil,' he said. 'He's a nice boy.'

Then she saw him on his way from the stadium and the medal ceremony. 'You've won!' she cried. 'You've won! Fantastic! Show me the medal. I'll take it with me as a good luck charm.' Emil handed it over and wished her luck. He was then shepherded away. 'They were trying to get him away because there were so many autograph hunters, but I had his medal in my bag.'

Emil could not get away from the hordes of people and instead found the luxury of a shower. Then one of the Czech team directors broke into the changing room and shouted that Dana had just thrown the javelin 50 metres. The actual mark was 50.47 metres, a new Olympic record. It was only the first round, and a trio of Russians toiled and screamed but none could match

Dana. 'There was a Soviet who was only 46 centimetres short on her final throw,' Dana said. She did a cartwheel to celebrate. All those repetitions of 40 x 100 metres, the endless throwing of a one-kilo iron bar, the runs with Emil in thick snow and that time she had collapsed and said, 'No more,' only for him to tie a rope to her waist and drag her home, had all paid off in one perfect arc of the javelin. Within the space of a few minutes the couple had won two gold medals.

Emil was waiting for her by the bus. 'It's all down to me,' he joked. 'With my victory you got so fired up that in your enthusiasm you threw two metres further [than normal].'

Dana was unimpressed by his claim on another gold medal. 'Well, go and inflame some young girl since you are so clever,' she barked. 'See if her enthusiasm can make her throw 50 metres.'

It was a remarkable Sunday. There were only three days until the marathon and Zátopek let it be known that he would be running in it. He joked that he needed to regain the initiative from his wife now that their medal tally lay at only 2–1 in his favour.

Jim Peters' wife, Frieda, was at home. There had been a whip-round, organised by the local garage owner, to pay for her to travel, but she said it would be better if his coach went instead. And so Peters, Johnny Johnston and the coach's other runner, Stan Cox, sat down before the marathon and discussed Emil Zátopek.

'Do you think he's just doing it to help the other Iron Curtain runners?' Stan asked.

'I don't know,' Jim replied. 'But I don't know how he will stand up to doing the marathon after doing the 10,000 and 5000. That's lot to ask of anyone, even Zátopek.'

They deduced that Zátopek was serious and was going for a third gold. The pressure was mounting. On the Saturday Roger Bannister, another gold medal hope, was beaten into fourth place in the 1500 metres. Josy Barthel, a small man from Luxembourg, had won; Stanislav Jungwirth had gone out in the semi-finals. Salvation for the British team now lay with Jim Peters. The media was already turning. Pirie had been so disgruntled when he read the British papers, which had labelled him a bad sport for passing Chataway on the line in the 5000 metres, that he contemplated retiring. 'I was so furious that I flung my kit into the corner of a room and decided to give up running. How could men who could not run 100 yards have the effrontery to talk such damaging nonsense?' It took a long talk with Chataway himself to stop him from quitting, but Pirie never forgot the insult. Worse would follow if Jim Peters could not arrest the decline.

The omens were not good. The runners were checked over by the Finnish doctor. Cox had a fast pulse and was told he could not race. Only the intervention of an American doctor, who explained such pulse rates were normal before elite competition, earned Cox a reluctantly written pass note.

Jim was also suffering. He had developed a paranoia that somebody would try to nobble him. His kit was given the forensic once-over. Jim and Johnny made sure there were no loose bits of wool that might turn into a garrotte over 26 miles. Jack Crump, the team manager, did not allay Jim's fears when he explained that his water bottles would have Union Jacks on them, but he would be expected to stop at the water stations to find them.

Emil Zátopek was also unusually worried. He had never run the marathon and, although he was sure he had enough mileage in his legs, he was less confident about the after-effects of running 20,000 metres in a week and of keeping his natural desire to run fast in check. He kept telling himself about London in '48 and how the great Belgian, Étienne Gailly, had gone hard and fast all the way to the last lap, when he was bereft of all power and collapsed in an ugly heap. 'Gailly was staring in the void as if in a trance,' Emil recalled. It had been like that in 1936 too. Juan Carlos Zabala was no mean runner, setting an Olympic record when winning gold in 1932, but four years later he collapsed, pulled himself up and into the void and then retired. Of all the races in the Olympic programme, the marathon was still a voyage into the unknown. Some runners decided it was best not to drink at all before it. Others drank beer. Jim Peters had a lightly poached egg at midday and waited. His nerves were now hypersensitive; a mere twinge felt like a paralysing seizure.

Jim was the world record holder and had every cause to be optimistic, but the drip-drip of British failure had upset him. He had his plan and would keep to it, but he knew Olympic marathons could be unpredictable affairs. Each race was a mini-epic, a drama of broad scope and narrow margins. As the runners finally assembled inside the stadium, between the white tower and the orange flame, Zátopek looked for Jim Peters. He did not recognise him but knew he was No. 187 and so he decided he would follow that vest. If anybody knew how to run a marathon then it would surely be the man who had done it faster than anyone else. 'He'll do the thinking and I will just pip him at the post,' he told himself. 'All you have to do is push out your chest at the finish.' That throwaway comment from his army chief had germinated in his mind and now the marathon was an overriding ambition. He was the best long-distance runner so he thought it stood to reason that he should be the best at the longest. Contrary to popular myth, he did not decide to enter the marathon on a whim or to increase his medal haul in comparison with Dana.

Zátopek did some light jogging before the start and saw the No. 187 on a pristine white jersey, washed by Frieda and checked over by Johnny.

'How do you do?' Emil said. 'Are you Peters?'

'Yes.'

Emil shook his hand and felt reassured. This was his horse; imagine what he would have done had he picked the wrong one and ended up with a donkey.

Those at home hoped for the best but were not convinced that Zátopek could win his first marathon against the greatest distance runners in the world.

Ludvík Liška said, 'At first I have to say we admired him when he decided to do the marathon. But he was surely too tired. I think it helped that he did not take any refreshment for the whole race; he had tried that several times before and it was psychologically damaging to his opponents. He also talked to them, asking if they were fine, if he was running well. That disconcerted them. It was psychological warfare.'

Jan Mrázek, another runner who worked under Emil, said, 'Emil was thoughtful and sensitive. He would use his experience of observing his surroundings. So when he was running he could assess the strengths and weaknesses of opponents and adjust his tempo.'

Aleš Poděbrad, his deputy at ATK, said everyone was surprised that he entered the marathon, but pointed out that the signs had been there. 'Emil had tried a shortened step in training and he used that for the marathon.'

Perhaps most significant was that he had proved himself adept at running for an hour, and that he was now thinking not only of winning but of Olympic records. Zátopek reasoned that he needed to run 85 seconds for every 400 metres if he was to break a third record in eight days.

The 66 combatants began in a warm afternoon sun. Their first task was to run three-and-a-half laps of the stadium. A barefoot

Pakistani runner shot into the lead at sprinting pace, but was soon overhauled. With his fear of being jostled, Peters quickly ran into the lead, chaperoned by Zátopek.

The first five kilometres were a dream for Jim. He completed them in only 15 minutes 43 seconds, which gave him a huge lead from Zátopek and Gustaf Jansson, of Sweden. As he passed Johnston, who waved a Union Jack at him, the coach shouted, 'Take it steady, Jim.'

Jim was alone for ten kilometres, not far off a quarter of the race. And then Zátopek and Jansson caught up with him and the trio ran together for a few miles. The course was a straight out and in type and, just before the turn, Zátopek turned to Jim. He pointed to Jansson, mystifying Peters, and said, 'The pace? Is it good enough?'

Who knows whether that was a genuine enquiry from a novice marathoner or some of the psychological warfare that his friend, Liška, insisted he used. Whatever the cause, its effects were dramatic. Jim was struggling at that point, but he feigned strength and muttered, 'Pace too slow.' Later he would admit that he was 'absolutely shagged and knackered', but he was damned if he was going to let Zátopek know that.

Zátopek sought confirmation. 'Too slow? Are you sure?'

'Yes.'

It was the affirmative that would have hugely negative repercussions. According to Zátopek, he encouraged Peters to step up, but the Englishman was a 'bit irritated' and crossed over to the other side of the road. 'From then on he lost his freshness.'

A few seconds later Zátopek and his new ally, Jansson, took Peters at face value. They put on a spurt that crippled Jim and left him with a crushing emptiness. At the 13-mile mark, he was only ten yards adrift, but by 15 miles the gap was 150. Jim was now struggling with severe and worsening cramp. 'To my utter dismay I realised my strength was going.'

Jim did not know it but Emil was struggling too. Indeed, 'a terrible tiredness' overwhelmed him and it felt like his legs and ankles were made from wood: 'For the first time in my life I felt like retiring.' He later said the only thing that stopped him was the thought that he would be 20 kilometres from the centre of Helsinki dressed in only shorts and vest if he did.

Jim did not know that and it did not matter. After 15 miles he told himself that if he could just hang on then he would have an Olympic medal – not a gold one, granted, but still a legendary trinket for the humble son of a railway worker. Focusing on the end only precipitated it. After 20 miles his mind gave up moments before his body. He stopped and collapsed into the arms of Sam Ferris, the silver medallist in the 1932 Olympic marathon. He struggled up, staggered along the road for another 200 yards and then flopped down in the road. He was shepherded off it and into a ditch. 'I was in complete despair.' A press car full of journalists arrived on the scene and Jim suffered the added ignominy of being rescued by the very men who were damning the British team for their failure. Further back along the marathon road, Stan Cox was also collapsing. He was taken away in an ambulance. Poor Jimmy Johnston, standing further up the course, and eagerly anticipating a glorious finale, waited in vain, each passing runner a passing bell for an Olympic dream.

The race for the title was still going on. At the 25-kilometre point, the leaders were offered lemons. Zátopek did not take one, deciding that, even though his mouth was watering, he would wait to see if the refreshment had a beneficial effect on his Swedish rival. 'Then I would eat three lemons at the next station.' Without any sustenance, he felt exhausted but toiled away. By the next station at 30 kilometres, Zátopek was clear and so he ignored the lemons again. He felt dizzy, disorientated and even desperate, but he was restored when he heard the sound of the fans. The crowds grew as he neared the stadium, even if the white tower seemed to remain in the far-off distance. Suddenly, from the depths of the crowd he heard a familiar voice. Zátopek would become famous for his saying: 'I was not talented enough to run and smile at the same time.' But when he heard that voice, though, the smile grew.

'*Bravo, Emil, allez, allez.*'

He had taken two gold medals from Alain Mimoun and yet the Frenchman was there, urging him on. 'I was careful not to trip and spoil everything,' Emil said. The Czech broadcaster lost his cool:

Zátopek is the first through the gate. We declare to the republic: at these the 15th Summer Olympics in Helsinki, Staff Captain Emil Zátopek is approaching the finish line in first place.

'At the finish line I even smiled happily and opened my arms, as if to embrace that minute tape towards which I had slaved for 42 kilometres. On the podium I didn't have to think about the next race. The Finnish people waved their hands, shouting, '*Nakkemin*,' (goodbye) and by a miracle I held back the tears because it was beautiful and, perhaps I knew that never again would I live such beautiful moments.'

If that sounded almost apocryphal that was probably because Zátopek was too good to be true on the day. His time was 2 hours 23 minutes 3.2 seconds. He had won three gold medals and set three Olympic records, as well as seeing his wife win a gold medal in another Olympic record.

By the time Reinaldo Gorno, of Argentina, arrived in second place, Zátopek had already been hoisted onto the shoulders of the victorious Jamaican 4 x 400 metres relay team. Gorno was some two-and-a-half minutes adrift. Then came Jansson. Dana was watching and Emil went over to the spectator stand. She came down and kissed him.

Others did not fare so well. Later that night Jim Peters discussed what had gone wrong with Stan Cox. Their symptoms were similar. Jim wondered if it was all linked to the discomfort and cold they had felt on the flight to Helsinki. Others wondered if he had paid the price for running a world record so close to the Olympics. 'Hang out the crepe,' said the *Daily Express*. 'Lower the flag to half-mast.' Some pointed out that only a bloody horse, Foxhunter, won a gold medal for Britain. Only *Athletics Weekly* sounded a supportive note as an editorial opined, 'How good would Zátopek be if he had to do an eight-hour day first?' It added that Zátopek was an exception to almost every rule of law.

Stan Cox had been admonished by the same doctor who had declared him unfit to race. The Duke of Edinburgh visited them and then the two invalids took sleeping tablets, while Johnny Johnston started to open a letter to the AAA asking if the Honorary Medical Advisory Committee would conduct a thorough examination of his two marathon men in the hope of vindicating his 'severe training methods'. It had started with the Archbishop and had been an unholy mess for Britain's endurance men thereafter.

The Games, though, belonged to Emil Zátopek. Life could scarcely get any better.

15

The British

Ladislav Kořan had started running when post-Heydrich curfews forced him off his bike and he was still struggling to make progress.

He met Zátopek in 1943. Kořan was two years younger but would keep a picture from those days for decades. They met again in 1944 in Moravia and bonded over a girl Kořan liked. They remained firm, but distant friends. Ladislav had one problem, though. His father-in-law had a small business making fountain pens. He wanted him to work in the business but not in the factory. They bought a patent for an electro-magnetic pick-up from an engineer in Brno and Larry, as he would come to be known, developed an electric piano. He established a small laboratory and built guitars and basses too. Business was good and he decided he should expand. He wanted to sell a manufacturing licence to Australia and Canada. He had the contact. And that was the worst business decision of his life. 'I became a so-called capitalist,' he said. 'And this was a time when they were after everybody.'

At least he was informed that the StB were coming for him. Kořan was married with a small child, but knew that he had to get out immediately. He escaped to Germany and began making plans for a new life with his family. It was a long, complicated process to smuggle people across the border, but six months later

Kořan returned. He had paid a man in Germany to help him and they crept in darkness by the border between Bavaria and western Bohemia. 'I don't like to even think about it,' Kořan said. 'We heard these voices shouting, "Halt, halt." Then there were gunshots. A bullet hit my left arm and glanced my coat, but the man next to me took 27 projectiles in his body. It was a murder. It saved my life. That night they got me. They caught me and gave me 18 years in a concentration camp, for espionage. That was the end of my athletics career.'

That was in 1950, just as his old friend, Emil, was winning at the European Championships. The year before he had trained with Zátopek as he prepared for his first world record in Ostrava. Kořan had been there in 1947 too, when Emil had insisted on putting calcium in his water so as not to damage his teeth.

By the end of the Olympic Games in 1952, Kořan was into his second year in hell. 'Every concentration camp is hell. It was different in the Hitler and the Stalin camps, but in both everything was bad for you, for your life, your body, your soul. We were working very hard in the uranium mine and the equipment they gave us was not for miners but prisoners. We were slaves of the system. I have never seen so many dead people.'

Kořan was in camp with members of the Czech national ice-hockey team. They had been world champions in 1949, having missed the Olympic gold in 1948. They should have been heroes but were jailed in the belief that they had been planning to defect. Kořan got to know Gustav Bubník, who got 14 years for treason. 'They were all double world champions before they arrested them. It was horrible, but being a runner meant I was strong. That was something.'

Kořan found himself spending the Olympics in Jáchymov, that Stygian outpost, alongside corpses, withering hockey players, and Jan Haluza. The old trainer was now weary of the constant moving between camps. Each one was distinct in its horrors but shared a common inhumanity.

In four years Haluza was permitted only three visits from Věra. At one of the meetings, in Karlovy Vary, Věra felt an overwhelming sadness. Her husband entered the room, shackled and drawn, dressed in threads and emaciated to a deathly pall. A thick, wire mesh separated her from the cadaver. The conversation was monitored. She had been told not to ask about life in the camp. She was barred from bringing a book or any food. She would carefully compose the three letters that she was permitted to write a year. As time went on she wrote more and gave them to a civilian worker at the mines who remembered Haluza as a runner. They were both risking their lives in doing so. The letters and meetings were life-giving because several times the death toll read out on Radio Free Europe included Jan's name. She needed proof. Now, as she looked at her husband, the criss-cross mesh making scars of his bleached face, she wondered if he really was alive.

Ivan Ullsperger did not know Jan Haluza but he knew and loved Emil Zátopek. His father came from the Ore Mountains and his mother from Ljubljana. He was born in Bulgaria, close to the Turkish border, because his father travelled a lot. Unfortunately, his father drank a lot too and was abusive and, before long, he took three children to Bohemia while three more, including Ivan, were exiled in Slovenia. Ivan watched the rise of fascism and, by the age of ten, was having problems as he was perceived as a non-German. His elder brother helped by teaching him how to box, but when he refused to join the Hitler Youth, the locals turned on his family and took him away from his mother, saying she was unfit to raise children. And so Ivan had found himself in a children's home in Graz in Austria, where the people in charge tried to make him German. At the end of the war he was allowed to see his mother, who was now working in the household of a widowed photographer in Jablonec in Czechoslovakia.

One day, Ivan and his friends stumbled across a warehouse containing thousands of German books, including many by Karl May. His tales of the Old West had been delivered to German troops during the war under direct orders from Hitler, who confused the racial message and was a May fan. Ullsperger and his friends made a mess in the warehouse and were caught. His punishment was to work there, tidying and filing the books, and so he began to read Karl May. Then he read about science, medicine and, increasingly, sport. Most interesting of all were the magazines, and the young Ivan read with interest about the exploits of Paavo Nurmi. From there it was inevitable that he would grow to admire Emil Zátopek.

It really started after the 1948 Olympics: 'I felt sorry he was defeated by Gaston Reiff, but he was betrayed by the weather. I did not like the style of Zátopek, but I admired the verve. When I looked at his legs I saw they ran well, but his style was too hard-won. I did not like the hands and body position. I said to myself that I have to do something with my own style, so I made triangles that I attached to my hands while running so that they were fixed in the right position.'

He moved to ATK where Dr Ladislav Fišer, the coach of Stanislav Jungwirth, became his coach. Fišer was a talented but paranoid trainer who felt everyone was spying on his methods. When Ivan took all his records and training calculations to him, the coach threw them all away. However, the young runner failed to improve under Fišer's secret regime and, after a while, decided to train alone. He was not the only one suffering. 'In 1953 everyone said that Emil should train for speed. He had just won three gold medals, but now they made him chase the sprints. He did not improve. That was noticed by the head coach, Major Havlík, and so they decided that Emil should take charge of training of not only himself but all the endurance runners at ATK.'

Ivan enjoyed his tutelage. Zátopek lined up the endurance runners and gave everybody individual training programmes. 'Ivanek, you're young,' he said. 'You're going to run 5 x 200 metres, 20 x 400 metres and 5 x 200 metres. Run that way and you will improve.'

It worked. 'Gradually, others began to improve too and they wanted to try to compete with Emil. He always ran just a little bit faster to beat them, mainly to motivate them. It took me a long time before I dared ask to run with him. When we did he said, "Well, Ivanek, just come." We both ran really fast but we could have gone faster. We did not do it because we realised we wanted to be friends not rivals.'

Both Emil and Dana warmed to the young outsider. At one point he also went to live with them. That happened when Ivan let it slip that every time he left his hotel for more than 48 hours the manager put his stuff out of his room. It meant he would have to return from training camps just to be seen. Emil was incredulous when he heard. 'It's agreed,' he said firmly. 'You'll stay with me and Dana.'

During Ivan's stay his sister called from Austria and said she planned to visit their mother in Jablonec. However, when she tried to check into her hotel in Prague she was barred because she was a foreigner. She was distraught, but Emil sorted the problem by driving the sister all the way to Jablonec. It was a four-hour round trip and he did not think twice.

'I think Emil and Dana really loved me,' Ivan said. 'I don't know why; maybe because they never had a child.'

Ullsperger began to dream of the Olympics too, but already had a memento. Late for training one day, he asked Emil what time it was.

'You have your own watch, right?'

'I don't. I was saving for one but then they introduced monetary reform and suddenly it had a tenth of the value. I was pretty upset. When they asked me what I thought, I said that sort of thieving would not be possible under capitalism.'

Emil studied the younger man. If he had any deep-seated hatred of capitalism or western whims then it did not show when he turned up the next day and handed a watch to Ullsperger. 'It was the watch he had been given for participating in the Olympics in Helsinki.'

Time was ticking from one Olympics to the next, the pendulum swinging from the greatest to the next big thing, and in Russia the sternly tragic figure of Vladimir Kuts was emerging as a genuine threat to all.

Zátopek was hardly finished. He had just pulled off a treble that has never been matched and surely never will be. He ended his Olympic year with a string of runs that belied tradition which dictated that he should be slowing down. Instead, Zátopek, feeling energy and strength inside him, ran his fastest 5000 metres of the year after the Olympics in Opava, clocking 14 minutes 6.4 seconds. The postscripts kept on coming. Summer was drowning in the puddles at his beloved Houstka stadium in the forest on the northern limits of Prague when Zátopek entered the arena intent on breaking three more world records. This was his track. The soil was sandy here where the firs grew, and the groundsman used old oil to make it perfect. Often he would not allow anyone else to use the inside lane; that was reserved for Emil. The 15-mile, 25-kilometre and 30-kilometre marks formed a triptych. It was an oddly absorbing sight to watch this man who had achieved so much demanding more. It was the postscript in the afterthought. A contingent from Korea added to the colour, as devotees watched their icon run lap after lap. Nothing was changing except history. He broke the 15-mile mark of Mikko Hietanen of Finland with ease. A few minutes later he broke the same man's benchmark for 25 kilometres by a minute. He kept on running and broke the 30 kilometre record owned by Russia's Yakov Moskachenkov by a minute and a half. With Jungwirth, the man he had saved from Olympic exile, breaking the Czech 800 metres record that same day, Helsinki was neatly framed by the exploits of men who put everything on the line in every way.

Hints of impending trouble were plentiful, though. 'He was a brave man and not a man happy to do the propaganda of the state,' Ladislav Kořan told me in the summer of 2014. 'He was not a political man. He was a runner. That is what he lived for. That is what he breathed. He was a runner in his dreams.'

Yet Ivan Ullsperger knew that Helsinki had been a huge gamble for Zátopek. Run and win and he was forgiven, as evinced when he received the Order of the Republic, the highest honour that could be bestowed on citizens. Even the concierge in his block of flats had turned. Hitherto a committed sporting heretic, who lambasted Emil and Dana for the noise they made while exercising in their flat above – 'go to the park' – he was responsible for decorating their home as if for a wedding on their return. Emil was the first sportsman to receive the Order of the Republic, and it may have felt like balm to salve the wounds of his stance over Jungwirth. But Ullsperger knew the wounds could be reopened. 'If he had not won then it could have been very bad for Emil,' he said. 'The authorities backed down over Standa, but they did not like doing that. And they did not forget.'

On 5 August 1953 Emil was more worried about the white-haired former sailor standing across from him on a Bucharest track. It had been a relatively quiet year for Zátopek, who had started the year suffering from tonsillitis, which forced him to miss long periods of training. Now he was on a foreign track and his Russian friend, Aleksandr Anufriyev, told him the striking figure was Vladimir Kuts. 'He's good,' said Anufriyev. Emil studied the new rival. He felt his thick-set frame and the 40°C temperature would bother him. 'You won't enjoy it, my friend,' he said to himself. 'You are from Leningrad where it's always cold.' Zátopek felt Anufriyev and József Kovács, the promising Hungarian, would be his main problem.

Kuts defied logic. He set off at a terrific gallop, thudding his way along the track as if spilling anger and blood were his only goals. Zátopek was mystified. He thought about the concierge back at his block and how he would not be pleased if he came second. The only condition of his newfound patronage was continued success. 'Make sure you win everything,' the concierge had said before his trip to Bucharest. Emil had protested that it was not that easy and that, someday, possibly soon, someone would come along and beat him, but the concierge had dismissed that as heroic self-deprecation. As the concierge faded from his consciousness, Emil slowly managed to edge his way back to parity, whereupon Kuts immediately set off again until he had opened up a 30-metre advantage. A sagacious observer of tactics, Zátopek realised his best way to beat Kuts was to make the last two laps into a long-distance sprint. Kovács was in game mood, too, and the duo began running faster than ever with 800 metres to go. Kovács had been expecting that and so had done the mental preparation. The gap to Kuts, the ultimate loner, dwindled painfully. With 300 metres left, Kovács began to fall away. On the final bend Zátopek searched for Olympic leftovers and made his legs move faster. He was careful not to overstride, the tempting but flawed tendency to take longer steps, and he burst for the line. Kuts was beaten, but he was young and had plenty more races ahead. Zátopek took the plaudits but felt his 30 years. The time was 14 minutes 3 seconds, equalling his Czech record set in Brussels three years earlier. Gauntlets littered the track; the next two years would see them picked up. 'I had risked a lot,' Zátopek would admit.

The 10,000 metres was far easier, as Kuts again went off at a suicidal pace, chasing the equally bold Anufriyev, and suffered for it. Zátopek even had time to nurse a friend, an Australian named Dave Stephens, to a national 5000 metres record. As Stephens dropped out and sat on the verge, he marvelled as his friend overhauled the rest over the second 5000.

Kovács had already run the 5000 metres faster than Zátopek when he arrived in Prague to wrestle bragging rights from the Czech soon afterwards. The race was notable for Zátopek kneeling down on the start line to tie one of Kovács' shoelaces, which had come undone. Then Kovács came undone and Zátopek won again. However, there was a clear gathering of rival forces. It seemed ominous when he and some friends flung Dana into a river while enjoying an afternoon's swimming, only for her to fall awkwardly on a sandbank and break her shinbone. With her right leg in plaster, Dana kept training by chopping wood while Emil took to carrying her on his back during his training runs.

Forces were gathering in England too. Gordon Pirie and Jim Peters had enjoyed stunning summers in 1953. For Pirie life had started to change even before he left Helsinki after the Olympics. A delay at the airport resulted in a group of British athletes, including Chris Chataway and Roger Bannister, indulging in pleasant conversation with the German trainer, Woldemar Gerschler. Pirie tagged along with the group and the conversation swiftly changed towards how Gerschler had trained Josy Barthel, the man who had beaten Bannister in the 1500 metres final. When Bannister and Chataway moved on, Pirie stayed and, with typical boldness, asked Gerschler to coach him. He had been immediately seduced by the 'quiet authority' of the man who had worked with a heart specialist, Professor Hans Reindell, at the Freiberg Institute for 20 years. If Pirie was to beat Zátopek, he reasoned he needed the best help. Gerschler told him he could only work with Pirie if he came to Germany. It would take Pirie a year to save up the money to make the trip, but in the interim a monthly letter from Gerschler guided him. For the first time someone told Pirie that, instead of running less and burning himself out, he should do more. That was manna from heaven for a man with a masochistic work ethic.

His form improved. He was still capable of throwing verbal grenades at the sporting establishment – 'tripe' was his dismissal of the press' pre-Olympic predictions and bitter post-mortem – but now his actions were also speaking loudly. He still bristled at criticism and defended his new, even harder regime with a sneering honesty. 'You can't afford to rest if you're after Zátopek's records, which I am,' he said. He said he wanted to run the 5000 metres in 13 minutes 40 seconds, which sounded beyond bragging given that the world record was 13 minutes 58.2 seconds, and was distinctly un-British in its brashness. At the Southern 6 Mile Championships he boasted to Jim Peters' followers that he would lap him, and when he didn't he remarked on 'excellent running for a veteran'. He rowed with officials in Berlin when told he had to meet the British ambassador – 'competition should come first and social junketing second' – and admitted 'my lone wolf behaviour did not make me popular'. He did not care. He felt the approach of other British athletes was too relaxed. The 5000 and 10,000 metres would come his way. It was inevitable.

Other athletes were not convinced by his methods. Pirie ran 20 miles a day and he also bucked orthodoxy by believing he could run a huge range of distances. However, that summer it paid off. At the AAA Championships he finally broke Heino's six-mile record with a run of 28 minutes 19.4 seconds. He then threatened to pull out of the British Games unless he was allowed to run in the new Emsley Carr Mile, a race devised by William Carr to honour his father, a famous newspaper baron, and facilitate the breaking of the four-minute mile. The race was a big deal, with Paavo Nurmi, Sydney Wooderson and Gunder Hägg among those watching. The field was loaded too, but Pirie won in 4 minutes 6.8 seconds. It was two fingers to the establishment who said a six-miler could not run a mile. The papers were now convinced. Here was a tough-talking figure who liked bragging and ballet. He was interesting. He was box office, so they looked for gossip, claiming he had arrogantly signed his name on the winners' page of the Emsley Carr Mile's red leather book before they had even had the race, but also shouting, HAIL PIRIE – THE BRITISH ZÁTOPEK! Gunder Hägg, now 34 and long-banned for being professional, wore a shirt and suit as he watched. He still held the mile record but knew it was under threat like never before. He warmly shook Pirie's hand and told the press, 'He will be burnt out in two years.'

Jim Peters was faring even better that year. The Queen's surgeon himself passed him fit after the awful denouement in

Helsinki, and like Pirie he decided to adopt the Zátopek mantra. While people looked to his pre-Olympic schedule, and his attempt to run two marathons within six weeks, he decided the only way to win was to work harder. He expressed a desire to run 500 times and 4000 miles in 1953. The marathon world record was still his, until Keizo Yamada, of Japan, ran 2 hours 18 minutes 51 seconds in Boston; it was an incredible time that was almost two minutes better than Peters' best, and it would be years before it lost all credibility when it emerged the course was more than 1000 yards short.

Jim suffered terribly with blisters that summer. They really began to hurt when he missed out on the British allcomers one-hour record at White City. His feet were red raw and pockmarked by circles of hard skin and exposed areas by the end. The 85°C temperature did not help. Alf Shrubb's ancient record survived by 151 yards. Jim was adamant the only way to dispense with disappointment was to run. The press looked on aghast. The *News of the World*, remarking that he had run 3000 miles in only nine months, talked of his new labour – the forthcoming Poly marathon: 'To use his own words Peters is a worried man because he believes the White City barbecue may have burned his chances of winning the Polytechnic marathon for a third successive year.' They quoted Jim as saying, 'It's hopeless to sit back with my aches and pains. The only way to build myself up to take the punishment of the marathon is to keep running.' Referencing the criticism he got for Zátopek-like efforts, he added, 'Pirie works even harder.'

It paid off. He estimated a time of 2 hours 40 minutes due to his badly bleeding blisters and a strained muscle. He ran 2 hours 18 minutes and 40.4 seconds. It was another world best. The scale of Peters' pessimism was staggering, but he was becoming obsessive now. The next day he mowed the lawn, took his son out for a walk and then did an evening training run. Six weeks later he ran another marathon in Wales for the AAA Championship. At one point he was stalled by a herd of cows on the road and yet, despite his frail form and sickly background, he pushed the cows out of his way and charged on. His time was a world's best for an out and in course and, he noted, almost a minute inside Zátopek's Olympic record.

Frieda asked for a rare holiday and Jim complained to Johnny. Coach told charge that it would do him good, but Peters now just wanted to run. In his own head he decided that if he could train three times a day then he could rival Zátopek. They would meet again, of that he was sure, if not before then at the Melbourne Olympics in 1956.

In September 1953 he entered another marathon in Enschede, Holland. He clocked 2 hours 19 minutes and 22 seconds. He noted that this time was well over three minutes faster than Zátopek's Olympic mark. Still, he kept running. Three weeks later he went to Turku, home of the great Nurmi, and was amazed when he was told there were 17 cinder tracks in the city. His interpreter took him to a hotel and asked if he wanted a girlfriend for the duration of the trip. Jim thought of Frieda and what she would say if she knew what he was being offered.

The interpreter was surprised when he declined. 'You are so different from the Americans who came here,' he said.

It was different in Finland – from the girls to the rules, which permitted each runner to have his own personal attendant, who would cycle with him, sponge at the ready. Peters took some keeping up with. His time of 2 hours 18 minutes and 34.8 seconds was another world record. This was his second of the year; he now had three of the top five times ever run for the distance. He was a bona fide great and yet he seemed to fly under the radar – an unassuming, wiry dispensing optician whose natural métier was self-deprecation. When he got home only Johnny Johnston and his son were there. In *The Star*, an editorial ran: 'Had he been a New Yorker he would have had a ticker-tape reception. Had he been Emil Zátopek there would have been traffic jams and vast crowds in Prague.' Jim shrugged. The day after he arrived home he did six miles. Like Pirie, he was copying Zátopek to beat him.

Zátopek's record-breaking feats reverberated around the sporting world. He was the icon inspiring iconoclasts. The ripples crossed to Russia and, at the end of August, Vladimir Kuts ran a 5000 metres in a blistering 14 minutes 2.2 seconds. It passed to Hungary, where Kovács went even faster to beat Kuts.

For Zátopek, the year had started with him in hospital after having his tonsils out; it ended with him removing his lungs in a visceral act designed to stop the taunt of time. František Kožik told of the biting wind and drying leaves as a parade of cars and coaches and bicycles made their way to Zátopek's favoured forest track at Houstka Spa on 1 November: 'There were workers from Boleslav, there were students, soldiers, actors from Prague theatres, children, all people who are fond of him.'

The stage was set; the goal was beating his own 10,000 metres world record. The lateness of the date made it harder, as did the other runners, who inadvertently got in his way. He also struggled, as he often did, around the seven-kilometre mark, but he felt strong. He fed off the trees and the people, off the love and greenery. Emil Zátopek was a natural. The world was changing but he maintained a semblance of order and churned out fast lap after fast lap until he hit the tape in 29 minutes 1.6 seconds. It was yet another world record. 'They had seen one of the greatest sports records in the history of mankind,' said Kožik with a typical flourish. Pirie sent a congratulatory telegram. The sport smiled. As the calendar ticked over into 1954, the limits of distance running were being pushed like never before. They were into record season.

16

Record Season

'Does it sound impossible?' The question hangs in the air of Sir Roger Bannister's study. He has just stated that someone will break the two-hour marathon mark by the 2016 Olympics.

It will be 60 years on the Tuesday after we meet since Bannister forged his way into the book of sporting fables with his landmark turn in Oxford. No sporting milestone has caused such an indelible impression, dwarfing Nadia Comăneci's perfect ten or Sir Garfield Sobers' six sixes. Yet if he was now 85, the prized neurology award on the mantelpiece – by the picture of Bannister with Winston Churchill – proved he was a man of science as well as history. So there was method in what some would deem his madness.

'The person would need to run at 4-minute 35-second mile pace,' he said of the sub-two-hour marathon. 'That would be a 2 per cent improvement on the current record.' He pointed out that Bob Beamon had improved the long jump record by 6 per cent in Mexico City in 1968. 'The thing is nobody is attacking it like we did the four-minute mile. Runners run as fast as they need to, but it would be dead easy if they could choose the perfect day, on a straight track, with a prevailing westerly wind, with the temperature about 18°C.'

It was fascinating to hear Bannister talk of new records. In his book *The Perfection Point*, John Brenkus pointed out that the marathon world record holder set a mile pace that was 23 per cent slower than his best mile; so if Hicham El Guerrouj, the mile champion, had been able to run a marathon pace with the same percentage reduction, he would have clocked 1 hour 59 minutes 52 seconds.

Competition was the thing. 'You only get real progress when you have a rival,' Bannister told me. 'The reason I got there was I was kept informed of what Wes Santee was doing in America and what John Landy was doing in Australia. If I had not known they were running 4 minutes 2 seconds I would not have been driven to go faster.'

Landy had come close, running under 4 minutes 3 seconds on six occasions, and Bannister waited nervously on his results. He set the date for his own challenge – 6 May 1954 – but the wind made him consider postponing.

Then his advisor, Franz Stampfl, described by Bannister as a 'Viennese Rex Harrison', waded in. He reminded Bannister that Landy was soon to race again in Europe. 'If you pass it up today, you may never forgive yourself for the rest of your life,' Stampfl said.

'He said I could run 3 minutes 56 seconds, so I could still do it in adverse conditions. I did not believe him, but he knew a bit about pain because he'd been torpedoed in the war and was in the water for a length of time that would kill most people. I felt he was a survivor and so knew something.'

At Iffley Road, the wind was still up, but his pacemakers, Chris Brasher and Chris Chataway, were growing 'impatient and irritated' by Bannister's dithering. The flag dropped and the history makers ran. 'My mind took over,' Bannister would say. 'It raced well ahead of my body. Time seemed to stand still, or did not exist.'

It moves on. Bannister was good company and had trenchant views on sport. By the time he retired as chairman of the Sports Council in 1974 there were 400 multi-purpose sports centres in the planning stage, as opposed to the four that he inherited. He told me that Harold Abrahams threatened to sue him for defamation because of an alleged conflict of interest over negotiating broadcasting rights while working for the BBC. The *Chariots of Fire* hero versus the four-minute miler – now that would have been something. He recalled the meeting in which he convinced the Jimmy Carter regime to forget about Britain when it came to the 1980 Olympic boycott of Moscow. Sometimes he sounded of that post-Waugh, post-war age when everything was black and white – but he still exercised the grey matter. He was suffering with the early throes of Parkinson's disease, but nobody could accuse this octogenarian of being behind the times when he criticised the Olympic price tag or President Putin for fulminating against homosexuals.

Yet although he was up to date and would prefer to be known for his work in medicine and for being Master of Pembroke College at Oxford, it is 6 May 1954 for which Sir Roger Bannister will always be known.

After one and a half laps he was still worrying about the pace. 'Relax,' shouted Stampfl. He passed the half-mile in 1 minute 58 seconds. Soon afterwards Chataway took over at the front and began to lead his friend on. He passed three-quarters of a mile in almost three minutes exactly. Bannister had to do the last 300 metres from the front. He felt spent but said 'the physical overdraft came only from greater willpower'. He said he felt like 'an exploded flashbulb with no will to live'. He staggered into outstretched arms afterwards and then the announcement came.

'Three minutes and—'

The details were lost in the roar. The mythical four-minute mile barrier had been broken. Bannister grabbed Brasher and Chataway, his friends and pacesetters. 'I felt suddenly and gloriously free of the burden of athletic ambition I had been carrying around for years,' he said.

In his Oxford home in 2014, you sensed he was still amused by all this time-trial time-travel. 'I rate Olympic gold medals higher than time trials and records,' he said before we spoke of Emil Zátopek. Even then, decades on, Bannister was mystified by his work ethic and range.

Some had even wondered if Zátopek and not Bannister might be the man to break the four-minute mile barrier, but he had enough on his plate in 1954, which would become the *annus mirabilis* of record-breaking. Bannister started it, but Zátopek took up the baton within days.

Publicly, Zátopek was not offering too much hope in 1954. He said that he would only be able to compete in the 'short' long distances 'as a sort of guest artist'. He was looking to the 10,000 metres and beyond. He knew the global rivals had never been more threatening. 'Why shouldn't the world record holder of the ten kilometres one day be called Pirie? Whoever surpasses my training will also break my records.' He had developed a friendship with Pirie through letters they sent each other. 'I believe that he will be a success and will become the pride of his country. That is all I can say at this stage about Pirie.' Yet even Zátopek had a caveat for Pirie: 'As long as he doesn't burn himself out too soon, for Pirie is still very, very young and, at his age, one shouldn't force the longer distances too much.'

Vladimir Kuts, too, had a strong constitution, although Zátopek queried his tactics of setting off in every race as if he wanted to 'shatter the world record by at least half a minute'. He likened Kuts and his friend, Aleksandr Anufriyev, to racehorses that could only sustain so many terrible beatings.

His friend and protégé, Ivan Ullsperger, was also improving. Eight days after Bannister's epic run, Emil opened his season with a very fast 5000 metres. The time of 14 minutes 4 seconds made a mockery of his 'guest artist' statement. Ullsperger was a distant second, but was well aware of the pressure that was growing on Emil. He had seen it when the Communists had come to him and made him speak out against General Sacher because he was in charge of the Military Physical Association and they wanted to merge that into ATK. Emil was their innocent sledgehammer. The questions he received elsewhere went way beyond the remit of the average sportsman, not least in the aftermath of the execution of Rudolf Slánský, one of the most powerful politicians to be executed by the Czech regime. 'Once Emil was asked how it was possible that Slánský was executed,' Ullsperger remembered. 'Emil did not answer them directly. He did not hold up either the official line that Slánský was a villain and nor did he condemn his execution. He just started to speak about another topic; he did not want to talk too much about politics.'

Emil wanted to run and to teach, although he could be hard on Ullsperger. 'I had some problems with Emil,' he said. 'Emil once told the boys that I'm lazy. I confronted him and he said I used to train harder and now I had eased off and got worse results. I went to the bathroom and had red urine. So I urinated in a glass and brought it to Emil. He looked at it and when I explained what was going on in my body, he went pale: "Ivanek, I promise I will never chase you again."' Beneath the bonhomie, Zátopek was driving himself and others to the absolute limit.

Armour Milne was more impressed with Ullsperger. He noted Zátopek's opening time at the trials for the European

Championships at Houstka Spa and pointed out that others were now copying his methods. Ullsperger even wore the same long socks, albeit that he was mocked as a sycophant behind his back. 'The interesting point is that at long last Zátopek's training methods have been vindicated at home, where they have been confined largely to Zátopek himself. Another is that indications are there that a successor to Zátopek, although still very immature, can be seen in young Ullsperger.'

Three weeks after Bannister's run in Oxford, Zátopek went to Paris. He had already run there that year in the *L'Humanité* cross-country run. After winning that race he was asked by some acquaintances what he thought of Paris, and he gave an enthusiastic response before adding some 'less noble observations about the notorious Rue Pigalle'. It was in Brussels that he heard he was barred from France. The Belgian police told him it was because he had labelled Paris 'pornographic'. The Belgians were not bothered by that and offered to organise a race for him themselves. Then Zátopek got word to go to the French embassy at midnight. To his surprise he received his passport and headed for the airport at 3 a.m.

The plan was to run 5000 metres at Stade Olympique Yves-du-Manoir, named after a French rugby-playing aristocrat who had died in a plane crash. The stadium had been used for the Olympic Games and the 1938 World Cup final, but nobody was expecting too much as Zátopek lined up against only four other runners.

Emil craved the 5000 metres record above all others. It was the hardest to crack and the one he toiled for. Now he decided he had better put in a good performance given his bad reputation in France over the 'pornography' slur.

He took the lead from the start and after 300 metres had dropped the rest. The first four laps were sub-67-second circuits.

The last kilometre was completed in a thrilling 2 minutes 43.8 seconds. He had a lead of 280 yards at the bell. The time was 13 minutes 57.2 seconds. From almost nowhere, on a nothing night at a nothing meeting, Zátopek had broken the 5000 metres world record. Gunder Hägg's mark had stood since 1942, almost a dozen years. Hägg's mile record had stood since 1945, almost nine years. It could sensibly be argued that Zátopek's achievement was far more impressive than Bannister's, which had involved the use of pacesetters, but the four-minute barrier had captured the public imagination in a way being the second man under 14 minutes could not.

Nevertheless, fans mobbed him and women tried to kiss him. 'I was in good condition and perfect health,' he said before heading to a Communist-sponsored reception. 'The visa affair didn't bother me at all. I didn't get any times along the way but knew I was doing well.' He concluded that he could beat this time again. Ron Clarke would feel his intangible ache after setting landmarks in the future, but Zátopek regarded them more practically. 'To boast of a performance which I cannot beat is stupid vanity; and if I can beat it that means there is nothing special about it. What has passed is already finished. What I find more interesting is what is still to come.'

He moved swiftly back to Brussels for his 10,000 metres at Stade des Trois Tilleuls, a picturesque stadium with poplars forming a windbreak around gently sloping football terraces. Again, he was at his metronomic best. Zátopek showed he could run on his own at even pace or win titles by surging throughout. He was the running everyman. He passed halfway in 14 minutes 27.6 seconds. It seemed almost inconceivable that he would break two records in three days and yet he maintained his pace until he sprinted for a final kilometre of 2 minutes 46.8 seconds. He knew it was fast but had no idea quite how fast. The time of 28 minutes 54.2 seconds meant he was the first man to dip under 29 minutes. He had held the record for almost five years now. He had broken it five times in total. Each notch on history's bedpost was another mark of the man and the myth.

He went home and enjoyed his life and wife, training with Dana, gently goading and inspiring each other. He had a good role in the army and was left relatively free to work as he wanted. If there was jealousy from abroad, where even the self-effacing Jim Peters had questioned how Emil would cope if he had to fit training around a full day's work, there was simmering resentment at home too. Ludvík Liška remembered, 'There was a rivalry between the ATK and civilian runners. We at the ATK actually had it as a profession, and the civilians behaved very badly towards us. They said, "You don't have to work, you're fine." They perceived it that we were on a year-long training camp.'

The following month Zátopek was beaten. He had lost before but never over 10,000 metres. He had won 38 races in a row since his 1948 debut, taking in world records and Olympic and European titles. He was famous and influential, but as Ullsperger had warned, once intimations of mortality set in then his reach might recede.

József Kovács was the man who beat Zátopek by four yards in a time of 29 minutes 6 seconds. Neither man quavered in the race that was the highlight of the Hungary–Czechoslovakia match in Budapest. They were conjoined duellists. With 200 metres left Emil led, but then the ghostly figure of Kovács, his all-white kit standing out against the dark, floated past. To Emil's horror, he realised the momentum had swung away from him. The defeat inevitably hit him hard. As for Kovács, the Hungarian was in the vanguard of change and had needed to run the second-fastest

10,000 metres ever to gain his scalp. Inevitably, people began to wonder if Emil was nearing the end. 'Zátopek's first defeat over 10,000 metres naturally shook the athletics world, but I advise sanity in weighing it up,' Armour Milne wrote. He suggested Zátopek now lacked the sprinting speed and merely needed to change tactics, back to his famed habit of wearing the rest down. It was a serious setback for Emil, who had grown used to winning, but the slight figure of the angular Hungarian signalled a new rival to contend with. It also cemented Eastern Europe's status as the home of endurance men.

The summer of 1954 was turning into something special. On 21 June John Landy broke Bannister's mile world record. After all the effort and pain, the barrier had gone and now it felt easier. Bannister had the record for six weeks and, in the eyes of the wider world, six decades.

In 2014 Bannister would tell me that Chataway's presence in Landy's record race was pivotal. 'Landy had run five 4-minutes 2-second races and said it was like a brick wall,' he said. 'I can assure you from my medical knowledge that it was not a brick wall. The situation was one had to find something extra and John Landy did not have a pacemaker. The missing factor for him was competition, somebody he was frightened of. So he looked over his shoulder and saw Chataway. And he took off.'

As his wife delivered tea and biscuits, Bannister said that he believed Landy would have broken the four-minute barrier first had he used pacemakers. So why didn't he? Landy, himself, explained, 'I didn't want to be part of something questionable, which is how pacesetting was seen at the time.' Criticism of Bannister's 'schemed' time trial, with Brasher and Chataway clearly acting as pacemakers but being forced to say afterwards that they had been trying to win, festered through May of 1954.

There was even a debate about whether the world record would be ratified due to the uncompetitive nature of the race at Iffley Road. The disdain some had for time trials was reflected later that year when Chataway, rather than Bannister, won the inaugural BBC Sportsview award, which later became the BBC Sports Personality of the Year. 'I wanted to run the four-minute mile by myself,' Landy said, years later. 'I never saw it as a team business.'

Now Landy had clocked 3 minutes 58.0 seconds, destroying Bannister's mark. The pair would face each other in a massively hyped race at the Empire Games, the forerunner for the Commonwealth Games, in Vancouver. It was dubbed 'the Miracle Mile' and yet it would be a day that changed the life of Jim Peters above both men.

In a packed stadium Bannister and Landy lined up. Bannister was worried about hearing reports of Landy's training done in the stadium. By contrast, adhering to his Achilles Club ideals, Bannister had taken it relatively easy. 'If Zátopek ran 60 quarter miles in 60 seconds each, in a single workout, then it seemed only a man who could train still harder could beat him,' he wrote in *The First Four Minutes*. 'Where would it all end? Running would have lost its purpose.'

The last lap of the duel had the stadium in raptures. 'One of the most exciting and intense moments of my life,' Bannister said. Vancouver was his redemption after the post-Helsinki criticism. He drew up to Landy and noticed him look over his shoulder: 'I knew then I had him.' Bannister won the race in another sub-four-minute time. *The* so-called four-minute mile was now validated in Bannister's mind.

Sport is about getting there first, both as a race winner and pioneer. Few outside the athletics world know Landy's name, and in Australia he is best remembered for something else entirely. Two years later, already being touted as the face of the Olympic Games in his native Melbourne, he doubled back during the 1500 metres at the Australian National Championships to check on Ron Clarke, who had fallen. Landy explained that he had caught Clarke's arm with his spikes as he fell. 'Sorry,' he said as he helped him up, whereupon he rejoined the race and won in 4 minutes 4.2 seconds. A statue of the incident stands in Melbourne's Olympic Park.

Landy later became the Governor of Victoria and was never bitter about Bannister's triumph. Nor did he tell anyone that the night before the Miracle Mile he had stood on a photographer's discarded flashbulb and been taken to hospital with a profusely bleeding foot. After the race the wound became infected and he didn't run again in 1954. Bannister retired that year to focus on his medical studies. The pair never raced each other again.

The Miracle was over but not the drama. The 33,000 people in the stadium were still in uproar when Jim Peters entered the stadium after completing almost 26 miles of the marathon. He had been the overwhelming favourite, as he had broken the world record for the marathon again the previous month, clocking 2 hours 17 minutes and 39.4 seconds at the Poly. The lure of facing Zátopek at the next Olympics hovered in the distance, but now he was after another medal.

He had been edgy in Vancouver: the obsession with the Miracle Mile meant no officials were out on the course; Johnny had not flown over; there was concern over the paucity of drink stations; the temperature was hot; and there was a strange incident at the start when a man had emerged from the stands dressed in a white running vest but with no number. Allan Lawrence, an Australian runner, heard Jim and Stan Cox shout, 'Remove this madman,' and was amused at how serious they were taking the interruption. 'Where's the bloody mounted police when you need them?' he quipped. Then he watched the man jump into the air and crash down on to the track head first, before punching an imaginary assailant and butting the grandstand fence.

Jim was certainly tense, not least because he had travelled the route and was firmly of the opinion that it was longer than the official marathon length. He had also got to know the Achilles Club men a bit more during the trip. Chataway was incredulous at his team-mate's work ethic. He had told his great friend, Bannister, that working like Zátopek was not human, but re-examined his words to see if they stood up. 'Here we are doing a third of the running Zátopek's doing this week. While he goes for a 20-mile training run on his only free day, we lie here panting with exhaustion, moaning that the gods are unkind to us, and that we're too intelligent to train hard.'

Bannister, Chataway and the Oxbridge set were dubbed 'the cads' by the likes of Peters, Stan Cox and team captain, gargantuan shot putter John Savidge. It was a good-natured barb but there was a clear split in terms of both class and work ethic.

Bannister was still celebrating as Jim neared the end of the marathon. He would say that he felt fine with 380 yards to go.

Allan Lawrence dropped out after 22 miles. The searing heat from the road had been unbearable and his blisters made every step agony. He slumped in the gutter and took off his shoes and then carried on, wondering if being barefoot would enable him to hang on for third place. He lasted a mile. Later he was aghast when he found out what had happened in the stadium.

At 25 miles Stan Cox had careered off the road and run into a lamppost. Up ahead Peters entered the stadium in the lead, but almost immediately fell over. A hush descended over the jubilant atmosphere. Jim got up: 'I was completely bewildered. Then I made up my mind. I was going to finish. I didn't want to disgrace my wife and the kiddies.'

He fell again. And rose. And fell. John Savidge was crawling alongside Jim on the inside of the track, urging him on. He was a massive 15 minutes clear of the rest and merely needed to walk around the track. Chris Brasher, one of the cads, cringed. 'It was a hell of a scene and one of the most horrific in athletic history.' Bannister was heard to liken it to feeding Christians to the lions and shouted, 'This is dangerous; get him off the track.' It scarcely seems possible now, but at one point Peters collapsed beneath the main grandstand and lay there for several minutes. Murray Halberg, a New Zealander who competed in the mile, said, 'When a boxer is punched into that condition, the referee stops the fight.' He said he would like to forget the images but never would. It took Jim 11 minutes to reach the finishing line. There were reports of women crying and people vomiting at the awful spectacle. Jim was like a puppet – with each step taken another string was cut – and utterly at the mercy of the sun and his own frailties. The elite marathon world record holder was suddenly transported back to his sickly youth.

Roy Moor of the *News Chronicle* penned one of the most vivid reports of that afternoon: 'Children sitting in front of the Duke were told to hide their faces to shut out the pitiful sight. And if I thought such a scene was likely to be repeated I would clamour for the abolition of marathon racing. Men and women turned their heads away as Peters continually fell, sometimes lying spread out on the cinders. Twelve times he went down.'

To compound this visceral disaster, Jim fell into the arms of Mick Mays, the team trainer and masseur. He thought he had crossed the line, but he had actually just reached the end for the

Miracle Mile. The marathon finish was still some distance away. Some of the officials had not known that because they had missed the marshals' briefing to watch the mile. Receiving assistance meant Jim was disqualified and Joe McGhee won the race in silence. The highs and lows of athletics may never have been as vividly realised as by the juxtaposition of the Miracle Mile and the debacle of a dozen falls. 'Jim Peters was rushed to hospital and for 24 hours was close to death,' Lawrence recalled in his autobiography. 'He was not told he had been disqualified until three days later.'

The next day a radio broadcast stated that Jim had passed away. It was an error. A journalist who said he would get a message to Frieda in return for a scoop was allowed into his hospital room. The message was finally relayed to Frieda by Hampshire police. The *London Evening Standard* painted an almost gothic picture of Jim in an iron bed, '. . . blanketed in grey, whimpering like a wounded animal, his arms jerking convulsively, his plimsolled feet twitching a ghastly kind of tattoo on the wall, his pores oozing perspiration, saliva drooling from his colourless lips.' He was, however, alive.

Bannister stayed on in Vancouver to help Peters, due to his medical training. A man who worked with juvenile delinquents visited and asked if he could put his name on a trophy that would be competed for in a prison. A 'Jim Peters' fund was established to help boys and girls who were in trouble. He came home and hugged Frieda and said that was it.

'Jim, I'm convinced that you'll never retire until they take you out in a coffin.'

'I mean it this time,' he said. 'I'm retiring.' And he did.

For others the season was still to reach its peak, with the European Championships taking place in Berne just a few weeks later, at the end of August. The marathon was the first event this time, but the change in scheduling could not alter the chaos.

Ivan Filin, a Russian coal-miner, entered the small stadium with a comfortable lead. Then he turned the wrong way on the track. It meant that the Finn Veikko Karvoven took the tape. The Russians complained bitterly, saying Filin had been misdirected by an official. A four-hour meeting was held by race chiefs before they agreed with Filin, but decided to let the race result stand while the Russian would get a second gold medal that did not mention his placing, just his time.

That controversy detracted somewhat from the 10,000 metres. Gordon Pirie was absent from the field and so would have to delay his stated aims of breaking world records and beating Zátopek. Pirie had developed into a running machine with Woldemar Gerschler's scientific back-up. Already television audiences had been treated to the sound of Pirie's heartbeat as cameras filmed this high-tech programme. However, he had suffered a biting pain in his left foot while running in the woods and, as was his wont, chose to counter it by running harder. At the AAA Championships he trod on the edge of the track and cracked a bone. 'The accident to my foot cost me at least two or three years' progress. I had to fight from behind. I listened to the European Games on the radio.'

Zátopek got over his defeat to Kovács with few problems in the 10,000 metres. Realising he had made a tactical error during that defeat, he went to the front quickly and shrugged off the hint of a challenge. Herbert Schade put up some token resistance, but Zátopek was 100 yards clear by halfway. Frank Sando, of Britain, was having the race of his life, albeit in an entirely different race, while Kovács settled for a fight for silver. With more of a challenge Zátopek might have been pushed closer to his own world record, but behind him a battle was being fought with few holds barred as Kovács and Sando worked together to reel in Schade. Zátopek, meanwhile, continued to lap the best runners in Europe. He had made it past the sixth-placed man, the British number one Peter Driver, by the time he crossed the line in 28 minutes 58 seconds. That was only four seconds off his world record and had been run while negotiating stragglers and without any opposition. Almost half a minute behind, Kovács just got the better of Sando, who had run a lifetime best. The message was clear. Zátopek was still the undisputed star of the 10,000 metres.

The 5000 metres would be an altogether tougher proposition because Vladimir Kuts was now nearing his prime. Western suspicion of the Soviet Union remained deep-grained, led by Pirie, who opined, 'Russians are luckless people who are unaware of the wonderful world outside their dismal homeland.' A few years later an editorial in *Athletics World* alluded to Russia's £30 million drive to 'win the Olympics', which it claimed would not only produce champions but also benefit 'the drab lives of her own people'.

Kuts fitted the stereotype. He had an intensity that others, like Zátopek, left on the track. 'Emil had kids around him like flies,' Ron Clarke would say. 'He was like a pied piper with an infectious personality.' Kuts had no time for frippery. He was a late developer and lacked natural speed. He compensated by wringing his body for every joule of energy. He ran bruising races designed to pierce everybody else's psyche, going off fast and then maintaining it, creating the impression of a warrior when inside he was in utter agony. With his coach, Gregory Nikiforov, and his masseur, who worked on him twice a day and then followed him home, he had risen to the top by taking what Zátopek was doing and making it even more savage. So where Zátopek confined his interval training to 200 and 400 metre runs, Kuts upped it and did 800, 1200, 1600 and even 2000 metres intervals. Dave Stephens, the Australian who Zátopek had coaxed to a national record, ran with Kuts and was staggered by the workload. At one session he ran 25 lots of 440-yard circuits at a pace of around 63 seconds, jogging 100 yards in 33 seconds in between. Stephens managed 12 before he gave up, coughing, spluttering and spent: 'Kuts was strong as a bull. It was the hardest and best training session I had seen in my life.'

Kuts also took two days off a week, seemingly aware of the perils of his regime. And now he was ready for the 5000 metres final. Emil had scraped through his heat after almost being overtaken on the line as he hammed it up for the crowd and jogged in gently with one of the Finns. Pierre Page, a Swiss runner, had finished strongly and came close to overhauling the duo, and thus condemn Zátopek to an early exit. In relief, when he realised what had happened, Zátopek clapped his hands to his mouth.

Zátopek looked around and said a few helloes. Old foes were there in Schade and Chataway, but it was this new figure, this blond bulldog in the crimson vest, averting his gaze, who bothered him most, even more than the known threat of Kovács, who had beaten Emil in Budapest. The gun punctured the air of anticipation and Kuts went. He hit the front and kept going – that relentless bellicosity. Great runners like Kovács and Schade felt their belief evaporate and dropped out. Perhaps they did not realise that Kuts was a bluffer. He suffered for his tactics in the second half of races, with aching limbs and dangerous heart rhythms. He kept his stoic, iron mien and pumped his arms as a street brawler, but this was a hurting game for him too. His strength was his will. It may have been forged on a savage personal anvil of Nazi beatings and being a Red Army teenager, but it had produced, as Ron Clarke would eloquently suggest, a dogmatic belief in himself. Emil could not keep up. Worse, he could not get past Chataway, who was enjoying his career peak that summer. Worse still, Kuts took the tape in a time of 13 minutes 56.6 seconds. He had shattered Emil's world record.

Dana had won another gold medal in the javelin, despite being ranked only third in the world, but her husband sensed enduring problems. It was his turn to be reclaimed.

17

Duel

On 27 September 1954, as Emil Zátopek prepared for a meeting against Sweden in Prague, an escort came for Jan Haluza. The old coach was a crumpled man marinated in abuse, his face drained of colour. Now, as the guards transported him back to the camp's central headquarters, bound by American handcuffs, he was taunted once more. He almost smiled to himself. Like the hardest of endurance runners, he was beyond hurt now. These were the last attempts of the guards to torture him. Where once they had used weapons and electric shocks, now they just mocked him. Yet this was the day. He was given 2000 Czech crowns for his four years' work in the mines and released.

He was reunited with Věra and they moved to temporary accommodation in a school in a village called Biskupice. He was a 40-year-old political prisoner. He was trained as a lawyer but ordered to work on drilling for water. A friend helped him to get a better position working with debtors and dealing with tribunals. However, it was not long before the StB came calling once more. They drove him to their office in Uherské Hradiště and asked him to enlist as an agent. Haluza knew he could not accept, but also knew how painful the consequences of refusal could be. He politely declined and sought a stay of execution. They gave him a month to mull it over. He took two, then three and prayed that they had forgotten about him.

He needed money in order to build a house and could only see one way. Věra pleaded with him not to do it, but he signed up to return to the Ostrava-Karviná mines as a civilian worker. He reasoned that the pay was good for civilians and that he could buy cheap beams from the mine bosses. They bought a plot of land and began working on their own house. 'I worked in the pit for three years,' he said. 'None of the other miners knew I was a doctor of law. Eventually, they found out and were cross with me, but I told them they wouldn't have wanted anything to do with me had they known.' All these years on and the sinister machinations of the Communist regime were still having an insidious effect on the lives of those it had chosen to banish. It was only a halfway house to freedom.

It is doubtful whether Haluza's first thought was to see what had been happening on the sporting field, although he did say of Zátopek, 'It is sad that I could see his most famous Helsinki moments only through barred windows.' He had loved sport, but he loved his wife and God more. Running had been important to him, but he was now tainted and had the StB monitoring him. However, Haluza said that Emil did meet with him after his release and that he could not have expected him to do any more. 'Forgiveness is a Christian duty,' he said. 'Why would I hate? If I was killing by hatred I would not live to my current years. I felt no joy even when the judge who sent me to jail committed suicide. And Zátopek? I think he and Mrs Dana showed enough courage that they came into contact with us after my release in a friendly way. Because I knew so much evil myself, I know what would wait for Emil if he stood behind me. There is nothing to forgive. In 1948 he would have been mercilessly destroyed.'

Zátopek was dealing with a different taunt of time. He had broken a world record at 5000 metres and won a European gold at 10,000 metres, but Kuts had stolen some thunder and Pirie was still to return. Emil was ageing towards harder times.

On 13 October White City was packed, the crowd buzzing with excitement under the floodlights ahead of the meeting between Kuts and Chataway, first and second at the European Championships. It was an enthralling duel. Some in Britain, including team manager Jack Crump, believed Kuts' win in Berne had been 'fluky' because Chataway, in his obsession with Zátopek, had totally misread where the true danger lay. So, too, Pirie had listened to Rex Alston call the Berne race on the radio in mounting disgust. 'Was Chataway ill? A hundred yards behind? That day my foot really itched to get racing again.'

Crump now took up his place on the far side of the White City track to call out times to Chataway, who did not make the same error again. He stuck to Kuts as a relentless pace was sounded out to the backbeat of a party. 'This man seems unbeatable,' the voiceover on the Pathé film would say of Kuts. But coming off the last bend Chataway, belying all the criticism of toff training and playboy whims, drew level. Then he edged in front to the wonder of all watching. Chataway now sprinted for the line. This was his moment. An intelligent man, who became a polymath in later years with business and charitable interests, Chataway won in a time of 13 minutes 51.6 seconds. Kuts was a tenth of a second and a mile behind. Chataway was utterly spent. This habit of Achilles Club runners collapsing after races led to widespread suspicion in Russia where an interpreter would tell Chataway that all British athletes took drugs. 'Oh, yes, my dear,' the urbane Briton said. 'You're always right.' The eroding of barriers was clearly still in its infancy. A Manchester businessman had caused a row when he presented Kuts with a gold and diamond Czarist ring. The incensed Russian manager had demanded all the papers print a denial that Kuts had accepted the gift, and attacked the British officials as 'sly folk' who were trying to trick him into professionalism. Now Chataway had set the world record anyway, so there was no need to devalue Kuts' methodology. Kuts shook Chataway's hand but would later say that he thought the finish line was a few feet further on and, thus, had made a fatal miscalculation.

Ten days later Kuts was in Prague to face Zátopek. It was not a contest. In front of 50,000 people, Kuts ran from the front, opened up a 50-metre lead in quick time and then proceeded to pull away. Zátopek had broken the world record earlier that year but looked an ailing force. Kuts was now relentless in the way Zátopek had once been. Zátopek cringed and may have thought that he had created a monster. Inspired by Zátopek, Kuts now destroyed him and kept going hard enough to lower Chataway's new world record by four-tenths of a second. Zátopek was almost half a minute behind, just ahead of Ullsperger. It was that rarest of home defeats for him. The world record that he had wrested from Hägg after almost 12 years had now been broken four times in five months by three different runners.

Zátopek knew he was fading. 'My Paris record did not last long,' he recalled. 'It was beaten again and again. I followed without being involved, as if the thing had nothing to do with me any more. I started getting used to watching the record men from a rearguard position.'

He travelled by tram from his flat in U Půjčovny, just off Wenceslas Square in the heart of Prague, to his army office – he had been promoted from major to lieutenant colonel – and walked to the stadium. He trained and took the tram home to his two-room flat. Stalin had died in 1953, but that had served merely to strengthen the oppressive views of the state, and a huge statue of the Russian leader was erected on a spot that had once been set aside for Sokol demonstrations. Now a variation on Sokol was introduced, the Spartakiáda, designed to use vast numbers in Sokol-like demonstrations to boost patriotism and promote the power of the collective.

By the summer of 1955 Zátopek's mantle of invincibility was clearly slipping. A bid to break the 10,000 metres world record, his favoured distance, failed in the weather. Then Ivan Ullsperger further narrowed the gap until he began to beat his mentor.

'I wanted to be like him,' he said. 'When I trained with Emil at Houstka, he gradually increased his training – 40 x 400, 60 x 400, 80 x 400, 90 x 400. He said all this proudly to us and I thought I will try to be better and run 100 x 400.' That is close to a marathon in a day at pace, but Ullsperger felt that if he did more than Emil then he would be a match for anyone. 'I did 50 x 400 in the morning without any problem, but in the last 10 x 400 I thought I should die. My body was completely exhausted. Somehow I did it and then I ran the 1200 metres home. I just collapsed on the bed and lay there motionless.' When Emil heard what had happened he followed Ullsperger and shook him. 'Awake, awake,' he cried, worried that such a regime might actually kill him. Ivan muttered, 'I'm fine,' as Emil quickly brought him some tea and lemon and demanded he drink it.

Ullsperger beat Emil in a cross-country race to the crushing disappointment of all who saw it. Emil was a hero and Ullsperger a nobody. The young flower-girl tried to give her bouquet to Emil, but he redirected her to Ivan. 'No, him,' Emil said as he pointed at his protégé. And Ullsperger sent her back because he knew she wanted to give the flowers to the famous runner. 'I was disappointed because I never wanted Emil for a rival. I went home and my sister said I had upset her because she had wanted Emil to win too.'

That June Ullsperger beat Zátopek in Brno over 5000 metres. His time was good, 14 minutes 10 seconds, and Emil could no longer live with it. It was his first defeat by a compatriot over the distance since 1944.

'The next race was Rošický Memorial, and I wanted to run 5000 metres,' said Ullsperger. 'I knew I would probably not win, but I wanted to try it. Emil, as my coach, agreed, the doctor too, but the Communists did not like it. They wanted me to run 5000 metres, because it was the tenth anniversary of the liberation after World War Two and they wanted to showcase their best runners. Emil did not like it. He said, "He is young and strong, so he can run what he wants." The organisers were against it, and after half an hour Emil came to me and said, "We have received an official complaint. They've said that we have sabotaged the memorial, and they have handed it directly to the Ministry of the Interior." So I said, "I don't have to run at all," but Emil said, "Ivanek, unfortunately it's impossible. Brno saw the defeat of Zátopek and Prague calls for retaliation." So I had to run for political reasons and I beat Emil again. I don't know who had wished it, but our fights were desirable at that time.'

Zátopek was still good enough to get his last two of his 18 world records that year, at the novelty distances of 15 miles and 30,000 metres, and he was still the same, quirky individual. Every day Václav Chudomel, a marathon runner, went jogging in the Vinohrady Sokol gymnasium, doing 40 laps a day. Milan Svajgr recalled, 'One day Emil went there and just started running with him, still dressed in his civilian clothes. He did 15 laps and was talking to Václav as he went. He did not sweat at all, but just felt the need to run, even dressed for work.' Yet there was a gnawing sense among his followers that he was beginning the slow descent.

Jan Mrázek says it was the effect of all that relentless training: 'He took very high doses under adverse conditions. He wore those army boots – *komisňáky* – and laughed, claiming he ran more kilometres per month than most cyclists. But over the years he lost his speed, and that was confirmed by Kuts.'

Zátopek was still adored from the parliament to playground. He was made a Meritorious Master of Sport, and Karel Engel, then a 15-year-old schoolboy, was awestruck: 'Zátopek! It was something. When he had an important competition it was like a national holiday. After all those years of war, suddenly here was this man who was known to the whole world. It was fantastic. We listened in groups to the radio and we pretended to be Zátopek in the playground.'

Yet the pace of change in athletics was becoming thunderous. On 10 October in Budapest, Sándor Iharos, a weak-looking nine-stone Hungarian, broke Kuts' 5000 metres world record in only his third race at the distance. Iharos was the leader of a trio of Hungarians, the other others being László Tábori and István Rózsavölgyi, adding a new dimension to the global challenge. Eight days later Kuts took the record back in Belgrade. Five weeks after that Iharos stunned Kuts and Zátopek when he took another six seconds off the record and lowered it to 13 minutes 40.6 seconds. It was the sixth time the record had fallen since Zátopek had broken it the previous year. The wind of change was a full-blown gale.

Gordon Pirie was also edging towards Zátopek. Like Kuts, he had been motivated to run by Zátopek, and now his motivation was to hammer a nail in the coffin. Pirie had become friendly with Zátopek through their letters. There was a mutual admiration. Pirie had broken the world record for six miles, but the 10,000 metres was the Olympic distance that resonated around the world. He craved a victory over Zátopek and had a chance when he travelled to Prague for a Great Britain versus Czechoslovakia meeting. First came the 5000 metres. Pirie won by a yard, but he knew that Emil was saving himself for the 10,000 metres the very next day. It was a win over his long-distance motivator but a Pyrrhic victory. It was the longer race that mattered in Prague. Zátopek was in ebullient mood on the start line the following day, but Pirie had long dismissed this as kidology. He focused and concentrated on his pace. It was good enough to leave Zátopek somewhere in his wake, but by half-distance he was back: 'He had so much energy that as he came up to overtake us he ran alongside and urged me to go faster. I hadn't the breath to answer him.' Beating Zátopek in the 5000 metres was no consolation for Pirie, but it was hard to be annoyed with him for long. The following day Pirie trained with Zátopek at the stadium. Afterwards Emil brewed some Brazilian tea in a jam jar on a small heater and regaled Pirie with stories. He showed him his soldier's automatic pistol and told of how he had once stripped nude and gone swimming in the river in a section where it was forbidden. A soldier started shooting at him and so he swam for his life and ran for the bushes stark naked. The soldier arrived to find him straightening his tunic and cap, but Emil was still called before a disciplinary committee. 'They said, "You mustn't be a naughty boy,"' Emil had grinned. Zátopek travelled to the British team hotel the next day to say goodbye and said he would meet them the following month for the London versus Prague match at White City. Pirie knew that was his opportunity. He had to seize it.

But his prospects were not helped when he put his hand through a glass shower panel two days before their duel. It was only a flesh wound, Pirie reasoned. It would take more than that . . .

It was an epic race given an air of drama by the thick mist. Zátopek shot into the lead but Pirie and Ken Norris stuck to him. The British duo passed Emil, who then overhauled them. It was a game of cat and mouse. With four laps left, Norris took the lead and tried to break the two antagonists. By the bell Zátopek had a gossamer advantage. Jimmy Green made some notes but did not want to take his eyes off the action. From his scrawled memories he would later write, 'The crowd was tense with excitement. It was, "Zát-o-pek! Zát-o-pek! Zát-o-pek!" [then] "Pirie! Pirie! Pirie!" [then] "Come on, Ken!" . . . anyone's race.'

Pirie possibly wanted it most. He did not have the Olympic titles, the world records in the events that mattered, the global love and fame. Like Emil, he had been criticised over his masochistic training methods, with each injury being added to the case for the prosecution – but this was his opportunity; this was Emil Zátopek, morphed from the picture over the billet bed to the track. Pirie went with 300 to go. In *Running Wild*, he gave a vivid description of these moments: 'My lungs are protesting, my muscles numbing, the roar of the crowd is a mere murmur to me. I only hear the roaring exhaustion in my head. Fists working like a boxer's and legs pounding, I race for the line, afraid to look, for they are behind. My imagination dare not guess where they are and I accelerate against my body's pain. The tape snaps on my chest and I run easily to lose momentum. Senses flood back, washing out the terrible pains and exhaustion. I have won.'

Zátopek took the defeat well. He hugged his rivals and smiled more than many would have done in the circumstances. Pirie's boss at L. G. Wilkinson, a paint firm where he had taken a job in sales to fund his running, had left a note on his car windscreen. 'If you can't do better than that then you'll be fired.' Pirie had smiled as he turned the ignition.

Yet his troubled relationship with other writers continued. After his victory over Zátopek, the journalist John Fairgrieve wrote a glowing testimony in support of Pirie: 'Did you make a mental apology to Gordon Pirie yesterday? You were probably just one of thousands if you did, just one of those who called him a big-head, a windbag, a good distance runner but never a great one. Just one of those who said he would be left floundering by Zátopek, the Iron Man. Some people said he never had time for sportsmanship either. If they meant he didn't like losing they were right. He aimed to be the best long-distance runner on earth and that sort of objective has no room for defeat. Now he is the best.'

Fairgrieve's piece on 'the ultimate triumph' was lost in the trail of sulphur that followed Gordon Pirie. Emil was a ringmaster whose natural bonhomie and intuitiveness enabled him to capture every crowd. Pirie was more difficult. The following year he raced Iharos, but a runner trod on his shoe at the start and it came off. Pirie threw it away and sprinted to catch the Hungarian, blood dripping from his foot. He dropped out to a chorus of boos and damning reports.

By then his reputation was a funeral pyre of burnt bridges. The nadir came at a plush awards dinner at the Savoy Hotel in central London that December. Pirie picked up two awards, including what is now the BBC Sports Personality of the Year. Pirie stepped up to the microphone in front of the great and good of British sport and broadcasting. It was an occasion for platitudes and mutual back-slapping, but a lot went through Pirie's mind as he took those last steps. He knew he had not been invited to the sportswriters' dinner, where they wined and dined their six nominees, but the public had voted for him after he had beaten Emil. The flashbulbs popped and the television cameras were fixed on him. He flicked with his tie. And then he stared into the crowd again, at the part-time playboys, the 'shamateurs' and the overweight critics. Momentarily, he wondered whether he should let bygones be bygones, but, Christ, he had just beaten Emil Zátopek. Bugger that. And so he began: 'Public opinion has vetoed sportswriters' opinions. Fleet Street sportswriters do incredible damage to British sport. In an Olympic year they should boost not denigrate British sport. A few unkind words will inflict more damage than they realise. I hope they will be kinder in the future.'

You could have heard a pin drop. As Pirie recalled it, '. . . a sensation, a murmur of surprise and consternation'. The journalists who had been attacked did not take it well. Peter Wilson was the doyen of sportswriters. With a moustache like a tumble-dried ferret, he wore a cape and wielded a silver-topped cane. Known as 'the man they couldn't gag', he was described by the writer Norman Giller as being able to 'sink a bottle of whisky without spilling a syllable'. Now he wished they had gagged Pirie. In the following morning's *Daily Mirror*, beneath a headline THE POISON IN THE HEART OF GORDON PIRIE, he wrote, 'Pirie made what I consider to be one of the most unpleasant, ungracious and utterly outrageous speeches it has ever been my misfortune to listen to.' After a sub-heading 'What Rubbish!', he wrote of 'overweening conceit' and said he was 'sick and tired of [Pirie] trying to cover up his arrogance when he wins and his excuses when he loses'. Wilson had actually been one of Pirie's more favourable scribes, and had even landed him his job with L. G. Wilkinson.

A few days later Pirie was given the chance to make amends. The *Daily Express*, then a huge-selling newspaper, gave him the forum for justification via a first-person column. His attempts at mediation were limited. He said he had not meant to attack all journalists, but any conciliation was drowned out by the first line, 'I am unrepentant.' He added that unkind and cruel words could kill. Perhaps he was thinking of the way some had almost lampooned Jim Peters' shocking fate in the Empire Games marathon, describing him as 'running like a rather bad comic on the stage burlesquing a drunk. Two steps forward, then three to the side. So help me, he's running backwards now. The roar of the crowd dies to a hushed whisper and then to a silence in which you can hear a pin drop only it is not a pin that is dropping; it is Jim Peters.'

Even in the 1950s the famous were fair game. Pirie had become the biggest star in Britain and the writers felt they had played a part. 'The press claims to have made me famous,' Pirie countered, 'but I did not seek fame. I run for the sheer love of it. Any fame I have was pressed upon me and due largely to my own efforts. The press did not do my running for me.'

Pirie kept running. He had two major goals: he wanted world records over 5000 and 10,000 metres, and he wanted an Olympic gold medal. Perhaps he also wanted revenge and, if so, he got it the following summer in 1956 in a sooty, industrial town in Norway. Pirie had told journalists that he was going on a fishing trip. Instead, he headed to old friends in Norway and plotted a duel with Vladimir Kuts in Bergen.

It was a nothing meeting. There were few stars and, in truth, it was a warm-up for Russia ahead of the Olympic Games in Melbourne. Pirie and Kuts were poles apart and yet cut from the same cloth: obdurately good and ferociously competitive. For the next 14 minutes all that mattered was being more obdurate and ferocious than the other man. They did the first lap in 60 seconds and exchanged the lead. Kuts trod his usual attritional path. Pirie kept pace. The times were shouted out in Norwegian, so Pirie had no idea of splits, but he was in the flow. He felt he could go slightly faster but bided his time. He bartered with his bravery and then hit the front with around 250 yards left. He did not look but sensed Kuts had nothing to come back with. All that could beat Pirie now was losing his momentum – but it was beautiful for him that night, despite the ugly gas cylinder by the track and the modest environs. He hit the tape in 13 minutes 36.8 seconds. When they checked the three watches and announced the time Pirie mused that he could have been four seconds better. Still, it was the world record. And not a single British writer had been there to see it. He had gone fishing and they had taken the bait.

Perhaps they were still upset when he got married to Shirley Hampton, a British sprinter, and emigrated. At the time the William Hickey newspaper column in the *Daily Express* was an avidly consumed source of celebrity gossip. In truth there was no 'William Hickey'. The column was established by Tom Driberg, who would later be accused of being a double-agent working for the KGB, but now William Hickey turned 'his' attention to Pirie's marriage: 'Well, Gordon Pirie, the wonder boy of British athletics, left us for good last night. He drove into London Airport in that Hillman Minx – once used by the Duke of Edinburgh – loaned to him for his Isle of Wight honeymoon.' The column allowed Pirie to explain why he was leaving. 'Shirley and I think we have a better chance of setting up a home in New Zealand,' Pirie said. 'There are a lot of reasons but basically it is one of economy. We feel Britain is overburdened by taxation.' He was quoted as saying his aim was an Olympic gold and that he might return to Britain one day to run for New Zealand. The tone was designed to inflame Middle England.

'A flurried receptionist took him to the wrong plane – one bound for New York,' continued the columnist. 'Pirie muttered, "An American conspiracy to keep me out of the Games." A few minutes later he had gone. That was Pirie, that was.'

18

Love Over Gold

Olga Fikotová has a different name now. She is in her eighties but still works in the health and fitness industry in California. She has a good story to tell, but is initially hesitant about doing so. The years have passed. Things have changed. But it is still an enduring story of love and gold, even now, over half a century on from the day that she climbed the long, sloping hill up to the Strahov Stadium in Prague.

'I navigate life as it rolls along, paying little attention to statistics,' she says in reference to her age in a long and thoughtful email. 'Emotional highs and lows don't leave one's mind, nevertheless. They are lessons from which to learn. Meeting Dana and Emil for the first time was certainly such a high-impact experience. In fact, the beginning of my life-changing [experience]':

> My youth dream was to become a doctor and work for Albert
> Schweitzer [German, missionary physician who founded
> a hospital in Gabon] in Lambaréné. But when a medical
> student, I found myself spending more time wearing sports
> jerseys than hospital gowns. So I gave up time-demanding
> team sports, but my body felt miserable. Consequently,
> I decided to work out again, but on some individual effort
> where I could have my own schedule.

I was not built as a runner or jumper, or strong enough for shot-putting. I had a friend who was a discus thrower, but javelin throwing seemed to me more elegant. Especially, when watching Dana Zátopková. 'Maybe I should talk to her,' I thought, as I knew where she and Emil were training. At that time, though, Dana and Emil were demigods. And deservedly so. Seeing Emil Zátopek, people would whisper, 'Look, that's Zátopek!' Nobody would think of shouting, 'Hey, Emil!'

Having the athletic credentials of representing Czechoslovakia in team handball and basketball, one afternoon in 1954 I climbed up the hill to the Strahov Stadium where the Zátopeks usually worked out. I did not know if they would be there, but good fortune was with me. They were both just finishing their sessions. A special feature of Dana was her graciousness. She swiftly stabled her javelin in the grass and smiled with her inborn elegance as she walked toward me. After I told her about my dilemma about what sport to do she reached for my shoulder, ran her fingers along its structure and, since Emil had also joined us, she said to us both, 'Olina's shoulder is built for the discus; her shoulder does not have the open structure needed for the javelin.' We talked for few more minutes and Emil said, 'Do the discus throw, but give it full attention . . . and the three of us will travel to Melbourne.'

'Melbourne? What's in Melbourne?' I said.

'The Olympics,' answered Emil, and, assuring me that I had the right proportions for a discus thrower, he said, 'Start working out right now and you will make the team. We all will.' I looked at him speechlessly. And I was even more stunned by Dana's pulling a beautiful green velour sweatshirt off her torso and saying, 'I wore this one when I won in Helsinki. So you put it on now and keep wearing it.'

That one meeting set the tone of my next two years of existence: training and study, study and training. I hardly saw them [again] until our departure to Australia. But while I was doing my own small thing, Dana and Emil were spending lives dedicated to representing Czechoslovakia all over the world. And the world loved them. They were not representing the political aims of the government. They were representing the very best qualities of Czechoslovak culture and people. But Emil paid for that representation with his health. The wear and tear of training and competitions in long-distance events caused him awful damage, with two hernias.

It was not only the mileage. It was true that Emil sometimes carried Dana on his back when he trained and there was the time he had thrown her in a river and she had broken her shin. The hernias were debilitating injuries for a man who still harboured ambitions of adding to his four Olympic gold medals. As the weeks ticked by it seemed that Emil might not even make the team. He had carried his wife and his nation, and now he was suffering for his methods.

Olga had lived a complicated life up until then. She was only a teenager when people came to the door seeking Frank Fikota. He assured his little Olushko that everything would be fine and that the men were merely doing their jobs. But their apartment was declared 'military property' and his wife and daughter were evicted. Frank Fikota, who had served his country in the First World War and been part of the president's personal guard, was charged with idle vagrancy. On the way out of prison his daughter asked him how he felt and, with tears in his eyes, he said savagely, 'How do I feel? After 25 years of devoted duty I feel like a shit in the grass.'

The secret police came calling again a year before the Olympics. A tall man in a brown leather coat kept appearing as an incongruous comma to Olga's daily life. Finally, he approached and said he needed to talk to her. He took her to see a Comrade Douda, who told her the security of Czechoslovakia was threatened by a vicious network of reactionary spy rings, and that if she had any suspicions about any Olympic team member she should report them at once. She declined becoming an agent but, sensing her Olympic dream hung in the balance, said that of course she would tell the authorities if she heard of anything that threatened their country. Later she realised that the formulaic nature of the recruitment suggested all the Olympians had been through the same process; that there would be internal spying in Australia and that all citizens were regarded as potential traitors. And she thought about her father feeling like a shit in the grass.

In Melbourne she shared a room with Dana, two generations of great Czech field eventers. Dana was the European champion and had come close to the world record in 1955, but this had not been her best year. Olga was young and up against Nina Ponomaryova. The Russian discus thrower was the Olympic champion and had just been in the midst of a global diplomatic incident before the first official visit of a Russian team to London. The C&A store in Oxford Street accused her of stealing some hats worth £1.65. Ponomaryova was aghast, at least publicly, and after a warrant was issued for her arrest, spent weeks in the Russian embassy while special branch staked out the docks and the British ambassador was summoned to the Kremlin. The scale of the fallout shows just how precarious relations were. The cancellation of the athletics meeting was a financial and diplomatic disaster. Galina Ulánova, the prima ballerina of the Bolshoi Ballet, then threatened to pull out of her visit to London as people worked overtime to quell the fires. The papers dubbed the story 'Nina and the Five Hats' and it finished with her paying a three-guinea fine before getting on the steamship *Molotov* and heading home.

The long lay-off while holed up in the embassy had affected the fitness of Nina Five Hats, but Olga threw like never before. She twice broke the Czech record and even set a new Olympic one. Now she just needed to wait for the great Russian's last attempt. Olga buried her face in the grass and could not watch. The cheering did not explain the outcome either. She opened her eyes and the chief judge smiled. 'You won,' he said. It was an unbelievable rush. One of her team-mates handed her a thermos of tea. Crowds flocked around her.

Olga may not have realised it but in 1956 she was a stunningly attractive woman with searching dark eyes and a smile hitched to high cheekbones. One man who had noticed was Harold Connolly, the American hammer thrower. The pair had met in the village before the Games started and felt an instant attraction. Olga felt herself falling for him but knew it was hopeless. East–west relations were not allowed, not with spies in the camp and the team attaché warning them on their arrival that the 'imperialistic world judges you without mercy'.

She signed another autograph and noticed the men gathering for the start of the 10,000 metres. Emil should have been in it. The gun sounded and the race started. Olga thought about how Emil had been fêted on their arrival. Everyone wanted a story or a picture or an anecdote – press, public and peers. Emil smiled and, catching her glance, occasionally raised an eyebrow. He was charming company, fiercely intelligent with his penchant for languages, good fun with the two bottles of Pilsner Urquell that he unwrapped before dinner; it was a badly kept secret that Emil drank a glass of beer every day, even in an Olympic village. Olga thought about Emil and Dana and their fame and relative wealth, the car and nice apartment, and the plush villa they were building, and reasoned 'these two gold medallists would never cease being important representatives of Czechoslovakia'. On that point she would be wrong.

Ron Clarke was also watching that 10,000 metres. The 19-year-old was the junior mile world record holder and had lit the flame at the opening ceremony. He had been told not to tell even his parents until 1.30 p.m. on the day and, when he did, he threw down a couple of tickets on the kitchen table to their bemusement. 'They'd been planning on going to my aunt's.' When he entered the Melbourne Cricket Ground, burning magnesium was falling from the torch on to his arm as 102,000 people cheered. He could scarcely stop and wipe it off, so he carried on, trying not to grimace. He reached the stairs leading to the copper bowl with seven minutes left before the flame extinguished. Alex Jamieson, the man in charge of the relay, had a spare, just in case. Their eyes met and Clarke could see that Alex was a mess of nerves. Clarke had never felt that he was destined for the Olympics and would say even these Games did not have a deep-lasting emotional impact. Yet, briefly, as he climbed those stairs, he felt an 'eerie sensation of omnipotence' and 'an almost mystical identity with the old Greek gods'. By the time of the 10,000 metres those feelings had gone. Clarke's role did not give him entry rights to the events and he joined five friends, who had hatched a scheme of passing one ticket back and forth through a fence and then posing in the press seats. He watched Vladimir Kuts and Gordon Pirie duelling, and noted how the Russian's constant surges made it hard for Pirie to establish a rhythm.

Out on the track Pirie was feeling it too. Kuts ran lacerating strips and then would slow up. It was uncomfortable and, on a couple of occasions, he did it so abruptly that Pirie nearly stumbled. Yet with four laps left Pirie still felt he could win: 'I had passed the danger point and thought that it was only a matter of covering this last short distance before the gold medal was mine.' Clarke might not have felt like he needed gold, but Pirie did. These laps were the culmination of a life's mission.

Olga watched and realised there were little miracles taking place all over the Olympics. Zátopek was unable to defend his titles as he nursed injuries from his hernia-inducing schedule. He hoped that the extra days' rest would aid his prospects in the marathon, but now, out there on the track, Pirie was 'forging Vladimir Kuts into another of the immortal Olympic distance runners'.

Kuts beckoned to Pirie to take the lead. Pirie did not want to. It was another of those looks – as had been exchanged between Bannister and Landy, and Peters and Holden – that changed everything. Kuts was almost gone, but he did a forensic search of Puff-Puff Pirie. It was a career reduced to a nanosecond's poker game. Kuts could bluff better. He later admitted he was on the verge of quitting. It was that fast and totally destructive. And now these two men were forerunners of the great Ali–Joe Frazier fight when both men were close to death and it was a question of who blinked and sagged first.

And, Jesus, this sandy track was bad. By the time Pirie had taken his eyes from Kuts he was sinking into it. His belief drained and, from feeling he was going to win, he knew he couldn't. Kuts had killed him. He went past him and dismay and panic segued into slower steps. Kuts romped to his triumph and Pirie laboured home in eighth place. Clarke wondered whether Pirie had lost little morsels of power by diverting energy to monitoring Kuts. The press just sharpened their knives.

Emil gave Olga his last bottle of beer that night. His withdrawals from the 10,000 and 5000 metres were huge blows to the athletics programme, but he would still run the marathon. He would have his swansong.

The next day Harold Connolly won the gold in the hammer throwing, setting an Olympic record to beat archrival Mikhail Krivonosov. It was no mean feat given Harold had a withered left arm due to an accident at birth. When the pressmen asked him to raise his arms in triumph he raised only his right one as his left was actually four inches shorter. It was a rare achievement and odd for Olga to think that she and her new boyfriend were a golden couple, just as Emil and Dana had been in 1952.

On the Wednesday afternoon, Dana was only fourth in the javelin final. When Olga tried to sympathise, Dana was phlegmatic. 'Olina, don't let it bother you,' she said. 'I'll get up there again.'

Later that day came Pirie versus Kuts take two, in the 5000 metres. Derek Ibbotson felt the best tactic was for him, Pirie and Chris Chataway to form a three-man tag-team and box in Kuts. Pirie felt that was an extraordinary suggestion given Kuts' form and pace. He had his own plan this time and would ignore Kuts' attempt to run with surges while he just ran even pace. The teenage Ron Clarke already knew that was a tough thing to do. It involved incredible strength of will to ignore the senses of sight and sound, to run in a vacuum. 'It's extremely difficult to run at even pace if someone else is surging,' he said. It was a tactic that worked well enough for Pirie until he was overtaken by Ibbotson and Chataway too, and suddenly became embroiled in a different sort of fight. By the time he got past them, Kuts had opened up a fatal ten-metre lead. Pirie's heart sank when he saw that. This was the premature end of his Olympiad. He kept going and passed Ibbotson with 40 metres left. He crossed the line in second place. Ibbotson blamed Chataway afterwards, suggesting both he and Pirie could have caught Kuts had their putative team-mate not got in the way. Pirie was an Olympic silver medallist, which is a momentous achievement for the rank and file but a crushing disappointment for a man who would be king.

The victory ceremony was 15 minutes later and Pirie noticed that Kuts was in a stupor. Pirie even had to turn the Russian around so that he was facing the flag. It might have been dismissed as the disorientating effect of achieving goals, of that fleeting affinity with Greek gods that Clarke had felt as he ignored burning magnesium on his lap of adoration, but Pirie had other ideas. He caused another sensation when he later said he believed it was standard practice for Iron Curtain countries to use performance-enhancing drugs. He claimed a doctor had once called him a mug for being one of a minority that was not cheating. He said cyclists were 'souped-up' to dangerous degrees, and blamed the poor health of many Russians on their nefarious methodology. Allan Lawrence, from Punchbowl in Australia, had come third in the 10,000 metres and thought Pirie grew obsessive about his drug theory. They spent some time together the following year and Lawrence said Pirie always steered the conversation to his defeat by Kuts. 'To his dying day Gordon believed that Kuts was on drugs,' he said. Pirie would talk of the colour of Kuts' face on the victory dais. In his autobiography, Lawrence wrote, 'Gordon Pirie's view of the world was simple: no runner in the world was capable of running him into the ground as Kuts did in the 10,000 metres in Melbourne. The fact that Kuts had done exactly that was the only evidence Gordon needed to conclude Kuts was obviously drugged.'

***

It sounded like the knee-jerk conclusion of an unbridled ego, of the abnormal confidence so reviled by Jack Crump and others, of the bad sportsmanship so gleefully documented in the press. What none of them knew at the time was that Kuts had not wanted to run the 5000 metres. His pulse had been dangerously high and he had found blood in his urine. He was not a well man. He only ran because the Russians promised him a general's pension if he did, but time would prove Gordon Pirie right on many of his suspicions.

Kuts did get the 5000 metres world record back from Pirie the following year, in 1957, and, after the domino effect of incredible feats, this time it stood for eight years until a grown-up Ron Clarke claimed it one day in Hobart.

Kuts had always had it hard. At the Olympic winner's press conference a woman approached the front table and emptied a bag of painted rodents in front of him. 'Red rats!' she shouted. On a trip to Moscow for the Third International Youth Games in 1957, Zátopek took Lawrence for dinner at the Kuts' house. Lawrence remembered the night best for Kuts' wife, 'a somewhat overweight journalist', regaling him over the Australian press calling her 'fat' in Melbourne, and then Kuts storming out to the balcony in jealousy at his wife dancing with Emil. The arch diplomat, Emil brought them back into the same room, but later confided in Lawrence that there was tension in the marriage because Kuts wanted a child and his wife did not. Raissa Kuts had met her husband on her first assignment after graduating from the Faculty of Journalism at Moscow University. Her notebook had remained blank during several days of interviews. Now she would have plenty to write about.

Kuts' work was done in Melbourne by the time the Olympic athletics programme neared its end. It might have been different had Emil been in the races or, indeed, Sándor Iharos. That summer Iharos had ended Emil's seven-year hold on the 10,000 metres world record. Iharos, though, was not in Melbourne. The Hungarian revolution was taking place and the Soviet Union had invaded the country again. Thousands died as Hungary made a brave and bloody stand against Communism. Iharos was officially absent with a dislocated ankle, but he knew more important things were taking place at home. The brutality of the Soviet response and the way Iharos' sporting life would be consumed by his wider one were prescient markers on the way to Zátopek's own fight for freedom.

In Melbourne, all that was left was for the marathon to tie up the strands. Jim Peters was now long retired, but the Russians presented a powerful threat, as Emil well knew from having led a few training sessions with them. He found his old friend Alain Mimoun, now 36 and on the way back from a serious sciatica problem, and warned him that they had been running 2 hours 13 minutes pace in practice. Mimoun told his old sparring partner that he, Zátopek, was still the favourite, but Emil shook his head. 'No, Alain,' he said. 'This time it's you.'

Emil had been feeling pain in his groin since the spring and had undergone surgery when he should have been training. While in hospital he had monitored the rise of Kuts and Pirie. He was facing a race against time, and even took to jogging on the plane on the way to Australia. Initially, he had been surprised by the cold of Melbourne, which left the athletes with nowhere to dry their sweat-stained tracksuits – but soon a tropical wind blew the chill away and, by the day of the marathon, a heatwave had descended over the Melbourne Cricket Ground.

People still expected Emil to win. In the grandstands Olga watched with Harold. She pointed out Zátopek in his red shirt and white cap. A Frenchman overheard their conversation and said Mimoun would win because the French had won the marathon in 1900 and 1928 and so the passage of another 28 years made it a natural cycle. Olga wanted Emil to win, of course, but she turned to Harold at one point, as times and placings were read out over the loudspeaker, and said, 'It sounds awful but I almost wish Mimoun would win. At least once.'

Mimoun had suffered for his place in Melbourne. Three times he had finished runner-up to Zátopek in Olympic finals, and now he was running his first marathon. He was too old and had also seemed too fat after putting on 20lbs due to his sciatica problem. In *The Destiny of Ali Mimoun* Pat Butcher recounted his troubles: how a fan took him to dinner twice a week because he knew Mimoun could not afford it; how he went to Lisieux because he had heard how the young Edith Piaf had been taken there by the prostitutes at her grandmother's brothel and had miraculously recovered her sight; how he went to the Basilica of St Thérèse even though he was an atheist; how he knelt down, prayed, cried and was cured.

There was more prescience around Mimoun's last Olympic appearance. He told Butcher of his dream before his comeback race: 'I was in a farmhouse, in a room with a bare earth floor. It was empty except for a coffin, a glass coffin in the middle of the room. And what do I see? My grandmother's corpse and suddenly the corpse opens its eyes and says, "Don't worry, son, everything's going to be all right."'

He won that race and lost 20lbs. He also got married to a shy woman named Germaine, whom he had met at the European

Championships in Berne. Embarrassed by his impoverishment, Mimoun gave his address as the National Sports Institute, but it was only when Germaine read about his comeback and 'The Resurrection of Alain Mimoun' that she got in touch. They married, conceived and, on the eve of the marathon, a telegram arrived: wife and new child were 'doing well'. Mimoun was overjoyed and frustrated. He was a father.

The temperature rose to 80°C. Athletes covered their shoulders in Vaseline and scarves. Bizarrely, for the marathon, there was a false start. When it began in earnest runners criss-crossed the new dotted green line painted on the racing route in search of shade. Emil was not bothered by the early pace of the African runners and settled into a bunch including Mimoun, Franjo Mihalić, his friend from Yugoslavia, and an American named John 'the younger' Kelley. Nobody spoke to each other, which Emil knew was a sign that everyone was afraid and did not know what to do. The only sound breaking the quiet patter of herded feet was the relentless swearing of the Finnish runner Eino Oksanen. After 15 kilometres, Emil began to hit trouble as the soles of his shoes began to stick to the burning tarmac: 'I kept sliding back and forth on the lumps that formed underneath.' He said that was the end of his fluid style and every stiff landing and insecure push-off hurt his groin. By halfway, Emil knew that it was over.

Mimoun turned to his old friend and knew that he was gone – but Mimoun was struggling too. Almost every marathon involves a crisis and he hit his close to the turn for home. Then Kelley, who had trained with Mimoun, slapped him on the shoulder and shouted, 'Come on.' Mimoun followed him, but almost immediately, Kelley slowed. Mimoun realised he had not been challenging him but provoking him to a revival. 'He did it to jump-start me,' he would recall. 'How great is that?' Now, rejuvenated by brief competition, he set about the end, knowing the Russian, Ivan Filin, was coming just as Emil had warned.

Mimoun was so befuddled that he took the bridge that was 12 kilometres from the end to be the one that was barely a kilometre from the finish. The horrible realisation that he still had miles to go nearly destroyed him. 'It's at points like that, if you'll excuse the expression, that you need balls,' he told Butcher. 'I started to insult myself: "Arsehole, you haven't come this far just to fuck it up."' He thought about Germaine and his new daughter. He tossed the white handkerchief from his head to the crowd because it felt a burden. He noted a pretty blonde girl pick it up. 'My throat felt like a needle eye,' but something told him to ignore the drink stations. He prayed for his mother, his mother-in-law, his wife and his new child.

And then he was through the crisis and through the Marathon Gate. Olga leapt to her feet with the 102,000. 'The veteran Frenchman no longer toiled to run.' For Mimoun it was as if 'an atom bomb had gone off' as he did his final circuit. He crossed the line in a time of 2 hours 25 minutes. He walked off the track and on to the infield and immediately looked to the Marathon Gate. 'I wanted to see where my buddy, Zátopek, was,' he said. The next man was Mihalić, a minute and a half behind. Then came Veikko Karvonen. Olga noted that Mimoun ignored these runners and kept looking towards the entrance to the stadium. He counted them in. 'Jesus,' he thought, when the fourth and fifth men had arrived in the coliseum. And then, finally, the bobbing figure of a balding veteran arrived. 'The spectators applauded my sixth place but I didn't deserve it,' Zátopek said. He was lost in his own inner delirium at that point and doubled over. Then he noticed the familiar, friendly visage above him. 'Emil, I did it. I'm the Olympic champion.' That roused him. Zátopek smiled. He stood up and hugged Mimoun. They held each other. 'You did it, Alain. I'm so happy for you.' Then he kissed Mimoun on the cheek. 'He had a face like a saint,' Mimoun would say. 'I was his shadow, but now I was the sun.'

Zátopek wanted to congratulate him for ending their rivalry in such a way, but his old foe stopped him.

'Emil,' he cried with wide eyes. 'I've got a daughter.'

Zátopek was delighted. He felt Mimoun had never had much joy from their communal encounters, but now he had a double dose. It made the pain worthwhile.

At home in Czechoslovakia, Ivan Ullsperger was glad too. He had been heading to the Olympics until he fell ill and was taken to the military hospital in Prague, where they found he had been struggling with meningitis: 'I had to wait a long time before I could get back to high-class athletics. I became weak. I could not stay in the sun.' Now he heard of Mimoun's success and was happy: 'I'm not normally a believer but suddenly I felt, "God is fair," because he had been unlucky for such a long time and was always second to Emil. And then I thought that if I'd been there and run the marathon then maybe I would have beaten him. And then it would have been unfortunate for him because if he was not defeated by Emil he would have been defeated by Emil's disciple.'

Mimoun said the kiss and congratulations were worth all the money in the world. He had realised his life's ambition, and the French flag stayed raised for 48 hours because the marathon was the last event. He christened his daughter Marie (but called her Olympe). And the man who had been ignored and marginalised by his adopted country went home to be fêted by General de Gaulle, who told him they shared a similarity. 'We endure,' the general said.

When she got back to the village after the marathon, Olga found a note from Dana: 'Olina, immediately report to the headquarters. They're up in arms that you're always gone.'

Her relationship with Harold was causing suspicion in the camp. Both Emil and Dana warned her of the consequences. 'Connolly seemed a good guy but you shouldn't be taking your little romance too seriously,' Emil told her. 'It can't lead anywhere.'

Despite those words, Emil would come to play a major role in the romance, but first they had to get home. The Czechs boarded the Russian ship *Gruzia* and made the long journey to Vladivostok. The Russians had said the gold medallists would fly home, but Kuts was stuffed on to the boat and took solace by getting blind drunk for three days. The Czechs heard that Kuts faced a disciplinary hearing for his crime, to which he turned up drunk and swaying before offering to resolve it with a fistfight. He was reportedly dismissed after a fit of incurable hiccups. The one plus point from the incident was that it softened relations between the Czech and Russian contingents on the long voyage.

When they finally made it home to Prague, Olga visited the Zátopeks where Dana was upset that her young friend had received only 3000 Koruna as a reward for her gold medal. 'They're cutting you down over this Connolly business,' Dana said. Olga told Dana she had received a letter from Harold. 'Olina! Remember what you have at stake.'

In February 1957 Harold travelled to Prague on a visa he had obtained on account of a series of athletics camps he was putting on. The authorities had made it clear that they disapproved of this relationship between a Czech gold medallist and a cursed capitalist.

Dana then made a kind and courageous gesture. Olga retold the tale in her book *The Rings of Destiny*. Dana said the authorities might try to keep her and Connolly separate and that it would be impossible for her to visit him at his hotel.

'Bring him here,' Dana said.

'No, Dana, you're taking too great a chance.'

'Unless you two have an opportunity to talk undisturbed you're prone to do something emotional. Bring him here.'

The couple decided to get married anyway. When they told Emil and Dana, the elder gold medallists expressed their concern. Emil said Olga had to finish her schooling otherwise she'd be doomed by the regime. Dana, a practical woman, said she did not see how they would pull off an east–west marriage in the current climate. Olga noted that Emil was smiling, though. 'I'll think of ways to put in a word for you,' he said. She thought the situation suited 'Emil's love of controversy'.

It was not easy. At what was known as the 'Marriages to Foreigners Department' of the Ministry of the Interior, the referent said they must be joking. 'We're not about to let our Olympic champion run away.'

The paranoia about westerners surfaced when Olga and Harold visited her parents at their chemical plant in order to get a signed financial statement. Her desperate mother told her that it had been a terrible mistake to come here. The phone rang and they realised the armed guards had not initially understood Connolly was an American. Her mother tried to explain that no, he did not have a hidden camera with him. Then she told them to run.

At the Smetana concert hall, Emil Zátopek sat close to the president. So far President Zápotocký had ignored the furore and the letter that Olga had sent to him begging for help. Now Emil risked his status and reputation by intervening again. According to Ludvík Liška, Emil had some sway: 'Emil did not relate to politics but when they needed him to go somewhere he went. They used him often as a symbol. When President Zápotocký had to go to some foreign country they sent Emil first to prepare the atmosphere. There were many times people did not know whether our president was Zátopek or Zápotocký.'

The president listened to Zátopek's protestations but, according to Olga, then 'slapped his wrists'. Olga was told by the marriages department that 'being in love' was too elusive a concept to be a valid reason for marrying and that she must not sell herself to the capitalists. Yet something shifted thanks to Emil Zátopek.

Six decades on Olga Connolly wrote to me and gave her memories of the love and gold of Melbourne. 'There were tears in thousands of eyes when Zátopek entered the stadium,' she stated. 'People stood up shouting his name, giving him standing ovations. Emil crossed the finish line, and collapsing from exhaustion, was caught by Mimoun's arms, keeping the two standing together, softly speaking. Words cannot describe that Olympic moment. The love, the brotherhood, the nobleness of the two champions, the true embodiment of the Olympic spirit.

'A couple of months later when Hal Connolly visited Prague and he and I asked for a permit to marry, Dana and Emil invited Harold to stay in their home, a daring act in that time's political situation. Harold and I wrote a letter to the president; at a sports conference where the president was a keynote speaker, Emil asked him to support our request. I was present at that conference. Harold was waiting in the lobby and was surrounded by so many conference attendees that the organisers asked me to send him away. The president did not speak to me, but after a couple of days granted me an audience in his office. The president then allowed our wedding and my emigration. Some 30,000 wonderful people filled the Old Town Square on the wedding day, but it was not only because of the two of us, but also because of Emil and Dana, who were our best man and woman. They truly were the demigods, the superstars of the day.'

It was nearly over for Emil. Nobody would ever match his feat of doing the 5000, 10,000 and marathon treble at an Olympic Games. It may be the most remarkable feat of all in the pantheon of parameter-pushing. He broke world records at 5000 and 10,000 metres among his total of 18. He did it all with a smile while juggling complex politics. Few sportspeople have ever been so loved or admired. He also came up with some of the most abiding mantras of sport: 'If you want to run, run a mile; if you want to experience a different life, run a marathon.'

After Melbourne he said he did not have the will to pack his running shoes in another suitcase. He did not like living on past glories and he felt that keenly when local athletes waited for him in –35°C temperatures in Omsk. Why else would they be there if not for the old Zátopek?

It ended in San Sebastián in 1958. He travelled to the ancient Basque town of Irun for a race of five laps of a 2.5-kilometre circuit. There was a steep climb, a strong wind and a deep bog, as well as a strong field. For the last time, Emil dug in and won. 'I was happy to be able to give to those kind Basques the joy of having won my last race in their country. They lifted me up on their shoulders, they poured wine from their leather gourds and embraced me till sunset.'

As he left, a sports enthusiast and local café owner, Patchio Corte, gave him a present. Dana remembered, 'It was a little, white dog, like a fox terrier. Emil did not want to accept, but the train was leaving for Paris so he took the bag. The dog caused a lot of problems and peed everywhere.' Pedro lived with the Zátopeks in Prague until he died. Then Corte sent a woman all the way to Czechoslovakia with a basket containing three more dogs. They called each one Pedro and gave two away, one to Ota Pavel and another to Arnošt Lustig, two family friends and eminent writers. Pedro, Zátopek said, was his last trophy. The race was run.

19

Reclaimed (Prague, 1968)

The lieutenant colonel fastened a button. His wife was in the kitchen. These were the last acts of normality because, today, their lives would change irrevocably. The hum had grown from a barely imagined murmur to an ominous rumble. Voices of anger and defiance merged outside. Through the glass he looked out over the cold, bleached streets and shivered. And he thumbed another button through its hole.

The Russians had come. Everyone knew that now. Dubček's Action Programme had promised a better life for Czechoslovakia, but that was frightening for those in Moscow. The '2000 Words' had demanded reforms. Lord knows, people were aggrieved. They had suffered for a long time – both out on the farms and in the factories, where the people were denied a voice by the state-controlled censors and the great Bear in Moscow; and down on the track and in the athletics clubs, where organised sport had been corralled into one state-owned project. Emil was a Communist but, before that, he was a nationalist, and so, as the streets began to shake and the sound of tank on cobble drowned out the hiss of dissent, he fastened another button. He scanned the front page of the newspaper. It was dated 20 August 1968. It was only a few months since Alexander Dubček had taken over the Party after a vote of no confidence in Antonín Novotný. Back then, in that first optimistic flush of change, he had not foreseen the problems that had brought them to this point. The '2000 Words', written by an old Zlín associate Ludvík Vaculík, stated allegiance to Moscow and the Warsaw Pact, but called for the totalitarian regime to be liberalised. The full title was 'Two Thousand Words Which Belong to Workers, Farmers, Officials, Artists and to Everyone'. The impact when it was published in four newspapers was sudden. An emergency meeting of the Presidium was called and it was widely condemned by the government.

Zátopek sighed. It was 20 years since he had gone to the Olympic Games in London and become the pride of his nation. He had been championed by the hierarchy on his return to Prague, rewarded with his rank and given a good living. He had run and won and destroyed the very best athletes in the world. 'The pitiless race of elimination,' that French journalist had written. He himself had explained why he had worn a tortured expression throughout his entire career: 'I was never talented enough to run and smile at the same time.' Another writer had said, 'He ran as if each step was his last.' He had got through all that and become an internationalist, beloved by people all around the world – and now this.

Years later, in an interview in her tiny flat in Prague, his wife explained why they had signed up to the '2000 Words': 'It was about all the things that were going on,' she said. 'And because we were in sport, we could travel and see how other people lived. At home everything was damaged and destroyed, and we believed in a better socialism. So we signed. Maybe we applauded Dubček too much. We did not see the danger.'

They could hear the tanks now. He looked at himself in the mirror. Thin and bald, he had been like that in his prime, too, with an appearance out of kilter with his athleticism. Some things changed and some things stayed the same. He loved his wife and, for all its ills, he loved his country. He said goodbye to Dana and walked out of the door.

The Old Town was a mess. Hundreds of youths had made barricades from disgorged trucks. They built obstacles. Among the student protesters was Václav Havel, a playwright from a rich family, who had been denied an education by the state because of his bourgeois leanings. Havel would go on to pen politically risky plays and then, one day, become the president, but he was there as just another protester. They all knew that Dubček had reassured President Brezhnev that Moscow had nothing to worry about from his reforms, that the 'politics of conscience' would not undermine the Warsaw Pact. But now people were passing on word-of-mouth reports that tank battalions were rolling into Prague. One farmer had spotted them five miles to the north as he ploughed a field and had then outrun them in his truck in order to spread the warning. The Party broadcast lies on the radio to calm the masses, but the truth was an estimated 175,000 Russian troops were marching into the capital. Reports of deaths were coming in. Machine guns had been fired.

The tanks rolled across the Vltava river and the lieutenant colonel knew that he would never get to taste his dinner. The protesters cowered behind the barricades and waited. In the days that followed the Czech people would find fresh ways to undermine the Russians. A boy on a motorcycle would deliver rebel newspapers to those encamped in Wenceslas Square, braving the Red Army soldiers and the helicopters dropping Moscow propaganda. A student would chant slogans into his megaphone. Anti-Russian graffiti would spring up on the roads out of Prague, and statues of national heroes were blindfolded as if to spare them from the shame. As the Russian machine crawled forwards girls hitched up their skirts to distract the soldiers while boys ran up to their vehicles and smashed their headlights. For now the people were living on a mix of adrenaline and terror. The tanks rumbled on and then, briefly, the cries stopped. Megaphones were silenced. All eyes turned to an old soldier who walked out into the street. As a tank shook its noisy course down the street, its antennae sniffing opposition, the lieutenant colonel stopped and raised a hand.

'Who is that?' a voice said from the safety of the barricade.

And another said, 'That's Zátopek.'

***

Around 4,600 Warsaw Pact tanks rolled into Czechoslovakia on 20 August 1968. It would signal the end of the brief hope that the country would become more liberal while keeping its socialist heart. Luděk Pachman, a chess grand master, saw Zátopek holding court in Wenceslas Square. 'He dominated the scene on the first evening,' he said. 'I was with him as he literally hurled himself into groups of (Russian) soldiers, introducing himself by name, plus all his sports titles, then adding an invitation in Russian, "Now let's talk!" At once a crowd would gather and there would be an impromptu meeting.'

Emil's country was on the precipice and all he could do was rely on his sense of justice. Paratroopers had surrounded the Central Committee building and burst into Dubček's office. They were soon followed by KGB officers. Dubček lifted a phone but the line had been cut. A soldier tore the phone from the wall and pointed a gun at the Party leader. As Dubček was taken away he whispered to his office manager to hide his briefcase, which contained important documents. When he got back a week later he found his briefcase empty and realised the manager had been a Soviet agent all along.

The invaders shut down the television and radio stations, but the Czech resistance began to run a clandestine service. Emil was heavily involved. The day after the invasion, four Czech soldiers woke him.

'Have you come to take me with you or to take me away?' he asked.

One of the officers replied, 'Emil, your country needs you.'

He spent the next four days sleeping in different houses in Prague as he sought to avoid arrest and get his message across. On 23 August Czech soldiers took him to the kitchen of the half-finished Dům Hotelového Bydlení building in the Petřiny suburb. When the Russians had burst into the television centre a team of production workers and the star reporter, Jiří Kanturek, had escaped out the back door. They commandeered an outside broadcast truck and drove into a forest where they hid overnight. Then they went to an apartment, high on a hill overlooking Prague, and blacked out the windows with brown paper. The parabolic antennae from the truck was mounted on the twelfth-storey roof, camouflaged with briers and dark blankets. The antenna was then aimed at the tiny village of Buková where a local television transmitter was situated. From there the signal was re-transmitted by a microwave link to local stations all over the country. The broadcast truck, meanwhile, was stripped and abandoned on the other side of Prague. This complicated intrigue baffled the Russians as they tried to locate the signal's source.

Emil gave his first broadcast on that Friday night, preaching a message of defiance. Luděk Pachman, a journalist as well as a chess master, followed him. The Russians finally realised that these secret broadcasts were coming from Buková, but some television technicians threw them off the scent by directing them to Bukovany some several hundred kilometres in the wrong direction. Zátopek enjoyed his broadcasts until they upped sticks and moved to a new location. 'It was a hell of a lot of fun,' he would say. Outrunning the Russians came naturally.

Emil was ambivalent about his own safety in those days, even when other radio broadcasts maintained that he was in danger and must go into hiding. Pachman heard that Emil was still walking about town with only a Sherlock Holmes cap as a disguise. He went to find Emil. It was not hard. He was putting up an enormous anti-Soviet poster in Wenceslas Square. A Russian soldier approached him and stuck a gun in his back. Emil turned sharply and smiled. 'That's ok, *tovarish* [comrade],' he said and wandered away. No sooner had he got around the corner than he began putting up another poster.

Pachman wanted to take him somewhere safe, but warned Zátopek to keep quiet and not to provoke the Russians. When they were stopped at a checkpoint, Emil could not restrain himself. 'Even a dog wouldn't stand for what you've done to us!' he cried. Pachman lied and said Emil was drunk. They were allowed through.

Rumours quickly began to circulate that anyone who had signed the '2000 Words' manifesto was in grave danger. Emil and Dana were among 70 well-known people who had done precisely that. His old colleague, Aleš Poděbrad, knew Emil's fighting behaviour would cause trouble. 'Those who signed the "2000 Words" made their cadre situation very difficult,' he recalled. 'Emil signed it, as did the great gymnast Věra Čáslavská, but Emil was an officer disagreeing with military occupation. It was clear then that his fate as an officer was over.'

Bruce Maxwell was the *Sunday Mirror* man in Prague. On 8 September 1968 he ran an exclusive under the headline THE RUSSIANS JUST CAN'T KEEP UP WITH ZÁTOPEK. Maxwell said he had met Emil at a secret location where friends had whisked him after hearing the Russian Secret Service wanted to arrest him. Emil sounded a defiant tone. 'I think I should come out and face them and see what happens,' he said. Maxwell said he had seen Zátopek ignore jumpy young soldiers with machine guns to climb on boxes and address passers-by. He added he had noticed two Russian officers drive up in an army jeep and listen to his words. Then they drove away quietly. Maxwell deduced that Zátopek was a marked man.

Maxwell met Zátopek in a remote village. They sat in a bare room while guards paced up and down outside. Then Emil slapped a list of Russian demands on the table and cried, 'Look at this! See all these things they are doing to us!' Maxwell asked about his personal safety. 'I don't know what will happen,' Emil said. 'My friends rang today and said it was dangerous to return to Prague. I check with them each day. They say it is not good for me to go back, but I am not so sure. While you western journalists are here I don't think they will do much. Soon you will leave; then we will see. But I cannot stay in this room for ever.' He spoke about the forthcoming Mexico Olympics. The host Olympic committee had invited him and Dana as guests of honour. 'When all the countries march, I want to see what the crowd does when our Czech flag comes out – and what happens when the Russians appear.' Maxwell ended his piece wondering if he would ever see Emil Zátopek again.

Emil was prepared to take risks. A senior Czech officer told him that if the Russians arrested him then the Czechs would arrest them. It was bravado, of course, but Emil did come out in public again and did go to Mexico. It was a year of seismic change and sacrifice around the world. Emil left Czechoslovakia for a place where, ten days before the start of the Olympics, government forces massacred hundreds of protesting students in the Plaza de las Tres Culturas. During the Games, the American sprinters Tommie Smith and John Carlos would make their black-gloved Black Power salute on the podium. Avery Brundage, the IOC president and Nazi sympathiser, threatened the entire US team with disqualification unless Smith and Carlos were sent home. They were. Smith was sacked from his job washing cars and his mother died of a heart attack, distraught by the dead rats in the hate mail. Carlos' wife later committed suicide. Also on that 200 metres podium was Peter Norman, a white Australian who wore a small civil rights badge supporting his rivals and the Olympic Project for Human Rights. For that small show of solidarity, he would be banned from the next Olympics and barred from the 2000 Games in his native Australia. Speaking out always had repercussions.

Emil was turning 46 as he watched all this unfold, but he had been reassured when he heard the roar for the Czechoslovakia team at the opening ceremony in Mexico and the muted applause for the Russians.

Times and faces had changed. His old marathon foe, Jim Peters, was long retired and working happily as an optician in Kent, England. Alain Mimoun had run for longer, even winning the French marathon title in 1966, and was his adopted country's greatest ever athlete. However, the fragility of his hero status had been shown in 1961 when Parisian police shot dead hundreds of Algerians during a pro-independence demonstration. Mimoun, the man from Oran, had wept as bodies were dumped over ornate French balustrades and into the Seine.

The year before that bloodshed Mimoun had gone to the Olympic Games in Rome and come 34th for France in the marathon. Dana had been there too. She won the silver medal and, at the age of almost 38, became the oldest female athlete in Olympic history to stand on the podium. She won another European title and set a world record too before age finally began to catch up with her. 'Emil didn't like it when I was the number one in the house,' she would tell me. 'He was very jealous.'

The Rome Olympics also saw the last throes of Gordon Pirie's career. This time he was nowhere. The heat undid all the British, who had been refused permission to travel to Rome early and acclimatise, and he bowed out in the heats in the 5000 metres and was a shadow of his old belligerent self in the 10,000 metres. The British press had kept up their attacks on Pirie in the ensuing years. As Emil sat in his remote village hideaway, the media lamented the fact Pirie was again talking of emigrating (he had returned home from New Zealand) and taking up the new sport of orienteering to winning effect. Pirie knew he would never be accepted but had more pressing concerns. He had visited Prague and organised a petition deploring the Russian invasion of Czechoslovakia. He had insisted Russia and her supporters should be barred from the Mexico Olympics, and called on British sportsmen to stop being hypocritical. With typical Pirie forthrightness, he even damned the Prime Minister for his inertia, saying, 'Had Harold Wilson been down the Czechoslovak streets with us on Wednesday morning, with the tanks almost going over our toes, it would have been different.'

Emil watched the new era and briefly escaped. Two years on from giving a gold medal to Ron Clarke, he watched as his friend collapsed and almost died in Mexico. 'They didn't care about the athletes,' Clarke would say. 'Sure, they got upset about the horses and brought them down to sea level, but the athletes were treated terribly. Jeez.'

Sisu was no more. Ethiopia now ruled the marathon. First the barefoot runner Abebe Bikila had succeeded Mimoun and won two Olympic golds. Now Mamo Wolde won in Mexico. Bikila would be paralysed in a car crash the following year and would die of a brain haemorrhage aged just 41; Wolde spent six years in prison before going on trial for shooting an anti-government agent. He was sentenced to six years but had already spent nine in prison. He was released and died soon afterwards, buried next to his hero, Bikila. 'Run a marathon and experience life,' Zátopek had said. It was an event that seemed to encapsulate the highs and lows of human existence, with all its attendant dramas and tragedies.

Mexico was a temporary release but Zátopek refused to heed warnings from friend and foe alike to hold his tongue. He also refused offers from friends in foreign countries to quit Prague and join them. The British were particularly keen to offer him an escape route, but Emil said he had to go home. How could he desert his nation now with the Russians still in Prague?

Dana backed her husband but was naturally more cautious. 'People had started to be dissatisfied,' she told me of the genesis of the Prague Spring. 'Everybody watched you; everything was destroyed; everything was dirty. Then they started to build a better socialism and we joined in. For us signing the "2000 Words" was a tragedy. The Russian army came in one night and that was the end of liberty right there. The Soviets wanted to have Czechoslovakia in their hands. They said that Emil was against the state and society. He wasn't.'

On the night of the invasion Dana wondered if that was it. 'I cannot describe the feeling,' she told Leigh Montville, a writer from *Sports Illustrated*, when he visited years later. 'I thought we were all dead. That was the only thought: bye-bye. That we were all gone.'

The process of removing Emil Zátopek began slowly. He was still defiant at the start of 1969 and told a Viennese newspaper, *Die Neue Zeitung*, that, 'Czechs will arm themselves with anything that comes to hand – with stick and stones. They will attack Russian tanks with their bare hands if needs be.' He admitted that he expected to be arrested for saying what he had. Dana was frightened. She told Montville, 'I did not want him to go to jail. My father was in jail under the Germans. The Gestapo came in the middle of the night and took him away. He was at Dachau, Buchenwald, later in a prison in Brno. He was a colonel in the Czech army. The Nazis kept him as a hostage. He lost all of those years in jail. I did not want this to happen to Emil. I told him I did not want him to be a hero. What good is it if someone says five or ten years after you are dead that you are a hero? Maybe don't be such a big hero; maybe be alive, instead.'

He was not arrested but criticism grew. Ominously the Russian newspaper *Sovietskaya Sport* accused him of being a 'double-dealer' and a 'political careerist'. The paper said Zátopek had slandered the occupying Warsaw Pact countries and shown that he hated socialism.

On 16 January 1969 the *Daily Telegraph* carried a small report stating that Zátopek had lost his job as the physical exercise chief in the army and had been shunted into a minor coaching post. That news was overshadowed when, on the same day, a history student at Charles University set fire to himself in Wenceslas Square. Jan Palach died three days later and became an instant martyr. When it emerged he had written a letter saying he was part of a wider group of students prepared to burn themselves alive if Russian troops did not withdraw, there was widespread fear of more horrors. For Emil it got worse. Leaflets claiming that Palach's suicide had been organised by a group of five men began to circulate. The five were named as the chess master Luděk Pachman, the writer Pavel Kohout, the student leader Lubomír Holeček, the journalist Vladimir Skutina and the greatest ever Olympian Emil Zátopek.

The leaflets made their way to parliament, where an old hardliner named Vilém Nový said the five 'had a share in the death of Jan Palach'. It was a ridiculous claim and Zátopek and the others brought a defamation suit, although Pachman was already in grave trouble after initiating another document called 'Ten Points' which said the Communist Party need not have an automatic leading role in society.

In February 1969, Nový claimed that Zátopek and his group had been behind a sinister 'cold fire' plot. His outrageous allegation was that Palach had been told he could use a special sort of liquid to make flames without actually burning himself. Zátopek could sense antagonistic forces gathering around him, even if the StB files showed that Emil was very sympathetic to Palach. One of the entries states, 'Zátopek evaluates the act of Jan Palach as a moral act and the act of the brave man with a strong will.' Emil knew that it was a dangerous act to be taking on a hardline Communist MP against a backdrop of occupying Russian troops.

According to Pachman, Emil caused a sensation by backtracking and saying that he had never meant to imply any hostility to socialism and that he asked to withdraw his suit. He even shook Nový's hand. 'It looked as if they were about to hug each other in a double Khrushchev [a bearhug with kisses on both cheeks],' Pachman scoffed. Pachman clearly took this act as a personal betrayal. Later Emil would suggest the incident was twisted by the media. Some said he was angry with Pachman's portrayal of events. Meanwhile, Pachman's bitterness festered. While in prison he said his thoughts turned to Jan Palach and so he jumped off his bed headfirst on to a concrete prison floor. He had already rammed his head against a wall and said that was how Middle Age knights tried to kill themselves. He felt he was the scapegoat.

Olga Connolly had kept throwing the discus after emigrating and changing her name. She was seventh at the 1960 Olympics, where she competed for the USA. Her old friend Nina Five Hats won the gold medal. The former Olga Fikotová had just finished sixth at the Olympics in Mexico in 1968, but now penned pieces for the Associated Press and found her article about Emil syndicated around the world. In it she said Emil was disillusioned with the Kremlin and had been forced to wear a false beard and dark glasses. She said the Ministry of Defence had made *him* the scapegoat.

It was obvious that things would never be the same when Dubček was replaced as first minister in April 1969. His replacement, Gustáv Husák, had initially gone to Moscow to help with negotiations over Dubček's kidnapping, but now became a champion of those wanting to reverse the process of liberalisation. Meanwhile, the plaintiffs in the 'cold fire' case lost and the judge said Nový was right to criticise Palach.

Emil was dismissed as an army athletics coach altogether in April, but still he remained defiant, even as he studied the report into his putative crimes that lay on his desk at the Army Sports Club. He was accused of 'illegal political activities', spreading false information and disobeying orders from the Ministry of Defence. 'I didn't want to be a rat leaving a sinking ship,' he told a British journalist when asked why he had not taken up one of many lucrative offers to coach overseas. 'I believe in democracy and humanity, but if it is not possible I take life as it is. It is good that I am charged like this because everyone will hear what is happening. They know my name. They know I am not a counter-revolutionary or an enemy of the country.'

Emil was called before a disciplinary hearing and told them that he was prepared to go to prison. 'If you want to find me guilty then find me guilty,' he said. 'If you want me to sign a confession or statement then write it up and I will sign.'

He also gave an indication that his stance was more complicated than often portrayed. He refused to be a propagandist for the new Husák regime but he also revealed some growing dissatisfaction with Dubček. 'I told my general yesterday that I would do all I could to help Husák,' he said. 'He will use the whip which Dubček did not do. Husák needs the sympathy of the people and I can help him get that.'

It is easy to look back at history and realise that Zátopek had it coming. He had already admitted that he might be 'thrown out of my job', but neither Emil nor Dana knew that the StB files were filling up with reports on them. Their unique status as a married Czech couple allowed to western countries was a privilege that had long invited massive suspicion. People informed on them and passed on gossip, rumour and fact. So file 648808 details a decade of counter-intelligence dating back to the last race:

In January 1958, Emil and Dana Zátopek are thinking of staying in San Sebastián. They offer to join the Czech explorers, [Jiří] Hanzelka and [Miroslav] Zikmund, on their world travels [the renowned Czech duo would be blacklisted when they reported on poverty in the Soviet Union].

Zátopek says that Dana was afraid of the Russian invasion and discouraged him from signing the '2000 Words' Manifesto. Zátopek expresses his fear of the invasion.

Zátopek and Dana sign a proclamation for the preservation of freedom of the press.

On 13/11/1968 he co-organised with Dana an anti-regime meeting at which a foreign journalist is present.

Shortly after the occupation, Zátopek gives an interview to an English journalist and takes him to the places of 'resistance'.

He supports Dubček.

After his return from Mexico, Zátopek's movements were restricted and he was barred from speaking to journalists or westerners. Having been given a menial coaching role, he was then expelled from the Communist Party and finally sacked by the army in December 1969. His crimes were listed as possessing an anti-Soviet attitude, violating legal norms and making 'serious revelations' about the president and the first minister. Suddenly, the national hero who had previously had the ear of the former president, was *persona non grata*. He was told that he would be unable to get a job anywhere in Prague. And still the StB file grew:

Dana complains that Emil has to leave the army due to Lieutenant Colonel Novotný [not the president] and Lieutenant Colonel Černoch.

Zátopek speaks against the USSR army and the USSR in general at meetings and races.

Monitored by NKVD (People's Commissariat for Internal Affairs). Zátopek is afraid of monitoring.

Student Action Committee co-operates with Zátopek.

Zátopek was asked by a reporter whether he may publish his opinions about Russian danger. He allowed it.

Spring 1969 – Zátopek visits Moscow and the runner Vladimir Kuts, who complains that he is not loyal to the party.

Spring, 1969 – Overall Zátopek's attitude is less confrontational. He is trying to calm society down.

Zátopek is called by commander who asks him, 'Why did you provoke people?' Zátopek answered, 'I did not provoke anyone; I am defending the people against attacks coming from elsewhere.'

21/8/1969 – Zátopek is provoked by StB agent who says that Dubček was good; he does not seem to show any signs of disagreement.

25/8/69 – Interviews are given to foreign media, but which were not provided by Zátopek. He protests against these.

Lieutenant Colonel Novotný accused Zátopek of carrying radios from abroad and of co-organisation of Palach's demonstrative suicide.

1/10/69 – With the arrival of Husák, Emil is leaving the army.

Emil was now forced to live a half-life. He tried to get some other work, thinking his fame would help, but nobody would touch him. 'I kept looking and looking, but no one would hire me,' he recalled. 'I could not understand. Finally a man told me that everyone in Prague was afraid to hire me. He said I would have to find work outside the city.'

The only work he could get was miles away in the mines, where he managed to get a role with a geological survey team. He lived in a caravan for a fortnight and then would spend a few days at home. He dug holes and lifted 100lb bags of concrete. His crew boss mocked him and said this was good training for him. And the country went back to the way it had been, with pride and paranoia used to browbeat it into subservience. The Russians would stay for decades.

Many of those who knew and idolised Zátopek now turned away as he came to be regarded as an enemy of the state. The truth was Emil was always a Communist. He got that from his father. He just wanted a Communism that would work. Yet now he was regarded as a traitor.

The wife of Ludvík Liška explained: 'He was a bit worried that we had small children and he did not want to hurt them, but we were both knowledgeable of the sport environment, and friends of Emil, so we did not want to leave him in a bad situation. He talked a lot about friends who did not want to have much to do with him at that time, and would rather go to the other side of the street than meet him.'

Liška himself said he had lost touch a little with Emil, but when the regime turned against him, he made sure he stood by his old friend: 'I said to Emil, "What bothers you? Pack up and bring Dana and come and join us for a weekend in Stará Boleslav." I think Emil was grateful to us that we were behind him.'

Aleš Poděbrad, who had once worked beneath Zátopek in the army, said Emil's reduced status left people in a difficult situation: 'For a normal citizen it was not appropriate to care about him.

What if some party officials would report it? It would surely have a bad impact – you'd have children without education, or be given a labouring job and so on.'

To the wider world Emil Zátopek just disappeared, but he probably knew what to expect. He had hinted at what was coming in the media and had seen what had happened to others from his past, from Larry Kořan to Jan Haluza.

His old trainer was now 55. After working in the mines he had got a job with a crane company, but he was ostracised too. He was called a criminal, a slacker and the company director even labelled him 'the greatest enemy of the Communist Party and the people'. Haluza walked away from that job.

The StB monitored him too and repeatedly tried to enlist him as an informer. He stood firm. 'Gentlemen,' he said, finally. 'After all my experiences in recent years, do you think that I would be capable of doing something like that?' He was driven home and dumped out of the car. The official line was that the StB never contacted Haluza again. Somehow he had got away with defiance this time. However, for decades he and Věra would hear a mysterious clicking sound on their phone line and assumed their home was bugged.

In 1965, three years before the Prague Spring, Haluza finally got a job that used his law degree when he became the damages liquidator for the Czech state insurance company in Zlín. Štěpán Hrstka, the man who had first told him about Emil Zátopek, was working for the company and helped him get the job.

Everything seemed vaguely normal, until the aftermath of the Russian invasion and another investigation prompted by his membership of the K231 group (an organisation set up that year to help with the rehabilitation of 80,000 political prisoners). After another interrogation, the StB seemed to believe that Emil

Zátopek's old trainer and running partner was now too brow-beaten and crushed to cause them any problems, although his name would remain on the register of dangerous people for many years to come.

He had met Emil in the years since his release. Haluza's friend Božetech Kostělka said, 'When he was released, he met with Zátopek and he felt no malice towards him. After he nearly died in the camp from typhus, he said, "I was on the other side. I am in debt because I survived it all." Sometimes they met in the following years. Dana went there for wine and I think they met also at festivals on Radhošť' mountain. Haluza was not very active then. He knew he was being monitored and had to be careful. He liked his calm and knew that he could not provoke the state. The people [political prisoners] who were released still had threats hanging over them because they were basically released on parole.'

Haluza and Emil's lives had taken wildly diverging routes but now they were crossing once more. Haluza had suffered and been sent down the mines; now Emil was plummeting and had been forced to seek work in the same area. He was later quoted as saying, 'I ended up working 600 metres underground in a uranium mine in Jáchymov, 130 kilometres west of Prague with a miner's helmet on my head.' Haluza had lived through his Jáchymov hell; Emil was now going through his, but typically put a positive spin on his demise. 'The earth is not only nice from above but from inside.'

Larry Kořan, his old running friend who had served his time in the camps, was now in the USA after seeing 'a hole in the wall'. Through a friend in California, he received an invitation to go to the USA for three months. The brief hiatus of the Prague Spring gave him his chance. He got out, got an extension and, when the

Russians invaded and the country returned behind the Iron Curtain, he stayed put. 'I said to myself, "Ten years in a concentration camp is enough for one lifetime." But I never ever forgot what Emil did for me that day in 1961.'

The great amnesty of 1960 meant that more than two thousand political prisoners were released to a kind of low-level freedom in which they were shunted to the edges of society and their families were discriminated against. Kořan had been sentenced to 18 years after his capture that night near the Bavarian border. And then, after ten years, he was released, but life was not the same. The only peace he got, ironically, was going back to Jáchymov to work in the mines as a civilian engineer. He called it 'a republic within a republic'. Otherwise, he could find no employment and was a 'slave to the StB system'. A lifetime on and Ali, Emil and Larry had all suffered similar abuse.

Kořan was a ghost on the margins of society when the European Rowing Championships were held in Prague in 1961. Zátopek was fêted on the start line with a host of other dignitaries. The top-ranking Communist Party members were all there. It was an event to show off the state and the city in all its glory. Larry went to look out of curiosity: 'I was watching them and then Emil saw me. At that time all my previous friends did not want to know me. I was a political prisoner and that was very bad for anybody to be associated with. But Emil, in front of all these people, the Communist leaders and the rest, came to me, embraced me and said, "I thought you were dead." He did not have any fear. This is what made Emil such a friend. They said he was a propaganda man for the Communist system, but he was not. He was a runner with all his heart and thinking. That was it. Emil was a runner. The best. And then he signed the "2000 Words" and how they made him suffer for that.'

Kořan's old friend was still building the house in Troja in a plush northern suburb by the time of the Prague Spring, but after losing his job and post, it became an increasing struggle. Milan Svajgr, his former team-mate, asked Dana, 'Who designed this? It's terrible.' She told him Emil had. Milan sighed. When Emil returned from the boreholes, they would keep on building. 'It was drudgery,' Dana said.

Svajgr was once at a train station where he bought the wrong ticket and ended up having heated words with the cashier as he tried to change it. 'And then some guy comes up to me and says, "Milan, why do you argue?" I just thought here is some strange man, but then he asked about Věra. Suddenly, it dawned on me. "Emil?" I said. He was already working at the boreholes and living in a caravan then. I was leader of the athletics club in Opava and often went to Prague and I visited a club and met Dana. She told me that Emil was then living in very bad conditions in the Vysočina region, coming home only twice a month, and still their house was not finished.'

Ludvík Liška said that Emil was actually proud of the manual work that he was doing: 'He'd say, "Look, all my life I did nothing and now I have calluses – I finally know what it is like to do physical work."' However, the environment on the geological surveys was not conducive to a healthy life. Out in the wilds, cast off from their families, it was common for workers to drink heavily. Liška said, 'People drank a lot and they always wanted to drink with Emil. He did not manage to have it under control. People would say, "We like him, we want to have a drink with him." And I'd say, "If you like him, don't force him to go drinking."'

Jan Mrázek was another old colleague who would ask Dana about Emil when he bumped into her, but found her 'evasive and sad'.

It got worse as Emil grew older. On one occasion, Emil was home alone when Liška rang him. He had a policy of making Emil say a tongue-twister if he suspected Zátopek had been drinking. This time he could not rouse Emil, so he drove over and knocked on the neighbour's door. He climbed the fence and found Emil lying on the floor. He rushed him to hospital where a doctor told him that he had arrived in the nick of time. 'We saved his life that day,' Liška said. But it was now a life of exile and alcohol. It was hard for his friends to feel that Emil had not been betrayed.

20

The Gift

It was a remarkable descent for arguably the most famous man in Czechoslovakia. Now, whenever western journalists asked if they could interview the great Zátopek, the answer came that he was not available. He just faded away – until, in 1971, Emil met Brian Freemantle, a journalist who would later arrange the evacuation of a hundred orphans during the fall of Saigon. The ensuing piece carried a headline 'The Will to Win is Crushed' and portrayed Zátopek as a broken spirit. 'I am reconciled to conditions in my country,' he said. 'Once I was unhappy, but not now. There seems little point.' Freemantle, deploying the authorial flourishes that would make him a hugely successful thriller writer, added, 'There was a pause while he sought for the correct expression. Then he said, "I exist."'

Freemantle said Emil was bereft of the old outspoken attacks on Russia and quoted him as saying, 'At first I tried to work as a dustman around Prague, but people would gather round and some would even try to help.' Now he was part of a three-man team travelling around the country making test bores for construction work. 'At first things were hard for me. I was stripped of my army rank and I lost my army pension. Now things are better. I am reasonably happy. I think Husák is a good man. He is very intelligent. He has said that Zátopek is a sportsman who should only talk about sport and not involve himself in politics, and perhaps he is right.'

Three months later the newspaper *Rudé Právo* carried a full-page article in which Zátopek recanted the last vestiges of his '68 spirit. For those to whom he was a sporting star turned folk hero, standing up for the common man, it was a depressing read.

Referring to Freemantle's *Daily Mail* article, he said it was shameful that he had been portrayed as an enemy of socialism. Instead, the once defiant man who had put up posters in Wenceslas Square and ignored Russian guns was quoted as saying, 'I am sorry that I behaved like one of those who poured oil on to flames which might have become a danger to the socialist world system.' But, already, it was easy to detect the voice of the propaganda writer. He then said the '2000 Words' would have been a catastrophe had the manifesto become reality. He denied reports about his degradation and withdrawal of his pension and claimed that he was still a colonel of the reserve. Husák was described as 'realistic, efficient and able'.

Freemantle was not taken in. 'There is no doubt that the interview in *Rudé Právo*, from a man still regarded as a hero in his country, stems from government pressure to make the present regime acceptable,' he wrote, in a subsequent article. Freemantle's palpable anger was more with the state than Zátopek, but clearly he was saddened by the emasculation of a man who once wanted to fight with his bare hands but was now crushed and subdued.

As he had done before, Emil had just signed when given something. 'Emil made two mistakes,' Dana would admit to *Sports Illustrated*. 'First, he did not read what he signed. The journalist who wrote the story was not able to capture Emil's . . . what is the word? Heart? Maybe not heart. He did not capture the meaning of Emil. Second, Emil did not talk with me before he signed. If he [had] I don't think he would have done it.'

For all the attempts to hail him as such, Zátopek was not a political animal. He had a basic sense of right and wrong and lived by that. Sometimes, in such an aggressively black and white world, that made him malleable.

He was still barred from leaving Czechoslovakia at the same time as Dana. One of them would always remain at home as a hostage to fortune should one choose to defect. And, regardless of 'his' words in *Rudé Právo*, the StB continued to watch this fiftysomething with suspicion.

File 960319 details his time working on the geological survey team and features numerous reports from people and co-workers out in the remote villages where he now undertook what *Rudé Právo* insisted was 'new and absorbing work'.

Emil is satisfied outside of Prague, outside of people's attention. People recognise him, walk up to him for autographs, invite him to meetings – Zátopek doesn't want it. He does not lose his sense of humour – he draws cartoons of Dana chasing him with the spear.

He has no car.

People see him as a martyr.

When washing, cooking, etc., he is the most active of the group.

He resolves to stop drinking.

He rarely comments on politics: Dubček is a wretch and not a politician. He would have handed everything away and wasted money.

Openly admits that he had an opportunity to leave Czechoslovakia, but he did not.

He knows he is being watched.

Zátopek declares that he is in a worse situation than others – Jiří Raška [the skier] also signed the '2000 Words' manifesto, but he can continue doing sports. Zátopek cannot because he is a soldier.

Zátopek meets active athletes, but does not want to talk about politics. He is afraid of processes. He estimates his sentence to be 20 years.

He admits that entering into politics was a mistake, which Dana had told him.

He complains that his old friends avoid him.

Emil did make it to the 1972 Olympic Games in Munich, however, although the Palestinian terrorist attack made it a sombre event. Nevertheless, Karel Engel, once an infatuated schoolboy who had pretended to be Zátopek, now an Olympic wrestler, was delighted to see him there. Engel had been present at Houstka Spa when Emil had set his world record for the hour and was now standing next to him as the Czech flag went up in the Olympic Village. It was the first time they spoke and marked the start of a friendship that would last for the rest of Emil's life. 'We were so happy to see him because we had heard that he was back in prison,' Engel said. 'Nobody knew where he was or what he was doing.'

It was the same around the world. One of the most famous of all Olympians had apparently vanished, but then in 1973 the International Olympic Congress was held in Bulgaria and Antonín Himl, chairman of the Czech Olympic Committee, found himself harangued from all sides about the fate of Emil Zátopek and Věra Čáslavská, the gymnast who had also been ostracised after staring at the floor as the Russian anthem played when she won at the 1968 Olympics.

Before long Emil was recalled from the field and given a job in the documentation section of CSTV, the umbrella organisation for sport in the republic. He did not like the work. 'There was nothing to do,' Engel said. 'He just collected magazines from around the world and made press cuttings.' Some journalists tried to glamorise the task by dubbing him a sports spy, but it was overstating his small, bureaucratic role.

Others claimed he was more than a mere sports spy. In 1975 the US Judiciary Inquiry into Communist Bloc Intelligence Activities in the United States met Josef Frolík, a Czech spy who had defected. His testimony on the workings of the Czech intelligence forces was remarkable. It was straight out of a John Le Carré novel, with agents called Lucifer and plots to poison Radio Free Europe workers by replacing the salt cellars in the staff canteen. There were assassination attempts and Operation Rubber Dummy, in which they tried to blackmail a flirtatious secretary at the US embassy by using a spring-loaded dummy filled with 'blood' to make her think she had killed a man while driving. There were other cars with rotatable number plates, 'reserved' restaurant tables that were bugged, and a special room in the basement of the Directorate of State Security – those called for questioning were made to walk by this room containing an StB executioner with an axe and fake blood on the walls. Frolík said everybody talked after seeing that.

He accused lots of people of being agents and informers and said every sporting event was monitored by Czech intelligence and that a 'so-called' Olympic attaché would join the team at the biggest event on earth. Among the examples of 'sports contacts' listed was the name of Emil Zátopek. Frolík claimed, 'Emil Zátopek has been an agent from the early 1950s. During the period of the Prague Spring he was an *agent provocateur* who, through his own activities and through participation in other operations, was supposed to help compromise the regime of A. Dubček and his supporters. He comes across like an anti-Communist and as being very liberal.'

It hardly stacked up. If Zátopek truly was an informer then why would he have been sacked by the army and hounded out of Prague after Dubček was replaced? Would he have helped Olga Connolly emigrate? Contrary to Frolík's claim, Zátopek had also never tried to come across as anti-Communist at all; merely fair. Frolík told a juicy tale, all right, and his testimony had plenty of detail as he also name-checked politicians, royals and film stars. It may have been a coincidence that he had a book out that year.

Zátopek never professed to be a liberal but was happy to buy into 'the new socialism with a human face' during the Prague Spring. If he was trying to compromise Dubček, he did a remarkably poor job of it. It also makes no sense that the StB files made no reference to this supposed work. However, it is certainly plausible that the StB would have tried to recruit him, probably as an informer rather than an agent, and that, like Olga Fikotová, he may have palmed them off by saying he would pass on anything he heard that might be damaging to his country.

Quite what he was going to 'inform' anyone about after 1968 is also a mystery. It took years after the Prague Spring for the authorities to let Emil travel freely again. The first trip, fittingly, was to Finland, the original spiritual home of distance running, for a memorial race for Paavo Nurmi.

'The public was shocked to see how Emil was punished,' said Jan Mrázek. His faithful friend Ludvík Liška said, 'He was not much interested in politics. I think he just met someone who gave him it [the "2000 Words"] and he signed it.' Karel Engel, who became a great friend and help to Dana in later years, said the enquiries from abroad helped him. 'The great thing for him was the interest of foreign journalists.'

Dana kept on coaching and they retired to their home in Troja in the early 1980s. Dana found that her pension was substantially lower than expected. 'I told them I had worked for this country for 35 years,' she told Leigh Montville. 'I said I have been a coach, a teacher, a winner of medals. There were people who worked far less than me who had received much better pensions. The officials said, "Yes, but you signed the '2000 Words'. You never apologised. This is your pension. You will get no more."' They eventually sold the house they had painstakingly built and moved to a small flat in Prague.

The banishment of Emil Zátopek is an ugly stain on Czech sporting life. He was, and still is, the country's greatest sporting star. To imagine similar scenarios in the USA or Britain is incomprehensible.

Others suffered for their stances. Václav Havel was barred from travelling abroad in 1969. Despite her four gymnastics gold medals, Čáslavská failed to gain a job coaching with the Czech national team. Every January for five years she went to the same office to ask for the same job, until she was told she would only get anything if she said she had never signed the '2000 Words'. Even Juan Antonio Samaranch, the IOC president, was told he could not meet her.

It took another 20 years for things to really change, and Emil learnt to watch his words for fear of further reprisals during the interim. Then, in 1989, the Velvet Revolution took place and Communism collapsed. The first free elections in 44 years took place. Havel, the student protester and co-signer of the '2000 Words' with Emil, became president. And in 1990 Emil received an official apology from the Defence Minister for being thrown out of the army. After a 20-year exile it was too late. In 1998 Havel awarded Emil the Order of the White Lion, the best a Czech citizen can get. He had previously been stripped of his Meritorious Order of Sport. It may all have felt a little hollow, more political tit-for-tat. Nobody could give him back his years.

Zátopek was used to getting awards by then. The United Nations had given him the Pierre de Coubertin prize for promoting fair play in the 1970s. Later, the IOC would commission a statue to be built outside their offices in Lausanne. For all the prizes and platitudes, it was impossible to erase the betrayal.

Jan Haluza, too, was rehabilitated after the Velvet Revolution and, in 1994, at his 80th birthday celebrations in Luhačovice, Emil and Dana were among the guests. Emil called him Ali, as of old, and said, 'If there was no Haluza, there would be no Zátopek.' That may have been overstating the case but the kindness was heartfelt.

These two men had been there at the beginning, during those first track meetings in Zlín, and they had both been spat out by a society for daring to be different. Now they were ageing men but they were bonded by their feats of endurance.

Like Emil, Jan Haluza would also get an award from the Czech president, although Havel had served his two terms by 2010 and had been replaced by Václav Klaus. Jan and Věra had spent years working for young people and promoting Orel. He was 96 when he travelled to Prague Castle to receive the Medal of Tomáš Masaryk for outstanding contributions to the development of democracy, humanity and human rights. He died ten months later.

Emil had to watch as his rivals also fell. The first was Vladimir Kuts. He died in 1975 at the age of only 48. He had suffered severe stomach problems after Melbourne and retired in 1959. He studied at the Leningrad Institute of Physical Education and later dreamed of training a new Olympic champion. That never happened but he had his pension thanks to his deal cut before the 1956 Olympic 5000 metres. Yet there was no happy ending. Kuts drank heavily, once allegedly downing 15 bottles of vodka in three days, and his wife left him. He put on weight and disappeared. In 1970, Ron Carter, a journalist with *The Age* newspaper in Australia, travelled to Moscow to find him. The headline began 'He's 42 and Fat' and Carter wrote of how this pipe-smoker's size had almost doubled from his fighting weight to almost 17 stone. 'I have put on 2lbs for every 1000 kilometres I ran during my seven-year career,' he smiled. Rumours remained until the end. Gordon Pirie was convinced that drugs or hypnotism were behind Kuts' success, although he exonerated him and said it would have been forced on him by coaches. Zátopek, too, pondered whether Kuts had used 'enhancers'. Kuts himself had spoken of how damaging the regime of his coach had been: 'Nikiforov seemed like an executioner determined to break me down, body and soul, to make a warrior of me.' He suffered heart problems for the rest of his life. Embarrassed by his size, he shunned the athletics world and the Soviets returned the snub, with officials banning the publication of any photographs of the first great, but now decidedly portly, Russian runner.

Carter went home and Kuts' name only resurfaced in August 1975 when it was reported that he had quarrelled with his ex-wife and taken a dozen sleeping pills. He died that night, 16 August, with nobody sure whether it was suicide or an accident.

Gordon Pirie decided to continue running after the 1960 Olympics to 'ram it down the selectors' throats' and prove that they had taken the team to Rome too late. He won the 1961 AAA three mile title in a British record of 13 minutes 16.4 seconds, but was dropped for turning up late and then refusing to explain why. His strained relations with the media endured. In 1962 he accepted an offer to train England's cricket team ahead of the Ashes series and then accepted money from an Australian newspaper where he called the England players an 'unfit, paunchy bunch of barflies'. The Duke of Norfolk, the MCC tour manager, said England would have no more to do with him. The athletics hierarchy said the same when he ignored amateur rules and offered money to a young high jumper to appear on television.

He trained athletes with some success but there was criticism about the severity of his methods. He ended up living back in England, without his wife, and worked as a lumberjack in the New Forest. He was diagnosed with bile cancer and remained unorthodox and spiky until the end. In one of his last interviews, he said, 'For some time now I've purified all the water I put in my body and I also sent away samples of my hair for mineral and vitamin analysis.' He was nearly bankrupt and living off friends, and planned to blow his last savings on a trip to San Diego to undergo wheat-juice therapy. He was more bitter about his treatment by the establishment than his illness. 'What incenses me is that any inferior Tom, Dick or Harry can pick up a knighthood, yet I have received nothing, not even an MBE.' He said he had once phoned *Wogan*, Britain's premier TV chat show at the time. 'Gordon Pirie?' said the girl on the line. 'Who are you?' Pirie explained that he had run more miles than any other human being in the world (Pirie would make the *Guinness Book of World Records* for covering an estimated 260,000 miles). 'Well, have you been invited on the programme?' the BBC voice replied. Pirie concluded, 'There are some situations you just can't win. I only hope this cancer isn't one of them.' It was. He died ten months later in 1991, aged 60. An *Athletics Weekly* poll in 1965 voted him Britain's greatest ever athlete, ahead of Bannister, but his status has rarely been appreciated in his homeland since.

Jim Peters was diagnosed with terminal cancer in 1992. The doctors told him to let nature take its course, but he pointed out he had been a fighter all his life and paid for three shots of chemotherapy and it cleared up. He remained happily married to Frieda and always refused to regard the Empire Games disaster as a defeat. In 1967 he went back to Canada to be inducted into the British Columbia Hall of Fame and, in front of 15,000 people, he covered the final 220 metres. It was a PR stunt because he always maintained that the 1954 course had been measured wrongly and had actually been closer to 27 miles, meaning he had covered the marathon distance before his dozen falls. When told that a new book, *The Lore of Running*, had hailed him as 'the greatest marathoner ever', he said, 'I'll be blowed.' He was a genial, much-loved figure to the end, in 1999, but occasionally wondered what would have happened if he had been able to take on Zátopek one more time.

Chris Chataway would also succumb to cancer in 2014. He is remembered for more than a bit-part in Bannister's story and the 13 minutes 51.6 seconds that he took to beat Kuts at White City in front of a Europe-wide television audience of 15 million. After athletics he was a newscaster, reporter, politician, banker and chairman of the Civil Aviation Authority. His altruism extended to running for fun in aid of Vicky's Water Project, set up in memory of the fiancée of his son Adam. Chataway was knighted and reflected on how he had bristled at the work ethic of Zátopek but had grown to enjoy running in his later years. 'Joe Stalin has turned into Dixon of Dock Green,' he said of a sport that had been a tormenter but was now a 'friendly old codger'.

By the turn of the century, Emil was struggling with his health too, but he was allowed out of hospital to watch some of the Sydney Olympics in 2000. 'I was glad to see how he revived, especially when watching the 5000 and 10,000 metres,' Dana said. 'But he wasn't as sharp as in the past. He didn't count laps and didn't follow the times as he would do in the past.' He had suffered a stroke, pneumonia and a heart attack by the time he finally died on 21 November 2000, aged 78. The Czech authorities wanted to give him a state funeral but Dana requested something smaller. She also asked for the eulogies to be concise. Karel Engel helped organise the send-off, which was still held at the National Theatre.

Alain Mimoun came from France. Once marginalised by his country, he received the Legion of Honour four times and had scores of schools, streets and sports centres named after him. He would have been a true sporting legend had it not been for Emil Zátopek, but he loved his old foe, and their clashes defined his life. Mimoun did go to the 1960 Olympics, where he came 34th in the marathon, and was running well into his eighties. He remained never happier than when talking about Emil, and continued to do so until his death in 2013.

Zátopek's guard of honour included old team-mates Jindřich Roudný and Václav Čevona and, when they took Emil's coffin out on to Národní, the street often hailed as the genesis of the Velvet Revolution, the trams stopped and the bells began to ring. 'It was not planned,' Engel said. 'It just happened. It was noon and the Ursuline church bells started. There were thousands of people in silence apart from the ringing. It was just majestic.'

Everyone agreed there would never again be anyone like this simple man made complicated by his life and times. Liška did not hesitate when asked for a legacy. 'Outstanding man, abnormally cheerful, witty and intelligent,' he said. 'Handy for a lot of things and a good friend.' His oldest friends still meet occasionally and there are now races named after Zátopek held annually around the world. Accolades have kept coming since his death, *Runners' World* magazine voting him the greatest runner of all time in 2013. He is described as the founder of modern interval training and is held up as the template for driving yourself to the very edges of reason and possibility. More than that, he had what Gordon Pirie called 'the happiest and gayest' home he had ever been in.

Four gold medals won are perhaps only topped by the one he gave away. Ron Clarke set 18 world records, the same as Emil, but he never did get his gold on the track. After getting back on that plane from Prague in 1966, the nearest he got was four years later when he won a silver at the Commonwealth Games in Edinburgh. Self-pity passed him by. He had a good life and became the Mayor of the Gold Coast. He put Emil's medal in a museum and treasured the memory. He had received the greatest gift in Olympic sport and gave the greatest epitaph in return: 'There is not and never was a greater man than Emil Zátopek.'

Emil Zátopek: The Records

World records

1. 11 June 1949: 10,000m (29:28:2) – Ostrava
2. 22 Oct 1949: 10,000m (29:21:2) – Ostrava
3. 4 Aug 1950: 10,000m (29:02:6) – Turku
4. 15 Sep 1951: 20,000m (1:01:15.8) – Prague
5. 15 Sep 1951: 1 hour (19,558m) – Prague
6. 29 Sep 1951: 10 miles (48:12) – Houstka Spa
7. 29 Sep 1951: 20,000m (59:51.8) – Houstka Spa
8. 29 Sep 1951: 1 hour (20,052m) – Houstka Spa
9. 26 Oct 1952: 15 miles (1:16:26.4) – Houstka Spa
10. 26 Oct 1952: 25,000m (1:19:11.8) – Houstka Spa
11. 26 Oct 1952: 30,000m (1:35:23.8) – Houstka Spa
12. 1 Nov 1953: 6 miles (28:8.4) – Houstka Spa
13. 1 Nov 1953: 10,000m (29:1.6) – Houstka Spa
14. 30 May 1954: 5000m (13:57.2) – Paris
15. 1 Jun 1954: 6 miles (27:59.2) – Brussels
16. 1 Jun 1954: 10,000m (28:54.2) – Brussels
17. 29 Oct 1955: 15 miles (1:14:01) – Celakovice
18. 29 Oct 1955: 25,000m (1:16:36.4) – Celakovice

The medals

1948 Olympic Games: 10,000m Gold, 5000m Silver
1950 European Championships: 5000m Gold, 10,000m Gold
1952 Olympic Games: 5000m Gold, 10,000m Gold, Marathon Gold
1954 European Championships: 10,000m Gold, 5000m Bronze

Bibliography and Sources

Dana a Emil Zátopkovi vypravují – Emil Zátopek and Dana Zátopková, 1962, Sportovní a turistické nakl

Můj trening a závodění – Emil Zátopek, Vladimír Matoušek and Otakar Mašek, editors, 1955, Státní tělovýchovné nakladatelství

Zá-to-pek! Zá-to-pek! Zá-to-pek!: The Life and Times of the World's Greatest Distance Runner – Bob Phillips, 2002, Parrs Wood Press

Zátopek: The Marathon Victor – František Kožik, 1954, Artia

The Austerity Olympics: When the Games Came to London in 1948 – Janie Hampton, 2008, Aurum Press

Running Wild – Gordon Pirie, 1961, W. H. Allen

Running Fast and Injury Free – Gordon Pirie, 1998, John Gilbody

The Impossible Hero: A Biography of Gordon 'Puff Puff' Pirie – Dick Booth, 1999, Corsica Press

In the Long Run – Jim Peters, 1955, Cassell

Plimsolls On, Eyeballs Out: The Rise and Horrendous Fall of Marathon Legend Jim Peters – Rob Hadgraft, 2011, Desert Island Books

The Destiny of Ali Mimoun – Pat Butcher, 2011, Globerunner Productions

The Rings of Destiny – Olga Connolly, 1968, David McKay

The Kings of Distance – Peter Lovesey, 1968, Eyre & Spottiswoode

The Unforgiving Minute – Ron Clarke, 1966, Pelham Books

The Lonely Breed – Ron Clarke and Norman Harris, 1967, Pelham Books

The Complete Book of the Olympics – David Wallechinsky and Jaime Loucky, 2012, Aurum Press

Running: A Global History – Thor Gotaas, 2009, Reaktion Books

Checkmate in Prague: Memoirs of Ludek Pachman, 1975, Faber and Faber

Running – Jean Echenoz, 2009, The New Press

East Plays West: Sport and the Cold War – Stephen Wagg and David Andrews, editors, 2009, Routledge

Sport in Soviet Society – James Riordan, 1977, Cambridge University Press

The Frolik Defection: Memoirs of an Intelligence Agent – Josef Frolík, 1976, Corgi Books

The First Four Minutes – Roger Bannister, 1955, Putnam

Twin Tracks – Roger Bannister, 2014, The Robson Press

Olympus and Beyond: A Story of Life, Sport and Love on Four Continents – Allan Lawrence, 2014, Dorrance Publishing

A Gentle Cyclone: The Running Career of Sydney Wooderson – Michael Sheridan, 1999, Michael Sheridan

How They Train: Half Mile to Six Miles – Fred Wilt, 1973, Tafnews Press

Czechoslovakia: The State That Failed – Mary Heinman, 2011, Yale University Press

Born to Run – Christopher McDougall, 2009, Knopf

Chris Brasher: The Man who Made the London Marathon – John Bryant, 2012, Aurum Press

The Sports Gene: What Makes the Perfect Athlete – David Epstein, 2013, Yellow Jersey

1968: The Year that Rocked the World – Mark Kurlansky, 2004, Jonathan Cape

HHhH – Laurent Binet, 2012, Harvill Secker

Cold War, Warm Hearts: Two Life-Affirming Short Stories – Boris Starling, 2014, Kindle Direct Publishing

Acknowledgments

Many books, newspapers, magazines, documentaries, official reports, films, archives and interviews, both in English and Czech, were used in researching Emil's story.

I would particularly like to thank Dana Zátopková for agreeing to our meetings and being so hospitable. I am also indebted to the kindness of those peers who agreed to be interviewed or answer questions, especially Larry Kořan, Ivan Ullsperger, Aleš Poděbrad, Milan Svajgr, Ludvík Liška, Karel Angel, Božetěch Kostelka, Viktor Trkal, Jan Mrázek, František Fojt, Sir Roger Bannister, Ron Clarke and Bill Baillie. I am also grateful for Olga Connolly's email which showed that she is as good with a pen as she was with a discus.

It was sad that, during the course of writing this book, both Ron Clarke and Jindřich Roudný passed away. I am very grateful that Jindřich's daughter, Martina Smilková, gave me permission to use the memoirs that her father had been working on.

The book could not have happened without the interviewing, interpreting, translating and general organisational excellence of Zuzana Bílková and her husband Petr Bilek. I was blessed to find such talented researchers and, only through their work, did we get so much independent material. Equally, I would like to thank Anna Koucká for her help on one of my trips to the Czech

Republic and Daniel Skach for helping me plough through Radio Prague archives. Zuzana's father, David Kohout, was a huge help with his work in the State Security Archives.

As soon as I realised how the paths of Emil and Jan Haluza diverged and then re-crossed, I wanted to tell their parallel stories. Barbora Kreuzerová was very kind in allowing me to use information from the Memory of Nations, a brilliant oral history project co-ordinated by Post Bellum with its partners, Czech Radio and the Institute for Totalitarian Regimes. Klára Košářová's thesis on political trials in the Zlín region provided plenty of background information on Jan and Věra Haluza and the methods of the StB. At home, Dr Thomas Lorman, teaching fellow in Modern Central European History at UCL, joined me for a fascinating lunch in which I first became aware of just how bad life in Communist Czechoslovakia could be.

There are lots of other people who helped, advised, encouraged and raised eyebrows. Chris Turner at the IAAF gave me a nice anecdote about Viljo Heino and the Czech director David Ondříček gave me a DVD of one of his films and some insight into the Czech psyche.

Special thanks go to those great sages of the British athletics scene, Mel Watman and Stan Greenberg. Mel's office is an Aladdin's cave and I am privileged that he chose to let me into it and was then so helpful in loaning me books, pamphlets and carefully filed copies of, among others, *Athletics Weekly*, *Athletics World* and *World Sports*. It is people like Mel and Stan who make you remember that, for all the scandals and media negativity surrounding athletics, there are some wonderful people in it.

David Luxton did his thing with his usual calm, encouragement and skill – I am sure there is more to being a literary agent than hanging around Soho House, but he hides it well.

It has been a pleasure to work with a new editor, Charlotte Atyeo, and an old one, Ian Preece, and although they say you shouldn't judge a book by its cover, I think you can and should.

As ever, I thank Debs, Erin and Sam for letting me live with them. They are the best people I know and are always hugely supportive; one day I hope one of them reads something I wrote and then tells the others that I wasn't just surfing the web.

Index